1964-1974: A Decade of Odd Tales and Wonders

by Travis Edward Pike

This 1968 photo of me in Disneyland, Anaheim, California, with my baby brother Adam on my knee, is all the more poignant now, because Adam grew up to be my co-producer, co-arranger, recording engineer, and mixer on all the albums cited in this memoir. Thank you, Mother, for this great little brother.

1964-1974: A Decade of Odd Tales and Wonders

by Travis Edward Pike

Otherworld Cottage Industries
Los Angeles

1964-1974: A DECADE OF ODD TALES AND WONDERS

All appropriate lengths were taken to secure photo credits and permissions as well as attribution of quotes to editorial voices. Any omissions or errors are regretted and will be rectified upon reprint.

First Printing, September 2018

Copyright © 2018 by Travis Edward Pike

All rights reserved, including the right to reproduce this book or any portion thereof in any form, without the written permission of the Author, except that a reviewer may quote and a magazine or newspaper may print brief passages as part of a review written specifically for inclusion in that magazine or newspaper. For further information, email travpike@morningstone.com.

Pike, Travis Edward
1964 - 1974 A Decade of Odd Tales and Wonders

    1. Memoirs -- 1964 -1974. 2. American poetry -- Collected works.
    3. Stories in rhyme. 4. Music, Popular (Songs, etc.)
    I. Travis Edward Pike. II. Title.

920.8

ISBN-13: 978-1-892900-04-3
ISBN-10: 1-892900-04-1

Printed in the United States of America
Cover Design by Linda Snyder

Otherworld Cottage Industries
1746 South Kingsley Drive, Los Angeles, CA 90006

DEDICATION

I am most grateful to the friends and family who individually and together offered constructive criticism and encouragement as I wrote this book. Very special thanks are due to my youngest brother, Adam Christopher Pike, whose audio engineering, musicianship, tireless patience and extraordinary good humor made it possible to bring these songs and rhymes into the 21st century, and to the many notes from my daughter, Lisa who lived through these times with us, but was so young that much of this book came as a revelation to her, and to my wife, Judy, who contributed mightily to the research and editing of this book in an attempt to assure the accuracy of its timeline in the hope it will prove as interesting to pop culture historians as to fans past, present and future.

I owe a particular debt of gratitude to the students and military personnel of that vital, turbulent decade from 1964-1974, whose actions and activities form the backdrop for this memoir and inspired many of the songs and rhymes in this collection. Some are gone, and some are not, but these memories will linger on.

Lastly, I acknowledge The New Playwrights Foundation, The American Red Cross, The Hollywood Foreign Press Association, State Records, Stormy Forest Records, Alma Records, and Pike Productions, for their contributions to my saga.

ACKNOWLEDGMENTS

I shall surely miss some of the names of people who influenced my early career, or discovered and supported my efforts in the present. I shall endeavor to correct any such omissions in subsequent editions. These are people who made a difference, especially as related to the years covered by this book.

Adam Pike, Alana Shannon, Alice Pike, Andrea Snyder, Andy Pearson, Angus Kenneth MacAskill, Arthur Korb, Aurelius Skapars, Barbara Jordan, Benny Melanson, Bill Somers, Bob Doria, Bob Smith, Bobby Caron, Brent Backhus, Brian Houston, Bridget Shannon, Bruce Bradley, Buddy Brundo, Dick and Camille Turner, Cathy Palmer, Charly Ross, Chorty West, Chris Woodcock, Chuck and Beverly Monda, Colleen Stratton, Daniel Gregory Gunner, Danny Gravas, Dave Connor, David Carr, David Kessel, David Pinto, Dick Moran, Judith Stanton, Dr. Robert Bailey, Edward Plumb, Eileen Whitney, Ellen Hibler, Elsa Shannon, Elsie Christison, Emily Papa, Enriko Lomdardi, Erik and Susi Pike, Ernst-Gunther Schröder, Flo Selfman, Frank Dieter Andres, Frank Werner, Gary Schneider, George Brox, George Popadopolis, Gerard Alcan, Gordon G. Lightfoot, Gregory Pike, Harvey Kubernik, Herman Velarde, Ian Grinham, Jack Hibler, James A. Pike, James M. Pike, Joann Sittinger, Joe "Fuzzy" Gay, Joe Kondash, Joe Saia, Johnny Ferro, Jon DuFresne, Jonathan Hayes, Judi Reeve, Judy Pike, Julie Long, Karen Callahan, Karl Garrett, Kaththea Sias, Kent Kotal, Kim Schillereff, Kris Snyder, Lauran Doverspike, Laura Garafalo, Lee Garafalo, Lee Grimshaw, Lee Joseph, Lee Pennington, Lee Zimmerman, Lenny Helsing, Leslie Burnham, Linda Snyder, Lisa Gunner, Lois Tozer, Lonnie Snyder, Lynda Christison,

1964-1974: A DECADE OF ODD TALES AND WONDERS
ACKNOWLEDGMENTS (CONTINUED)

Mark Roth, Mark Edwards, Mary Moyers, Mel Davenport, Michael E. Fletcher, Michael Moores, Michele Hart, Mike and Anja Stax, Mike Dugo, Mike Valente, Mole Lambert, Nancy Friedman, Natalie Gravas, Norbert Wechselbaum, Pat Granger, Pat Prince, Patricia Ewing, Paul Holzwarth, Peter Bergman, Petra Davidson-Keasberry, Phil Cataldo, Phil Vitali, Phil Yeend, Philip Moores, Raoul Alteresco, Ray Fornier, Rob Cavicchio, Robert Maxwell Gunner, Roberta Edgar, Roger LaChance, Ron Stafford, Shay Burbridge, Squire D. Rushnell, Stephen and Diana Thompson, Stephen Cooper, Ted Charach, Teddy Stanhope, Terry Hagerty, Terry Ney, Tim Perlich, Tom Cooley, Walter Cooper, Wendy Christison, Werner Hingst, Wilfried Kühn, Dr. Woody James, and Zinthus Skapars.

TABLE OF CONTENTS

Chapter I: Prelude 1

Chapter II: My Year in Germany 29

Chapter III: Forty Songs and a Movie 55

Chapter IV: Coffeehouses, Concerts, Campuses, and Clubs 85

Chapter V: Everything Changed in 1968 111

Chapter VI: Knowing When the Party's Over 141

Chapter VII: From the Valley to the Basin 169

Chapter VIII: Getting Into Hollywood 195

Chapter IX: Afterword: An Interview with Harvey Kubernik 213

INDEX OF LINER NOTES, LYRICS, AND RHYMES 233

About the Music 235

Feelin' Better 239

Odd Tales and Wonders: Stories in Song 254

Reconstructed Coffeehouse Blues 268

Travis Edward Pike's Tea Party Snack Platter 283

Outside the Box 297

Odd Tales and Wonders: Stories in Rhyme 315

The Twaddle and the Gurck: An Interpretation 353

1964-1974: A DECADE OF ODD TALES AND WONDERS

PRELUDE

I don't know what year my saga starts, only that it resides in my earliest memories. I always loved to read, but like most children growing up in the 40's and 50's, my imagination was also fired by radio dramas like *Captain Midnight, The Shadow, The B-bar-B Riders,* and *The Lone Ranger.* Their dialogue, music, and sound effects kept me glued to the family radio. In the mid-50's, my father, James A. Pike, film director at WNAC-TV in Boston, launched *Cinema 7,* a Sunday afternoon double-feature program that established the standards for screening theatrical movies on television, all carefully selected and lovingly edited to include the sponsors' commercials with the least possible disruption to the film's dramatic continuity.

He not only screened movies all day long at work, but regularly brought some home to try out on the family. He hoped our reactions would help him anticipate how TV viewers at home might react. In fact, we seldom saw movies as a family. My father would be in the projection booth, my mother would be busy upstairs with the twins, and my older brother would be out with his friends, so my friend from next-door, Jimmy Riggs, often joined me, and we had the entire screening room to ourselves. Together, we must have seen hundreds of uncut versions of 16mm black and white prints of movies transferred from their 35mm, often color originals, rendered in black and white especially for television. And if we were quiet, while my father marked the edit points he selected for inserting the sponsors' messages, he'd forget we were there, and we'd catch a double feature. Without realizing it, I was being introduced to the rhetoric of film: dramatic structure, lighting, set design, camera angles, special effects, costume design, film scoring, acting, and directing by some of Hollywood's greatest filmmakers.

This newspaper photo, taken in late 1954, shows my father, Jim, and mother, Elsie, seated in the front row, with my sister Diana, (six), between them. In the back row, left to right, my brother, Milton, (13 and then going by his middle name); me, (11, nicknamed Teddy); and Diana's twin brother, Gregory, also six.

PRELUDE

I was a straight "A" student in the Sarah J. Baker elementary school, and followed my older brother into Boston Latin School. The oldest and one of the most prestigious public schools in the country, it only accepted the best and brightest boys from all over the city -- a model for what Los Angeles calls "Target Schools" today. The seventh grade curriculum was challenging. In addition to Latin, we studied history, geography, science, and even read Shakespeare in English classes.

I had to take buses to get to school and back, and was given lunch money to eat in the school's cafeteria. With so much commuting time on my hands, I began spending my lunch money on paperback books I could read on the bus, in the cafeteria, and in study halls -- or so I thought. No one objected to my reading on the buses or in the cafeteria, but during study halls, I ran into trouble for the first time since I started Kindergarten.

In that all-boys bastion of classical education, outside reading material was forbidden, and putting a Latin School book cover on the paperback failed to fool the monitoring professor. He confiscated my contraband. Whether he kept it or not, I don't know, but it was never returned to me.

I stopped bringing paperbacks to study halls and instead, began writing poetry and short stories. More trouble. The professor seized my notebook and reproached me for doing homework in study hall. Study hall was for studying. I protested that I wasn't doing homework -- the contents of the notebook were original compositions. Alas, my protestations not only failed to get my notebook returned, but talking back resulted in five misdemeanor marks.

1964-1974: A DECADE OF ODD TALES AND WONDERS

Six misdemeanor marks would result in a censure, and two censures in a single term could lead to expulsion, so although furious over the confiscation of my personal property, faced with possible expulsion should I protest, I held my tongue. The professor may have fancied that he brought a maverick student into line, but he had gone too far. In my mind, the perceived injustice fomented rebellion, and I remember, quite vividly, mentally paraphrasing the immortal words attributed to Captain Parker of the Massachusetts Militia before the battle of Lexington, and determined that "If he meant to have a war, let it begin here!"

My reaction was necessarily passive-aggresive. Outwardly, my demeanor belied the fury within. I sat quietly in study halls, staring at an open book, seeing nothing, entertained by my imagination, and refusing to study. Worse, I brought that attitude home with me, steadfastly refusing to study at all, concentrating instead on reading historical novels and fantasy adventures. I never skipped school, paid attention in class, and managed passing grades, but was regularly penalized for not handing in homework. The end result was that I only made it through my second year at Boston Latin School by the skin of my teeth.

Suddenly, in 1958, my father, then a Vice President of RKO General, left Channel 7 to start his own film company, Pike Productions. He sold the townhouse in Roxbury, a neighborhood of Boston which was fast-becoming an East Coast version of the notorious Los Angeles neighborhood of Compton, packed up the family and moved us all into a Queen Anne mansion on Lake Avenue in Newton Centre, arguably Boston's answer to Beverly Hills.

PRELUDE

THE CONFESSION OF THE FIRST MATE

No inheritor shall ever he be,
For he captain'd a ship and put to sea
And favour'd much by the Admiralty
Soon a fleet to command had he
Bound for the coast of Barbary
To put an end to slavery.
He carried no duty, no ransom, no fee.
No part of his philosophy,
Allowed for treating with piracy.
For him, only death or victory,
And so, in the midst of the dreadful melee
When finally he fell, wounded mortally
Shouting "If die we must, die free,"
His baleful eye drilled into me,
Seeing what no living man can see.
The crew responded desperately.
Each man battled ferociously,
Expecting no quarter, nor amnesty,
And as our dead sank in the sea,
In a way that only the dead can be
Of responsibility he was free.
'Twas I surrendered the ship, not he.
He was, after all, the son and heir
         to a greater part of the Kingdom.

I was 12- years-old when I first wrote this in a study hall at Boston Latin School. If I was caught, my writings and drawings were confiscated and I suppose, destroyed. They missed this one.

1964-1974: A DECADE OF ODD TALES AND WONDERS

My father's house in Newton Centre, Massachusetts

His new screening room with tooled Moroccan leather wainscotting.

PRELUDE

This undated entry for WHO'S WHO IN MOTION PICTURES AND TELEVISION, taken from his unfinished memoirs, provides a useful sketch of my father's career.

PIKE, James A. : b. Boston. MA Aug 15, 1922. e. Boston University. US Army WWII, Film Director, WNAC-TV, Boston, MA. Vice President RKO General. Movie Producer: Feelin' Good, Demo Derby. Founded Pike Productions in 1958. Produced TV Commercials for national clients such as Ford Motor Co., Silly Putty, Hasbro.
Produced special sales films for companies that included Gillette, Raytheon, AT&T, Perini Corp, Boston Patriots.
Produced political films for major candidates including Pres. John F. Kennedy, Senator Edward Kennedy, MA, Gov. John Volpe, MA., Gov. Endicott Peabody, MA., Sen. Leverette Saltonstall, MA, Mayor Kevin White, Boston.
Company currently designs, produces and distributes special trailers for exhibitors in the United States, United Kingdom, Germany, Spain, Portugal, Mexico, Chile, Argentina, Australia, and New Zealand.
Member Variety Club of New England.
Presidential Citation, Variety Club International.
Thomas A. Yawkey Memorial Award, Jimmy Fund/Dana-Farber Cancer Institute.

Ted Kennedy's wife, Joan, campaigning for her husband while he was recovering in the hospital, sent this photo of my father, (left), herself (center) and my mother (right) and signed it "To Elsie, Hope we always look so smiling and happy when we get together!!" Joan Kennedy

1964-1974: A DECADE OF ODD TALES AND WONDERS

The move to Newton Centre and the founding of Pike Productions, marked the end of never-ending movies with Jimmy Riggs . . . and the end of my unhappy sojourn at Boston Latin School. No longer living in Boston, my continued enrollment would have required tuition, well-worth it for my older brother, only a year from graduation, but a waste of money for me. I was to have a fresh start in a beautiful neighborhood, with a school system claiming to be one of the finest and most progressive in the country.

However, unforeseen adjustments came with that magnificent Queen Anne. My father moved his business into the house, too, and I soon learned that having it there made most of the house off-limits to the rest of us on weekdays, and especially off-limits to me, even on weekends.

I suppose I had imagined, as the cameras, lights, and editing room equipment were delivered, that I would be taught how to use the equipment and experience the wonder of filmmaking first-hand. To my dismay, my father instructed me not to waste his employees' time by grilling them about their jobs and the equipment they used. After school, I was to come home, change my clothes and go out to play. If the weather was bad, I could stay in my room -- but I was not to play my radio or record player lest it disturb the crew. Furthermore, I was to come and go through the back door, use the back stairs, and stay out of the front of the house, a rule that precluded access to the grand piano in the parlor and effectively barred me from the screening room, except by invitation. Lastly, I was not allowed friends in the house during working hours, and later, only with permission. Small wonder that house was never really home to me.

PRELUDE

At the start of the summer, while Pike Productions was still setting up for operations, I was introduced to Dave Malloy, two years my senior, son of Jack Malloy, who worked at WNAC Radio and knew my father well. Dave showed me around the neighborhood, and in the fall, helped me get concession work at Boston College home games during football season. There, I'd be given a money bag to make change, load up with as much as I could carry, and work the bleachers. I was a bit under-size for my age, but I was strong. Still, I must have been a sight, stalking the bleachers, shouting "Popcorn, peanuts, potato chips, pennants and programs here!" At the end of the game, my returns and cash bag were tallied, and I received a percentage of the take. I doubt my efforts ever amounted to as much as $20.00 a game, but it was mine to save or spend as I saw fit.

I was enrolled in the nearby coed Weeks Junior High School. Having spent the previous two years in an all-boys' school, I was astonished by the changes I observed in girls, and confounded by all the unwritten rules governing interpersonal relations at that school. To be fair, the Newton girls were nothing like the girls I knew in my elementary school in Roxbury. Newton's ninth graders wore makeup, perfume, came to school in designer fashions, and traveled in packs. Being new, they looked at me like something the cat dragged in, whispered among themselves, and finally broke into fits of giggles. I didn't know how to react, so I decided to keep my distance, not because I wasn't interested, or even because they acted silly, but because whenever they came too close, their perfume made me sneeze. As for the boys, some were openly hostile and it seemed that once a week, some new native would invent a pretext to pick a fight. I suppose they were probably trying to see where I fit into their established pecking order, but at the time, I thought the local Newton Centre teens were the most horribly clannish, hostile, and over-privileged I ever had the distinct displeasure of meeting.

One spring day, as I was walking home from school, two boys drove to the lake, cut me off and asked me if I was Teddy Pike, the singer. I have no idea where they got the notion that I was a singer, because I didn't have my rowboat, yet -- but that's another story. I'd never seen them before, but they were big kids. As I contemplated abandoning my books in favor of a cold, wet escape into the lake, they introduced themselves as a rock band from Natick, Massachusetts, in need of a singer to play at a sock hop in a neighboring town. They were out-of-towners, "friendlies," and to prove it, they showed me the drum set in the back of the station wagon.

I still had to report home from school, drop off my books, and change my clothes, but I was intrigued by the opportunity and accepted their invitation. They drove me to the house, and duly impressed, while I ran upstairs to change, they introduced themselves to my mother, gave her the address and phone number where we'd be, and then off we went to my first rock 'n' roll rehearsal.

The guitarist's name was Teddy Stanhope, and big as he was, I think he was younger than me. His father had sound-proofed his garage and bought Teddy a Fender Stratocaster and amplifier. I didn't know much about it, but it all looked cool. I regret that I cannot remember the name of the saxophonist, who was waiting when we arrived and helped bring in and set up the drums. He told me he took clarinet lessons, because if you could play clarinet, you could play sax. When the drums were set up, I was impressed by their logo. They called themselves The Jesters, and had a fool's head copied from a deck of cards fitted over the front of the bass drum. The drummer's name was Bobby Caron. He was a senior at Natick High School, and the only one of us old enough to drive a car.

They plugged a microphone into the amp, handed it to me and we began "rehearsing," which meant that they'd ask me if I knew a song, and if I did, they'd play it, I'd sing it, and if we liked what we heard, Bobby put it on his list. The first song we tried was Chuck Berry's "Sweet Little Sixteen," and when Teddy Stanhope played the guitar intro, it sounded exactly like the record -- and when I sang it, so did I. In those days, if I sang an Elvis song, I tried to sound like Elvis. It didn't matter if the recording artist was Little Richard, Fats Domino or Paul Anka, I generally succeeded in sounding a lot like the original artist.

We landed the sock hop in the basement of a Catholic Church in Needham, the town between Natick and Newton. There, I was a complete unknown and in neutral territory. The gig was supposed to pay $5.00 ($1.00 for gas and a buck apiece for each of us). The priest's policy was that once kids paid the $1.00 admission fee, if they left, they had to pay again to get back in. The idea was to discourage kids from leaving and getting into mischief.

That night, a lot of the kids left during our breaks, but returned with friends, and paid again to get back in. When it was over, the priest said he'd never seen anything like it. He rewarded us by giving us $20.00 for the night. We split it $8.00 for the driver-drummer-band leader, and $4.00 apiece for the rest of us, which we spent on fried clams at the local HoJo's, where we rehashed the wonders of our first gig late into the night -- practically up to 11 o'clock! And that's how, at 14-years-old, I became a rock 'n' roll singer.

In all, I think we played a total of three gigs, at least one of which was at an Oddfellows Lodge. I'd never heard of them, so the name stuck. But then, the drummer found a girlfriend, and that ended my early musical career.

Billy Madden was almost as much an outsider at Weeks Junior High as I was. I don't know how that came to be, but the story going around was that he'd been in some kind of trouble and was only back in school on trial. I don't think either of us made a conscious effort to befriend the other, but we gravitated to the same semi-isolated table in the lunch room, and eventually started chatting.

A neighbor girl asked Billy to invite me to come with him to her birthday party. I was showing off, removing a Coca Cola bottlecap with my teeth, when the coke shot up into my mouth and pushed the bottlecap halfway down my throat. I could either choke to death on the spot, or try to swallow the bottlecap, so I swallowed it. I think Billy and the girl were the only ones who knew it happened. When, about a week later, I finally told my father about the pain gnawing at my insides, and how it got there, he didn't believe me, but under pain of death if I was lying, he took me to the hospital for an x-ray. I've never seen an x-ray to rival the bright, white circle and serrated edge that appeared in mine. I was admitted and cut open to have the bottlecap removed.

PRELUDE

Why is it friends who visit you in the hospital always try to cheer you up by telling jokes? There's a lot of truth in that old saying "It only hurts when I laugh."

Billy and I had become friends by the end of that first and final year at Weeks Junior High, and he invited me to work with him that summer on a junk truck, mostly hauling refrigerators, stoves and cast iron bathtubs out of old apartment houses in Boston. It only paid something like $20.00 a day, but it was something we could do together, and having some money was way better than having none.

The junk man's name was Russell. Billy called him "Jelly Belly" (probably not to his face). Most of our time was spent riding from one job to another, crowding into the cab, or "surfing" on the back of the stake bed truck, waving and whistling at girls as we passed by. But when we stopped to make a pickup, the work was hard and heavy, with most of the things we removed coming from the upper floors of the old apartment buildings.

Stoves were usually stone insulated and we had to disassemble them to get them out of the apartments. Cast iron porcelain tubs we turned upside down and pounded with sledgehammers until the cast iron began to break up. Then we'd take them down to the truck in pieces. Afterward, we'd have to clean up all the porcelain dust and shards. You've probably never seen an old gas refrigerator, but they were so heavy, we removed the gas pipes and took them down to the truck, separately from the boxes. It was hard and heavy work, but we were developing some serious muscles.

One day, surfing from ropes wrapped around the front stakes of the truck bed, I fainted and fell off the truck onto the road. I never felt it when I hit the pavement, and when the drum pounding in my skull began to fade, apart from a few scrapes and bruises, I felt fine. But Jelly Belly wouldn't let me work on the truck anymore, even though I'd been cleared to return to work by the attending physician.

That fall, I used the money I'd earned to buy a pram -- a small, leaky dinghy with a flat, snub-nosed bow. With my older brother's help, I wrestled it into the cavernous cellar, where I quietly set about scraping, caulking, repainting, and installing wooden grate decking to protect the seals on the two-piece bottom. I then bought oars from Sears-Roebuck and had enough money left over to buy a transistor radio.

One day in January, when I came home from school, the crew was set up to film in my father's office. The only other time that had been done was when my father shot the opening sequence for *John Gunther's High Road*. I had left one of my short stories on a coffeetable in the big living room, and Mr. Gunther had read it and wanted to meet me. He told me he enjoyed it and thought I had a way with words. That, in front of my father, really made my day, but later, when the shoot was over, my father told me to never leave my crap lying around in the front of the house again. He had to interrupt filming because John Gunther wanted to meet me, and he had enough trouble with the changing ambient daylight, without me causing unnecessary delays.

At the time, I apologized and said it wouldn't happen again, but now, with the office all set up to shoot, I wanted to get a glimpse of the man who had found me worthy of praise. I'm guessing it was sometime in mid-January, maybe soon after we'd gone back to school after the Christmas Holidays, because I don't remember having to look past the Christmas tree.

I was standing quietly in the doorway to the narrow hall leading to the back of the house, peering around the corner into my father's office, and jumped when a voice from behind startled me, asking if he could get by. I quickly got out of his way, fully expecting him to go on and join the crew. Instead, he turned to me, shook my hand and introduced himself. I can't remember if he said he was John F. Kennedy, or Jack Kennedy, but he ended by saying he was running for President of the United States. I may have wished him good luck. I honestly don't know, but he asked my name.

"I'm Teddy Pike," I blurted. "I live here."

"Oh, I've got a brother named Teddy," he said, and grinned broadly.

I think I excused myself, but I know I beat a hasty retreat, changed my clothes, and got out of the house.

That spring, as the ice melted on the lake across the street from the house, I launched my rowboat and began exploring the lake, accompanied by Spooky, the family dog, an English Setter, who took possession of the prow, constantly holding my quacking fan club at bay, as I tossed them bread crumbs, while I sang along with the hits.

The lake was my moat, the rowboat, my island, well out of reach of would-be trouble makers. In it, I practiced my rhymes aloud, experimented with character voices, and mimicked recording artists as I sang along with the hits on my transistor radio. Occasionally, if I drifted too close to shore, an irate homeowner would threaten to call the police if I didn't shut up or row over to the other side of the lake. I always complied, but the police were never a serious threat. They had no boats.

In the fall, I went back to writing, drawing, and being a schoolboy. At that time, there was only one Newton High School to serve all the Newtons. Billy and I both lived in Newton Centre (not a spelling error, but an official affectation), and were both enrolled at Newton High, but he worked after school with Jelly Belly, so apart from school, I saw less and less of him.

I knew that Newtonville, Newton Highlands, West Newton, and even distant Chestnut Hill were all part of Newton, but at Newton High School, I met teens from Auburndale, Upper Falls, Lower Falls, Newton Corner, Thompsonville, Waban, Oak Hill, and Nonantum, a broad cross-section quite unlike the monolithic crowd I'd met in and around Newton Centre. I made new friends, especially with teens from Newton Corner, where I was widely accepted, once they realized, home address aside, I was not a product of Newton Centre.

I only saw my new friends at school, or more rarely on weekends, when we might go bowling or to a movie, because getting there meant someone had to pick me up and bring me home, or I'd have to thumb my way down and back on Centre Street, or walk, if no one would stop for me. At fifteen, I had no "wheels" and no license to drive.

I bought a copy of Halas and Batchelor's *Technique of Film Animation*. I'd been practicing funny voices and making faces for years and was especially eager to try my hand, because Pike Productions had installed an Oxberry multi-plane animation stand and from time to time hired animators for commercial productions. It was off-limits to me, but I drew a strange, long-necked cat, and animated it to walk in place and turn its head from profile to full face, and one day, when my father was out of town, I asked the animation crew if they'd shoot it for me and have it processed along with their next job. They did, and less than a week later, I was in the screening room with my father, watching that cat walk! He lectured me about bothering his crew, but I could tell he was impressed.

One weekend, when I was playing with Spooky on the side lawn, an old guy driving a Newton Centre Market delivery truck beckoned to me from the curb. I thought he needed directions, but instead, he asked me if I'd like to make some money. He introduced himself as "Fuzzy," but his name was actually Joe Gay. A functioning alcoholic, getting on in years, Fuzzy had fallen on some stairs, and was having a hard time making his deliveries. I think he offered me $15.00 for the rest of the day, which when he spoke to me, was already approaching ten o'clock. He promised we'd be finished by three and he'd buy me lunch.

I asked him to come in and meet my mother, and then we went to work. From that day on, especially in winter when the footing was slippery, on days when I wasn't in school, he'd pick me up and I'd go on his delivery route with him. And when winter set in, he told me he had another job for me, if I was interested. In addition to driving the market delivery truck, he cleaned the store after hours. With all the winter snow, slush, mud, and salt tracked in, the job was too much for him alone. If I'd help him, he'd show me what to do and pay me $15.00 for that, too, every time we cleaned the store. He taught me to sweep, swab, wax, and buff the floors. At first, the industrial buffer was almost too much to handle, but he patiently showed me how, and by the second week, I showed him how I could do it, one-handed! And now that I was a fully qualified assistant janitor, he brought me along when he cleaned Bonozoli's Beacon Restaurant, as well. As the sapling is bent . . .

The new Newton South High School opened the following year, and I was reassigned to it. I had turned sixteen that summer, but although I was old enough to drive, I had no car, no license, and little in common with the more affluent student body. As before, homework would have infringed on my independent studies, so I didn't do it. I was writing the original book and music for an animated musical fantasy I called *Sir Smudge*. Today, no longer a musical, I continue to develop it as a dark-ages fantasy-adventure series, retitled *Long-Grin*. I recently recorded two songs I composed for that musical and now, both "The Sorcerer's Waltz" and "A Red-backed, Scaly, Black-bellied, Tusked, Bat-winged Dragon" are included in my *Odd Tales and Wonders Stories in Song* CD.

That Junior year at Newton South, I met Aurelius Skapars. Born in Riga, Latvia, "Sam," as he called himself, was a loner, from Newton Upper Falls, also reassigned to South High. His step-father was a building contractor and Sam was a highly-skilled finish carpenter. We frequently sat at the same "outsiders" table in a far corner of the cafeteria, and eventually became friends. He had a pool table in his cellar, and invited me over to shoot pool. He taught me how, but I was never skillful enough to beat Sam or his younger brother, Zinthus (aka Zeko). I taught them all about motion picture animation and they taught me all about finish carpentry, but I never became skillful at that, either.

Me and Spooky in the driveway of my father's house on Lake Avenue in Newton Centre. The date may be uncertain, but it looks like early spring to me, and I'll bet I'm thinking about launching my rowboat.

Sam's mother and step-father were most gracious, and his grandmother, who lived with them, always greeted me with a smile. She was quite old and spoke no English, so I asked Sam and Zeko to teach me enough Latvian to say "hello," "goodbye," "how are you," and answer when she asked the same of me. I'll never forget the look of joy on her face the first time I spoke to her in her native tongue. A good ear and my practiced mimicry came in handy after all.

That summer, Sam and Zeko accumulated a small fortune working as finish carpenters. I'd been cleaning the restaurant with Fuzzy for some time, so he recommended me for the summer dishwasher's job in the sweltering kitchen of Bonozoli's Beacon Restaurant, which gave me an opportunity to weigh the consequences of an afterlife in hell. I persevered, every payday bringing me closer to purchasing animation equipment and supplies.

The cook was a good and gentle man from Roxbury, and being from Roxbury myself, he tolerated my early morning sing-alongs. Mr. Bonozoli did not allow me to sing at mealtime, lest I disturb his patrons, a not unreasonable restriction. Lunch and supper were early for me, but came with the job. If the worst of it was going home at night smelling like garbage, the best of it was payday.

By summer's end, I had enough money to buy two metal light platters with clear glass windows and steel rulers with industry standard registration pegs that slid along grooves at the top and bottom of the platter, pre-punched registration paper for roughs, pre-punched cels, cel-tested paint, camel hair brushes, and Rapidograph pens, which Sam and Zeko helped me set up in their attic in Upper Falls.

PRELUDE

Autumn marked the start of my senior year, and at seventeen, I finally got my driver's license, but still had no car. When Sam wasn't working, I'd go to his house. On days he worked, I went home to Lake Avenue, wrote, sketched, or made faces in the mirror, teaching myself how to draw expressions that conveyed the text (or subtext), I desired.

In 1962, Pike Productions landed the Duncan Yoyo account, which called for a little animated character on a mountainside to holler "yoho," wait for the echo, then holler "yoyo" and begin playing with one. It also required an animated version of Duncan's new Shrieking Sonic Satellite Yoyo to whistle through outer space. The combined clips weren't very long and my fathers's regular animator was busy, so I landed the assignment on spec (short for speculation, which means you don't get paid until the work is finished and accepted by the client).

My Latvian friends were both excellent draftsmen, and I'd taught them enough about animation to assign the Satellite Yoyo clip to them. I took on the little man on the mountainside and when we delivered our efforts, they worked beautifully and we all got paid. Sadly, the pitiful amount they received for the hours they'd worked was so beneath what they earned as carpenters, it was embarrassing. Shortly after we delivered our "successful" animation, we dismantled everything, brought all my animation materials to Lake Avenue, and stacked them in my closet.

That summer, after graduation, going on eighteen, broke, and still without wheels, Fuzzy got me a job at the Newton Centre Market, driving the refrigerated market truck used to pick up meat from the downtown suppliers, and doubling as the extra driver for their second grocery delivery truck on weekends. With my earnings, I bought a pristine 1954 Studebaker Commander with a seized engine for $50. The radio worked, and I now had a private retreat where I could roll up the windows, turn on the radio, and sing at the top of my lungs, fair weather or foul, as long as I kept the battery charged.

One of my Newton Corner friends actually worked in a speed shop, another in an auto parts store, but all of them considered themselves top mechanics. I decided to try to enlist their aid to put the Studebaker back on the road. If it was running, I could get in and sing at the top of my lungs, here, there, or anywhere else the road might take me.

I managed to convene a number of them at a local coffeeshop and began telling them what I had in mind. Before I'd finished, they'd started competing with each other as to who was the most qualified, who had garage space, who had a chain-fall, who could get the best deal on parts, and before they finished trying to outdo each other, it had come around to me only having to pay for parts, and them supplying all the labor for free.

We formed a three car caravan and drove up to Newton Centre, where my car was parked behind the garage. It was getting dark when we arrived, but being mechanics, they all had flashlights in their trunks or glove compartments. Everyone agreed the body and interior were in mint condition. Then a guy who specialized in auto detailing began describing how he'd like to give it a "flame job," a treatment popular with hot-rodders, and the mechanics argued that flames would be dumb unless the car had a mill to back it up. (For non hot-rodders, a flame job means having swirling flames painted on the body and a mill to back it up would be a really powerful motor.)

One of the guys offered to throw in a pair of rippled lake pipes for free, and when another pointed out the engine only had a single exhaust manifold, his objection was quickly overruled by the Chief, a biker who managed a Midas Muffler shop and said he'd do the conversion free, after hours, but I'd need butterfly valves or it would never pass inspection. A new engine was out of the question, but the existing one could be bored and stroked, a 3/4 race cam was a must, and the excited guy from the speed shop thought the newest Paxton-McCulloch supercharger, like the one that came stock in the new Studebaker Avanti, might fit under the hood. What it boiled down to was that for a lot more than I could afford, they could turn my Studebaker Commander into a customized classic street machine.

When I said all I wanted was to get it running, it seemed everyone lost interest. I protested it would take me months, maybe a year to get that kind of bread together. Someone suggested I could pick up some extra cash singing requests in dating bars, and one of the bikers said I could get in as his guest, as long as I stuck to "Shirley Temples." About then, it all began to run together, I had no idea what they were talking about, but I smiled when I realized I wouldn't have to walk or thumb a ride home.

A few days later, I was still mulling it over when Sam appeared in his new black, dual-quad, Chevy Corvette. He took me for a ride, and out on route 128, put the car through its paces. He even let me drive it for a bit and I confess, I was thrilled by its unbridled power. We went to his house, where I saw Zeko's used, but immaculate 1959 rose-colored Cadillac convertible. That was the year Caddy sported those huge tail fins. I was genuinely happy for them, but I have to admit, I felt like a poor relative at a family reunion. It made me want to wait and get the job done right, at the same time it made me more eager than ever to get on the road. Then, out of a clear blue sky, Sam handed me the title to his 1954 Oldsmobile 98. It used oil and guzzled gas, but it should last me until I got the Studebaker up and running. All I had to do was register it and I would finally have wheels.

Things were definitely looking up, especially when, on weekends, my friends from Newton Corner began taking me around to the dating bars. Some nights and some bars were better than others, and one night I came close to a hundred dollars in tips. I was banned in some places because the house band or the management objected, but welcomed in others, where my requests inspired competition as patrons sought to have me sing a song dedicated to their special boyfriend or girlfriend. When one place wanted a piece of my action, my friends and I left and never returned.

With an extra eighty to a hundred and forty dollars a week, things were moving along faster than I ever imagined. There were questions about just how far we could go, and I'm not sure just how far we went, but I did get the 3/4 race cam and somehow they managed to get a Paxton-McCulloch supercharger installed under the hood. The Chief installed the dual exhaust system with bypass valves that allowed me to switch from muffled to straight out exhaust through the 3/4 length ripple lake pipes mounted below the rocker

PRELUDE

panels. I never did get around to the flame job. The car came with a shimmering goldflake-mint paint job, so I left it alone, but I did buy into a wheel treatment that included new blackwall tires, chrome wheels, with shiny gold lug nut covers, illuminated by custom green running lights installed out of sight in the wheel wells. I could hardly afford gas, but standing still, the car looked great -- and the radio still worked.

The gauges weren't hooked up, when I picked up a mechanic friend and we drove to a bar where I knew I could make some money. My glittering, low-slung chariot bottomed hard as I roared into the parking lot. Hours later, driving home on Soldier's Field Road, a Chevy 409 and a Ford 406 were revving up at a red light. I slipped into the third lane. My friend grinned and gave me a thumbs up.

When the light changed, I left the Chevy and the Ford in my rearview mirror. It was an exhilarating moment, but ahead, in a parking lot on the side of the highway, a blue and red light began to whirl. My triumph had been observed by Metropolitan District Commission police. (In the hot-rodder vernacular, MDC stood for "More Damn Cops.") I hit them with high beams as I approached, and turned off my lights as I roared by before they cleared the parking lot. And then, horror of horrors, my engine seized, so I threw in the clutch, and rolled to a stop at the side of the road.

I'd like to say I'd been misled by my evil companion, but it wasn't so. I hadn't set out to race, but when the opportunity arose, the temptation was too great to resist. I later learned that I had punctured the oil pan, probably when I bottomed out going into the parking lot at the bar.

1964-1974: A DECADE OF ODD TALES AND WONDERS

The repercussions were swift and terrible. Street racing cost me my license, my market job, and my car. Financially wiped out, grounded, and with no prospects in sight, a tour in the Navy sounded good. If you weren't in school, getting drafted was almost certain, but if you joined, you'd get your choice of schools. It was April and spring was in the air, so with empty pockets and the call to adventure ringing in my ears, I enlisted. Or you could say I followed an old Yankee tradition for young men down on their luck, and with no prospects in sight, ran away to sea.

My high test scores brought me to the attention of the Commanding Officer, but "boot camp" was mostly marching, washing, and folding clothes. The more challenging military-type things were fire-fighting, target practice, tear gas training, swimming, learning to turn your clothes into

```
                    RECRUIT TRAINING COMMAND
                   U. S. NAVAL TRAINING CENTER
                      GREAT LAKES, ILLINOIS
                                                    J23-03:dv
                                                    1650

                                                    20 JUNE 1963

From:   Commanding Officer, Recruit Training Command, Great Lakes, Illinois
To:     PIKE, Travis Edward, 693 22 07, Seaman Recruit, Company 125, U.S.NAVY
Subj:   Letter of Commendation

1.  The Commanding Officer takes pleasure in commending you for your out-
standing performance of duty while undergoing recruit training. During
the period of your training you have maintained the highest average score
of the weekly composite examinations given to your company. Your outstand-
ing performance attests to those qualities of initiative, perseverance and
devotion to duty in you that are the attributes of all outstanding Navy men.
It gives me great pleasure to extend to you a "WELL DONE."

2.  A copy of this commendation will be placed in your service record.



                              IRA N. KING
                           CAPTAIN U.S.NAVY
```

flotation devices, knot-tying, naming parts and types of naval vessels, and learning nautical terms like "port" (left), "starboard" (right), "ladder" (stairs), and let us never forget that "head" means "toilet."

After boot camp, I reported to Yeoman "A" school in Bainbridge, Maryland, where I learned to type and heard the drumbeat that drives my song, "Oh Mama," played by Fire Control Technicians as they marched to classes.

I had two weeks leave before I had to report to my shore duty station in Germany. My older brother (now going by "Pike," in the Army, and "Jimmy" at home), had one more week at home before he shipped out, bound for the Berlin Brigade. When he left, I felt marooned (note my use of the nautical expression made famous by Robert Louis Stevenson as the fate endured by Ben Gunn in his classic novel, *Treasure Island*).

That last week, before I left to go overseas, my father screened "dailies" of the demolition derby action he'd shot at Norwood Arena. Even without sound, it was exciting footage. I suggested it needed a good rock'n'roll title song, so he told me to write one.

I couldn't tell if he meant it or was being facetious, but it didn't matter. I recorded a demo for him, and forgot all about it. However, while I was stationed in Germany, Arthur Korb arranged and produced the song with The Rondels, and it became the title song to *Demo Derby*.

1964-1974: A DECADE OF ODD TALES AND WONDERS

James A. Pike presents

DEMO DERBY

A 28 MINUTE FEATURETTE with CRASH ACTION
filmed on location at Norwood Arena

with a music score that will ROCK YOU . . . featuring the sensational DEMO DERBY title song (Travis Pike - Arthur Korb) - recorded by the RONDELS.

PREMIERES JUNE 24th
at the following theatres:

☆ **PARAMOUNT** - Boston   ☆ **CAPITOL** - Worcester
☆ **ALLYN** - Hartford   ☆ **PARAMOUNT** - New Haven

A FIRST THEATRICAL FILM from the producers of dozens of special purpose films and hundreds of commercials for Network and Spot TV.

In 1958, James A. Pike formed Pike Productions to make TV commercials, documentaries and films for industry. In 1964, his first theatrical release, *Demo Derby* opened with Frank Sinatra in *Robin and the Seven Hoods*, Elvis Presley in *Viva Las Vegas*, and played on screens all across the country with the Beatles *Hard Day's Night*.

MY YEAR IN GERMANY

It was late October when I arrived in Todendorf, Germany, which, roughly translated, means "village of the dead." I was still settling in when news came of the assassination of President Kennedy. JFK had been very popular with the German people, and everywhere I went, I was received with heartfelt condolences, simply because I was American.

In early December, I bought a used Sunbeam Alpine sports car from a sailor returning Stateside, and set out to explore my surroundings. Toward Christmas, I was having supper in a restaurant in the picturesque little town of Lütjenburg, when a nun came through soliciting the diners. She bypassed me, so I called her back and tried to put a few *Deutschmarks* into her can. She quickly covered the lid and explained she was not collecting money. She was inviting people to draw slips of paper with the name and age of an orphaned child. The idea was to buy an appropriate gift for the child and turn it in at the German Army base so the orphans would not be left out on Christmas Day. I asked to be allowed to draw from her can. She seemed flustered. I suspect she was not supposed to solicit from foreigners, but I told her I was far from home, had no one on my Christmas list, and would be grateful if she let me help. She relented and I drew two girls, ages seven and nine.

I was sitting near a window. It wasn't late, but at that latitude, it was already dark outside. It began to snow and for a few moments, I felt like I was living in a Dickens novel. Then I realized it was close to closing time for the stores in the town square, so I quickly finished my supper and as I paid the check, asked the cashier where I would find a toy store. I was directed to a nearby store that had a toy department.

Outside, it was cold and the snow was really beginning to come down, so I hurried down to the store, slipping and sliding on the brick sidewalk. Inside, kicking the snow off my shoes, I asked where the toys were and was directed downstairs to the basement, where a salesgirl, no more than 16-years-old, asked if she could help me. I told her I needed gifts for two girls, ages seven and nine. She asked me what they liked to play with and I told her I didn't know. The presents were for two little orphan girls. She flushed, her eyes welled with tears, and she excused herself. I should explain that every conversation I have described since I saw the nun in the restaurant, was in German. In that moment, I was reviewing exactly what I had said, for fear I may have said something other than what I meant to say.

The girl returned a moment later with another sales girl, more composed, but about the same age as the first, who asked me, possibly in English, if she could help me. Continuing in German, I asked what toys were popular that year, for young girls. She remained artfully composed as she showed me a toy electric bake oven that came with a lightbulb heating element and a few packages of cupcake mix. I told her I didn't think that would work. The gift was for an orphan and I didn't know if she would be able to replace them when the cake mix was gone or the light bulb burned out. The new sales girl's eyes flooded, and she quickly excused herself.

I just now looked up the word for orphan in my Langendscheidt New College German Dictionary, and discovered that the word I used to explain my quest to the sales girls, *Elternlöse*, was not the regularly used German word for orphan, which is *Waisenkind*, and probably a word used by the nun at the beginning of our conversation. However, since I did not recognize that word, the nun wisely described their condition, *Elternlöse*, which I understood as parentless, and therefore, orphaned.

The first sales girl, now composed, suggested they might like to play with dolls. I thought that was a splendid idea, and chose two I thought would be appropriate, but both sales girls seemed to think they were too expensive. With the current exchange rate running about four Deutschmarks to a dollar, I bought them, anyway, and I think it only came to around $8.00 for both. The girls gift-wrapped them and taped on the sad little labels -- "Girl - 9" and "Girl - 7," and as I left, they wished me the most sincere Merry Christmas I ever heard.

By then the snow had coated the whole town with a soft, white glow which contributed to my overall sense of generous well-being. For the first time that year, it was beginning to feel a lot like Christmas. I climbed into my car, drove up to the German army base, dropped off the gifts, made a U-turn around the guard house, and feeling really good about myself, started back down the hill.

High-crowned cobblestone roads are notoriously slippery when wet, and that "White Christmas" blanket of snow hid just how treacherous they had become. I skidded slightly as I turned onto the road into town, so I downshifted to let the engine reduce my rate of descent. The downshift slowed the motor, but set the rear wheels spinning and I went into a sideways skid down the hill.

Being from Boston, Massachusetts, I had plenty of experience driving in snow. I steered in the direction of the skid and waited for the car to respond. I wasn't going very fast when the front wheels jumped the curb onto the sidewalk, or when the front end crashed into the brick wall of the restaurant. Nevertheless, my right headlamp was broken and my right fender was crushed against my right front wheel, making it impossible to steer. I'd stopped skidding, but I wouldn't be going anywhere soon.

All afternoon I had been thinking and conversing in German, but as a small crowd gathered, I reverted to thinking in English and failed to understand anything the natives were trying to tell me. I didn't see the salesgirls from the shop approaching arm in arm, but when they recognized me, they began pleading my case to the townspeople.

I wasn't injured -- just disgusted by my terrible luck. Suddenly, strong arms moved me aside, and the crowd pushed the car away from the wall. Someone appeared with a sledgehammer and began banging the fender away from the tire. I was told to get in the car and see if I could turn the wheels. I could. Would the car start? It did. With only one working headlamp, they sent me on my way, cheering as I, like Santa Claus, drove out of sight.

Frank Dieter Andres was the mechanic in the Mercedes shop where I brought my car for repairs. He told me that to get a good color match, the entire car would have to be repainted. I selected Mercedes Wine Red over the drab gray of the Sunbeam's initial incarnation.

We got to talking about cars, and I told him about *Demo Derby* and how the drivers deliberately smashed into each other until the last car running took the checkered flag. Of course, I told him about my modified 1954 Studebaker Commander with its bored out Bearcat V8, belt-driven Paxton supercharger, racing cam and the flames that could sometimes be seen issuing from the 3/4 length, externally-mounted rippled lake pipes. I also explained that custom car enthusiasts often named their cars, and I had originally planned to call mine "The Banshee," but was considering "The Poltergeist," when I blew the engine drag-racing, lost my drivers' license and ended up in the Navy.

Frank, fascinated by my hot rod stories and the concept of a demolition derby, was thrilled when I said I'd bring him some American Hot Rod magazines. He was 17-years-old and had a girlfriend in high school who studied English. He invited me to join them at an ice cream parlor after work. Up to then, we'd been getting by with my wretched German, but that afternoon, our conversation and the magazines I displayed, drew a crowd of teenagers to our table and my auto parts vocabulary grew rapidly. I told them about my custom Studebaker and they translated for Frank, which impressed him even more. Asked how I could afford such an expensive hobby, I told them about my singing rock'n'roll for tips in dance bars.

1964-1974: A DECADE OF ODD TALES AND WONDERS

I'm not sure which was more exciting to Frank. As crazy as he was about automobiles, he seemed equally as enthusiastic about American rock 'n' roll. That same night, he and his friends took me with them to a dance club. Frank made a big deal about introducing me to the band. I sang a few songs and before long, requests were coming in. I didn't get tips, but drinks arrived in abundance. Not being a drinker, I shared them with everyone at the table, but we discovered that my old paradigm of singing song requests for customers resulted in rewards, just as it had in the USA. The crowning event of the evening came when Frank invited me to join him for Christmas dinner with his grandparents. I would not be spending Christmas or New Year's Eve (Sylvester), alone.

Oma and Opa Holz, (Frank's grandmother and grandfather), were most gracious and delighted that I spoke some German. After dinner, they asked where I was staying. I had a room at Hotel Brückman. Too expensive, they protested. They had a spare room. From now on, if I was coming into town for the weekend, I should stay with them and that became my routine. I'd come into town, Frank and his friends would take me around to the dance clubs and I'd sing a few rock tunes. The crowds loved it and I enjoyed the attention. Before long, whenever we'd show up, the band would ask me to sing. Then, the club owners wanted to meet me. Suddenly, I was in business. I took bookings on my off-duty weekends with whatever band was playing, for which I was well paid, by local standards.

One day in spring, I heard that the town was to be effectively shut down for the weekend for its annual

Kinderfest (Children's Festival). There would be a colorful parade, and the German Army would host the townspeople to a day of feasting, drinking, games and dancing. Everyone would be there, and I was invited.

The kids and most of the adults were dressed up for the parade, including an old mustachioed policeman in full regalia, saber by his side, wearing a *pickelhaube* (an ornate spiked helmet), portraying a legendary and historical local hero, Hein Lüth. Frank and I fell in behind the parade and marched up the hill to the army base.

A trio of soldiers was playing pop tunes and German folk songs. I was barely out of the buffet line when I heard Frank announcing me as an American rock star. The crowd applauded enthusiastically, so I sang a few pop tunes, and was more wildly applauded as I returned to my seat. There, I was besieged by friendly natives, including some dance hall managers, everyone talking at the same time. When I agreed to a booking at one place, I think someone else, nose in his schedule thought I was answering him.

Somehow, I was double-booked. I never noticed the discrepancy, because when the posters went up announcing my performances, Gasthaus Schröder's poster showed the dates, but The Koralle's poster showed I'd be there on both *Pfingstagen*. In 1964, *Pfingsten*, (Whitsun in Britain, Ireland, and celebrated by Methodists and Anglicans worldwide), fell on May 16th. In England, in 1964, Whitsun was marred by bloody riots between Mods and Rockers on its southern beaches. Had my double-booking been in England, in clubs catering to those opposing subcultures, both evolved from England's Teddy Boys, this tale might have ended badly.

1964-1974: A DECADE OF ODD TALES AND WONDERS

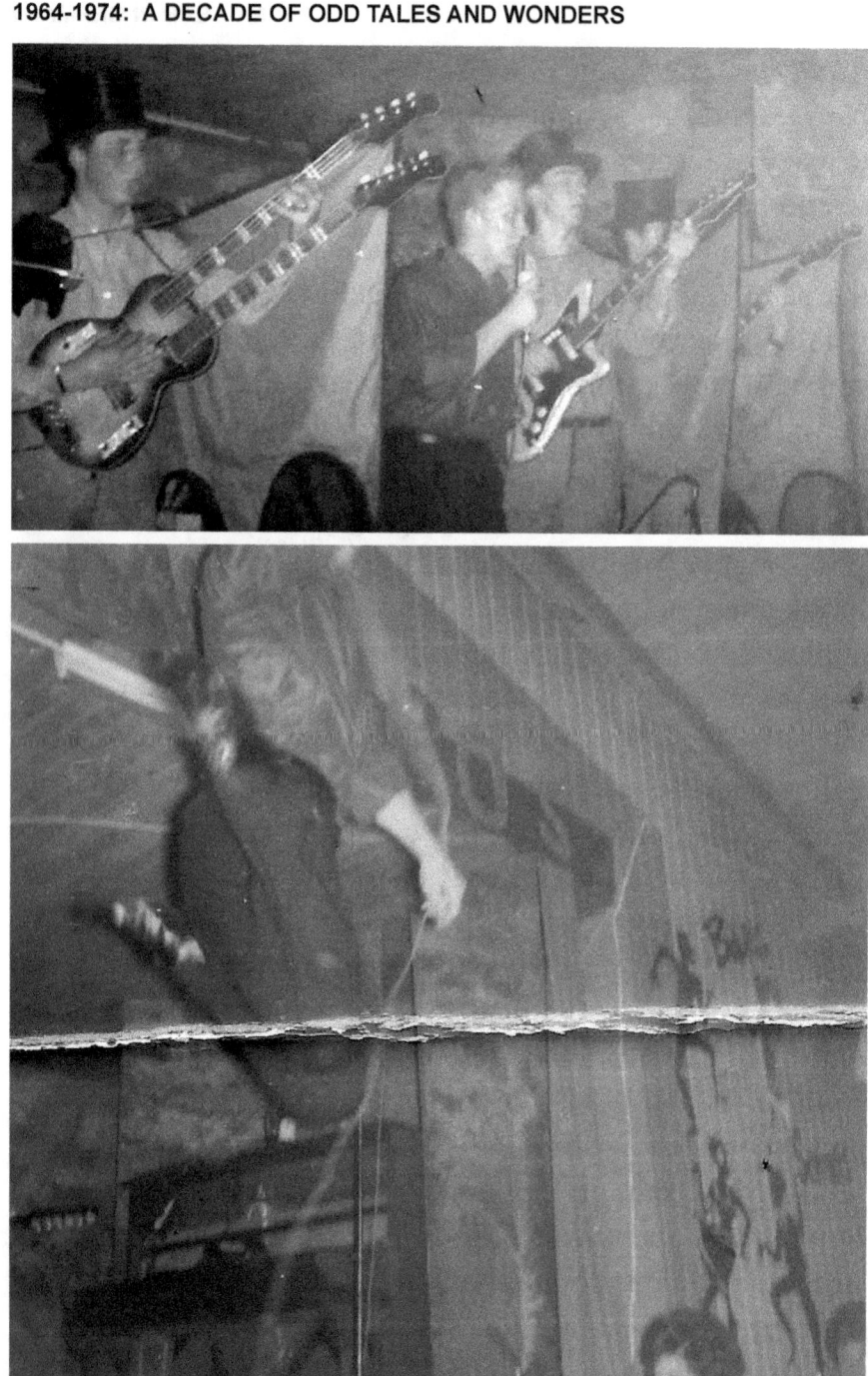

MY YEAR IN GERMANY

I regret the poor quality of the photos of me with the Vampiros at Gasthaus Schröder (left), but that leap is all I have to show how I earned my reputation as *Die Twistsensation aus U.S.A.*

Gasthaus Schröder Behrensdorf

The Vampiros

ALL-ROUND SHOW-BAND
IM RHYTHMUS DER ZEIT

Als Gaststar der Vampiros
Die Twistsensation aus USA
Teddy Pike
Sonnabend, den 16. Mai, 20.00 Uhr

KORALLE

The Nightstar's

in Plön

mit intern. Besetzung

Teddy - USA

Enriko - ITALIA

TANZ an beiden Pfingstagen

Die große Show-Band

Happily, Ernst-Günther Schröder, manager of the Beat Club in his father's Gasthaus, worked out a compromise. He drove me to my first set with The Nightstars at The Koralle in Plön, then to Behrensdorf to perform with The Vampiros, then back to Plön for a final set with The Nightstars and back to Behrensdorf for a final set with The Vampiros.

Rock promoter Werner Hingst rode with me in the back seat on that wild night. He offered to form a superband for me, and asked if I could have the best players from each band, whom would I pick?

Teddy - USA (left, holding his microphone in his right hand and facing the crowd), and Enriko Lombardi - Italia (center), perform at the crowded Koralle. The "stage" was a podium, two steps higher than the dance floor, and barely large enough for the band.

At first, I declined. My military duties had to come before the band. I could only be booked as a guest star. He readily agreed to that and more. His offer was worth considering. I didn't know if he could land the recording contracts he said he could, but it couldn't hurt to find out.

That night, during the shows, I evaluated the players in both bands, and after the final performance, told Werner who they were. He arranged for us to audition together at a hotel ballroom in Preetz. We all liked what we heard, and before I left, they named themselves "The Five Beats."

Teddy Pike - AKA *Die Twistsensation aus USA* (center), with the Vampiros at Gasthaus Schröder

1964-1974: A DECADE OF ODD TALES AND WONDERS

The Five Beats international showband

Besetzung

Teddy Pike
USA
Twist and Show Sensation

Enriko Lombardi
ITALIA
Gesang, Gitarre

Eddy Christers
Gesang, Gitarre, Klarrinetta, Baß

Charly Ross
Saxophon, Baß, Gesang

Ringo
Gesang, Schlagzeug

Chorty West
Gesang, Gitarre, Saxophon

Die Stationen dieser erfolgreichen Band waren:

Star~Palast~Kiel

Studio 62
Eckernförde

Schützenhof
Rendsburg

Demnächst auch **Star·Club**
Hamburg-St. Pauli

I agreed to appear exclusively as their guest star, whenever and wherever I could, when I was on liberty from the U.S.Navy.

As for me, I went by Teddy, my childhood nickname, because it was easier for Germans to pronounce than Travis, and it was decided I should continue to do so. Back then, I'd never heard of England's "Teddy Boys" subculture, but in those days, rock'n'roll was often linked to delinquency and danger, which is probably the biggest reason, after the music, that adolescents were drawn to it. Unbeknownst to me, my nickname, signifying youthful rebellion, may have contributed to my early widespread name recognition.

As I left that first audition, I was booed by a small crowd waiting outside the hotel. The young man who played the double-necked electric guitar and bass for The Vampiros confronted me. How could I do this? Who was I to say who could be in the band and who couldn't? Embarrassed by his anguish, I suggested he try to get together with The Nightstars, but he refused to consider it. He was one of the founders of The Vampiros. He'd be at Gasthaus Schröder to witness my downfall. He vowed the new band would be stridently rejected by fans of the Vampiros.

That Saturday night, I felt that "hole" in the pit of my stomach -- not stage fright, but guilt about cutting that young man out of his band, and his wounded expression haunted me. Never having formed a band before, I failed to consider the consequences of my agreement with Werner.

When Werner introduced The Five Beats, there were no wild cheers, just a murmur of anticipation -- perhaps even a suggestion of hostility. Both former lead singers sang before me. The music was tight, the vocals were superb, but the crowd withheld its approval. I chose to start with Ray Charles' "What'd I Say?" and signaled the band to start without me. At the last minute I leaped onto the stage and began to sing.

I kept the song going for more than 25 minutes, all the while springing, dancing, and even singling out the angry young man from the Vampiros in the audience, holding my microphone out to him, inviting him to lead the responses -- which he did -- and when I finished, the roar from the crowd was deafening. That one song completed the set and exhausted, I collapsed backstage with my heart pounding so hard I thought I might have a heart attack!

It was several minutes before I recovered enough to sit up. I left backstage to get a drink, and there stood the young man, grinning wryly, waiting for me to appear to offer me a glass of Sect (a German version of champagne). He embraced me and wished me the best of luck. He was a trained musician, and although it made him sad to admit it, he recognized superior talent when he heard it. He said The Five Beats were superb and sure to go straight to the top. It was a gracious, sincere and deeply appreciated gesture.

Gasthaus Schröder's success stemmed in large part from its sports camping grounds. The image shown (top, right), is from a postcard I bought there more than 50 years ago. Another old postcard shows its bright and comfortable dining area (center right), featuring the enormous jukebox seen between the windows on the left. The image (bottom right) is of its Great Hall today. This is the view I would have had from the stage, had I seen it empty, but I never did. When I performed there, it was always filled to capacity, the dance floor crowded with guests, and judging by the license plates, many were weekend campers from Hamburg.

MY YEAR IN GERMANY

1964-1974: A DECADE OF ODD TALES AND WONDERS

I can't be sure, but I think we played at Gasthaus Schröder through most of June, and it's possible that the first stop on what I now think of as Werner Hingst's "Northern Tour" was in Flensburg, right up at the top of the map on the German-Danish border.

Badewanne   studio 62
Eckernförde

Sensationsgastspiel

Internationale
All Round Showband

- **The five Beats**
mit den Schlagersängern und Schallplattenstars

- **Teddy Pike USA**

- **Enriko Lombardi ITALIA**

Sonnabend **4. Juli 1964** 20 Uhr

Zur Post - Kropp

Sensationsgastspiel

**Internationale
All Round Showband**

- **The
  five Beats**

  mit den Schlagersängern und Schallplattenstars

- **Teddy
  Pike USA**

- **Enriko
  Lombardi ITALIA**

Am Sonnabend - dem 11. Juli - 20 Uhr

    These posters show that we played in Eckernförde on the Baltic Sea, in the North-East corner of West Germany on the 4th of July 1964. As for Kropp, I don't remember if "Zur Post" was a Gasthaus, stand-alone nightclub, or the name of a hotel ballroom, but I do remember that everywhere we played we were well-received.

1964-1974: A DECADE OF ODD TALES AND WONDERS

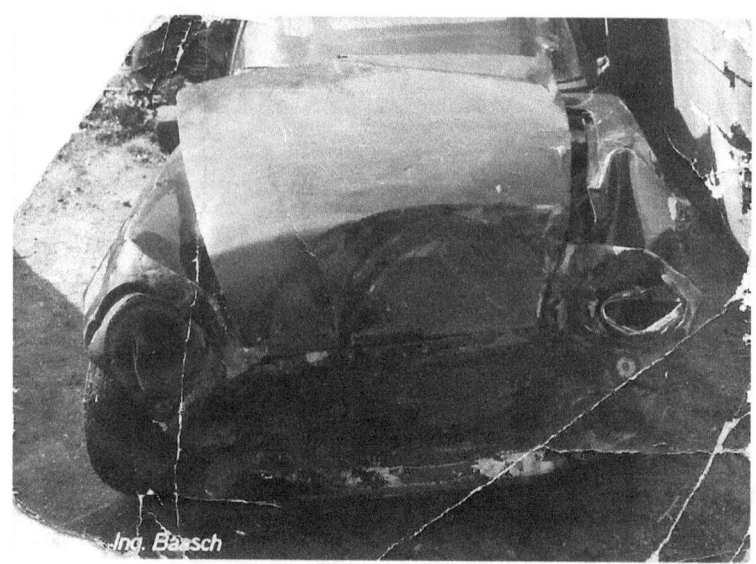

In mid-July, an armored truck skidded into my sports car. In the hospital in Preetz, I learned that in addition to cuts and bruises, I had a broken ankle, and some very unhappy vertebrae. The next day, I was transferred to the U.S. Army Hospital in Bremerhaven, and a week later, flown to the U.S. Army Hospital in Frankfurt, where my ankle was reset, put in a cast, and then I was presented with travel orders to return to Todendorf. The trip north by train took two days.

The Five Beats were booked at Gasthaus Schröder on Saturday, August 1st, so I went there for lunch to show I was back in town. I visited with the Schröders, and then sat in the dining room, listening to the jukebox, waiting for the band to arrive. Later in the afternoon, Regina and Hubert, honeymooners from Hamburg, introduced themselves and we passed the rest of the afternoon in pleasant conversation.

It was great to see the band again, and when I showed them that I could stand comfortably with my left knee on a chair, we decided that early in the evening, before the hall grew too crowded, I'd go on as a surprise guest, and sing a few songs. Word of my early appearance led to another few songs later that night. It was a real morale booster, but exhausted after that performance, I "left the building."

The next day, August 2nd, I turned 20. This card arrived, signed "wunschen Dir liebe Teddy, Regina and Hubert."

In the ensuing weeks, I hobbled through a few more guest appearances with The Five Beats, but I felt more like a curiosity than a performer. In mid-October, I was ordered to Chelsea Naval Hospital in Massachusetts for reconstructive surgery, marking the end of my year in Germany -- and my career as *Die Twistsensation aus USA*.

Happily, it was not the end for The Five Beats who went on to greater things, which suggests that I was, at least, good at spotting talent.

1964-1974: A DECADE OF ODD TALES AND WONDERS

| KIEL | Dienstag, 2. März 1965 | Seite 5 |

TRANSLATION: With banners and chanting, "The Five Beats" were celebrated when they won the band competition of the "Star-Palast" on Sunday evening with an overwhelming majority of the votes. The second and third place bands chosen by the audience -- "The Rebels" and "The Five Times" -- were also from Kiel. Altogether, over the course of several days, close to 30 bands from Lüneburg, Hamburg, Neumünster, Rendsburg, Plön and Kiel -- all part of the "Hard Beat Wave" -- competed for the grand trophy cup, which The Five Beats will have to defend again in the fall. The winners have only been together for three-quarters of a year; they used to be parts of two separate bands. The group is made up of three guitars, drums and saxophone. The "boss" is drummer Norbert Wechselbaum. So far, the two decorator apprentices, two students and the sales clerk make music "on the side." That's also how it is intended to stay for now. But who knows what the results of the demo recordings with two major Hamburg record labels, arranged for the winners by Manfred Woitalla, might portend?

MY YEAR IN GERMANY

Following is my translation of Ernst-Gunther's letter to me on page 51. He was not only the manager of the Beat Club at the family-owned Gasthaus, he was my friend.

Behrensdorf, 9 II '66

Dear Teddy,

Thank you for your lovely letter. I wondered if you were still alive, since you left Germany a year ago and this is your first letter. You write that you might come back to Germany this year, and it goes without saying that you and your brother, if he comes, can stay with us. If possible, don't come in June, July, or August, because, as you well know, that is our busiest season. Do you still drink "Screwdrivers?"

Frank, from Lütjenburg, (my auto mechanic friend), joined the (German) Navy. Our place is doing very well, especially the "Beat Club." You wouldn't recognize the dance hall anymore. We've redecorated it -- painted a silhouette of New York City on the back of the stage in day-glow colors.

A half year ago, I bought myself a Ford Mustang, but unfortunately, I totalled it when, a tree got in the way – not a truck, like your "Sunbeam."

The Five Beats have become really big around here, and twice won a Star Palace Battle of the Bands and are now Northern Germany's best Beat Band. They've signed a recording contract with Philips, and in June will appear on the TV show, "Showbands." Last week, I contributed to a newspaper article on the Five Beats and naturally, I wrote about Teddy Pike USA, too. I'll send you the article in the next post. *[Sadly, I never received it.]*

Last Saturday we featured a showband from Ireland called the "Mary Macs" -- a ten piece ensemble.

Werner (Hingst) now has a "Star Palace" dance club in Lüneburg, and never shows himself here anymore. Maybe he's become conceited since he bought an American Ford -- what kind I don't know, but it's very large and I think it's called a "Thunderbird," or something like that.

The Five Beats now have a singer with really good voice and on the 12th of February, played in Hamburg, Pinneberg in the "Bali-Beat-Club," and were paid 800 DM ($200) for the one night. You'd be surprised, but they now earn that kind of money.

Please send me a record or audio tape of you and write back soon if you are interested in meeting with me in America, and if later you need a manager for Germany, know that E.G. (Ernst-Gunther) can do that really well for you.

Greetings from Papa, my mother, and siblings.

Your friend. Ernst-Gunther

I've included a copy of Ernst-Gunther's letter for my German fans and German language students. I found it difficult to read, but I can't say if it's his penmanship or German Handschrift that made it so.

Behrensdorf, 9.II.66

Lieber Teddy!

Vielen Dank für Deinen lieben Brief, ich habe schon gedacht Du lebst garnicht mehr, denn schon 1 Jahr aus Deutschland und jetzt erst einen Brief. Du schreibst das Du in diesem Jahr nach Deutschland kommen wirst. Selbstverständlich kannst Du bei uns wohnen auch wenn Dein Bruder dabei ist. Wenn es geht komme nicht im Juni, Juli, August, denn denn haben wir ja Saison aber das weißt Du ja. Trinkst Du noch immer „Schraubenzieher"? Frank aus Sütjenburg ist jetzt bei der Marine. Unser Lokal läuft jetzt sehr gut überhaupt der

1964-1974: A DECADE OF ODD TALES AND WONDERS

II

"Beat-Club" Du wirst unseren Saal überhaupt nicht wiedererkennen. Dein alter Traum ist in Erfüllung gegangen auf der Rückseite unserer Bühne ist die Silhoutte von "New York" in Leuchtfarbe gemalt worden. Vor einem ½ Jahr hatte ich mir einen "Ford-Mustang" gekauft den ich leider Totalschaden gefahren habe, da stand einfach ein Baum im Weg, nicht ein Lastwagen wie bei Deinem "Sunbeam". Die "Five Beats" sind hier ganz groß herausgekommen und haben schon zwei mal einen Wettbewerb im "Star-Palast" gewonnen und sind jetzt Norddeutschlands beste Beat-Band. Die "Five Beats" haben jetzt einen Schalplattenvertrag mit Philips und

III

werden im Juni in der Fernsehsendung „Schaubude" auftreten. Letzte Woche hatte ich ein Artikel für eine Zeitung aufgesetzt wie die „Five Beats" entstanden sind und natürlich habe ich auch von Teddy Pike USA geschrieben, ich werde Dir diesen Artikel demnächst per Post zusenden. Am letzten Sonnabend spielten bei uns eine Show Band aus Irland „The Mary-Macs" in einer 10 Mann Besetzung. Werner hat jetzt ein Dance-Club vom „Star-Palast" in Lüneburg er läßt sich hier überhaupt nicht mehr sehen vielleicht ist ein Eingebildet geworden er fährt jetzt einen amerikanischen Ford welche Type weiß ich nicht aber er ist ziemlich groß

1964-1974: A DECADE OF ODD TALES AND WONDERS

ich glaube er heißt Thunderbird oder so ähnlich. Die „Five Beats" haben jetzt einen Sänger der hat eine unheimlich gute Stimme am 12. Febr. spielen sie in Hamburg-Pinneberg im Bali-Beat-Club die Gage für einen Abend 800,- DM - 200 Dollar. Du wirst staunen aber so viel verdienen die Five Beats jetzt. Schicke mir doch bitte eine Schallplatte oder ein Tonband von Dir und schreibe bitte gleich wieder denn Du weißt ja mich interessiert sehr was du so in Amerika treibst und wenn Du später einen Manager für Germany brauchst wirst Du ja E.G. kann sehr gut handeln und kennt sich überall aus. Schönen Gruß von „Papa" von mein Mutter u. a. anderen Geschwister. Dein Freund Ernst-Günther

FORTY SONGS AND A MOVIE

The infinitely kind Red Cross volunteers who bring books and magazines to servicemen on military hospital wards, brought me a guitar to help pass the time. I was not much of a player, but with nothing else to do, I improved quickly. I wrote "End of Summer," hoping, one day, to perform it in person for my German friends.

Word of that composition got around the ward and one day, a Red Cross volunteer asked if I would play it for her. I don't know if the song suddenly became more personal, or if it was just that I'd been asked to sing, that got to me. Whatever, I choked up half way through and couldn't finish. She told me not to fret. It was beautiful and she was sure Lorelei (the girl's name mentioned in the lyrics), would wait for me. I couldn't tell her there was no Lorelei. I took the name from Heinrich Heine's poem about the siren whose beauty so bewitched sailors that they failed to mind the rocks and were lost.

It's a sad song, but entirely appropriate for me at that time. The bright future I had glimpsed seemed lost. The song promises a reunion for the lovers, but a reunion for them seemed as unlikely as a comeback for me, even as Red Cross volunteers wheeled me from ward to ward to entertain other servicemen, many worse off than me.

The Five Beats inherited skits from the Vampiros, so thinking I might someday go back to Germany, I wrote "Till the End" for their Vampire show and "Ali Baba Ben Jones"

1964-1974: A DECADE OF ODD TALES AND WONDERS

for their Bedouin show and sang them on the wards. I wrote "Land of the Giant Bugs" more for the G.I.s, some of whom swore they'd seen the giant bugs in the jungles of Vietnam.

Early in 1965, at Lake Avenue on a weekend pass from the hospital, I was surprised by a visit from some high school kids. One was the younger brother of the drummer from The Jesters, now playing drums for his own band, The New Jesters. There was to be a talent competition at their high school where a rival band with a singer would perform. The New Jesters wanted me, the "legend" from the original Jesters, to sing with them, even though it would disqualify them from the competition.

I was flattered, but barely able to get around on crutches. They promised to provide a stool for me and my father volunteered to drive me there. One had brought an acoustic guitar, so we ran through The Everly Brothers hit, "Cryin' in the Rain," Elvis Presley's "Heartbreak Hotel" and, of course, the Ray Charles hit, "What'd I Say?"

On the big day, I hobbled onto stage and clinging to microphone stands, sang the songs. That night's high school audience reaction was as great as any I'd experienced with the Five Beats. Some of the audience leaped up out of their seats. The New Jesters were beyond ecstatic.

In a 1966 clipping from *The Boston Traveler*, on the day *Feelin' Good* premiered at the Downtown Paramount Theater in Boston, my father is quoted as saying that he "... had in mind doing another short film, somewhat the same as *Demo Derby*, a spontaneous exposition of the musical explosion which has swept the country." He wanted to do it in what he calls, sort of giggling, *"Cinéma vérité."*

" 'A father never listens to his kids,' said this father of five, 'so I really didn't know how talented he was. Then, when he was back at Chelsea Naval Hospital, I went to Natick High School to hear him.

" 'There he was with his leg in a cast, and 1200 or 1400 kids came alive when he sang. I said to myself--is that my kid up there making all this. It was a revelation that he could turn them on like this.

" 'THAT'S WHEN WE DECIDED'

"So Mr. Pike, took some of the 30 or 40 songs Travis had written down to New York to the 'tunesmiths,' and 'they said they were good. That's when we decided to make *Feelin' Good.'* "

That long-ago newspaper interview, helps me understand my father's approach to the movie, and why he began shooting at the First Massachusetts Jaycees Battle of the Bands in Weymouth, Massachusetts. *Cinéma vérité* "truthful cinema" is based on the notion that pictures don't lie (a statement today especially insupportable with the incredible advances in cinematography and special effects, which may explain why my father giggled when he said it). Taken less literally, it may be applied to the style of filmmaking employed by Richard Lester in *Hard Day's Night*, which captured spontaneous reactions and activities surrounding the Beatles, and conveyed a combination of rollicking tongue-in-cheek action, that appealed to non-fans (allowing them to continue to feel "above it all"), and simultaneously, brilliantly provided their millions of fans with intimate access to their idols.

1964-1974: A DECADE OF ODD TALES AND WONDERS

With a working title of *Rock Around the Hub*, filming commenced on a dismal day in 1965.

The Pike Productions crews had already proven themselves up to the task when they shot *Demo Derby* at night in Norwood Arena, so rain or shine, they were ready to roll, and shooting coverage of the First Jaycees Battle of the Bands was not only historical, but could provide thousands of feet of documentary-style, widescreen, color footage of excited crowds that could later be cut into the narrative film, (unless no crowds appeared and the event was rained out).

Beloved Bostonian, Arthur Fiedler, long-time conductor of the Boston Pops symphony orchestra, called upon to judge the event, had sense enough to stay in out of the rain, but resigned to the task at hand, doggedly kept his ears tuned to the musical performances nearby.

When the rain finally stopped, the sky remained overcast, and parts of the fairground remained a quagmire, but the hearty, early concertgoers rushed to line up at the solitary phone booth to dial their friends and tell them to come to the event. Today, it may be hard for youngsters to imagine their grandparents, (or parents), rushing to get in line outside a phone booth, but cell phones were still far in the future, and if the call was important, there was simply no alternative.

1964-1974: A DECADE OF ODD TALES AND WONDERS

The stands at the Weymouth Fairgrounds began to fill.

The sheltered Pike Productions crews, lights and cameras, came out from under cover and went to work. Here, my younger brother, Gregory, assists. He's the smiling guy on the left, helping to remove the tarp. The man in the center wearing the tailed Tam O'Shanter, is cinematographer Angus MacAskill, who generally went by his middle name, Ken. Behind him, on the right, is another Pike Productions cameraman, Paul Holzwarth.

1964-1974: A DECADE OF ODD TALES AND WONDERS

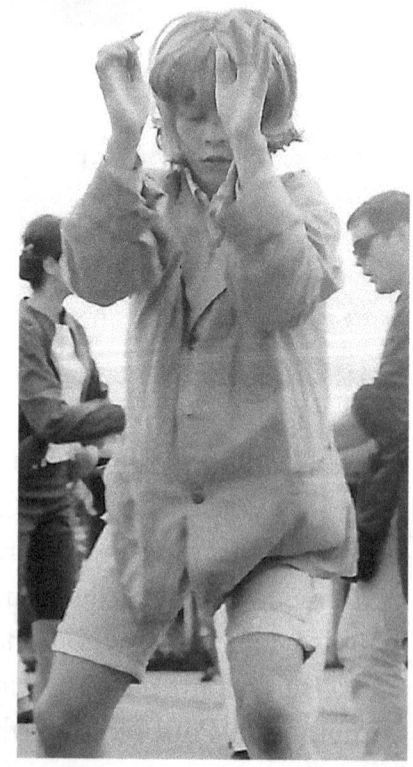

My father, James A. Pike (shown with the megaphone, above) produced, directed and co-wrote *Feelin' Good*. In this photo, he's targeting the most energetic dancers for cinematographer Ken MacAskill, and suggesting angles that should work best in the finished film. One lucky young lady who caught his filmmaker's eye was 11-year-old Judi Reeve, a dancing dynamo whose moves landed her a supporting role as Judi, the younger sister of my movie girlfriend, Karen.

FORTY SONGS AND A MOVIE

The Monclairs' first prize performance at the Battle of the Bands won them their appearances in the movie, and photos like this provided a reference for recreating the stage in the studio.

I didn't remember being there, but *cinéma vérité* proves I was.

1964-1974: A DECADE OF ODD TALES AND WONDERS

I arrived for treatment at Chelsea Naval Hospital on 23 October 1964 and cleared for limited duty, was transferred to Newport Naval Station in Rhode Island on 6 August 1965 to await further orders, which means that while I was undergoing physical therapy, I had plenty of time to write a number of novelty songs to entertain the hospitalized servicemen.

One liberty weekend, I met Arthur Korb, from the start personable, enthusiastic, and eager to share his knowledge and experience. Our first assignment was to run through a number of my songs, and prepare lead sheets. He did all the musical notation and I supplied the lyrics.

Arthur Korb's lead sheets for some songs I wrote for *Feelin' Good*.

I knew nothing about running the songs past the New York "tunesmiths" until I read the article in the newspaper, but Arthur could easily have played them on the big grand piano in the living room at the house on Lake Avenue, and my father might as easily have recorded demos of them.

My first official assignment from Pike Productions came in mid-June 1965. I was to supervise the recordings of the music tracks to my songs by Oedipus and His Mothers, (aka The Brattle Street East). The songs had been selected by my father, arranged by Arthur Korb, and the band had already rehearsed them when I met them for the first time for a Saturday recording session at ACE Recording Studios in downtown Boston. It was my first visit to the recording studio, too. As for me supervising the session, Arthur was definitely, and properly in charge of that. It seems to me, all I did was to say hello to everyone, and confirm that each song was in a comfortable key for me. I remember asking Arthur if there would be a saxophone on the final recording, but my father, on the control room talkback, quickly killed that idea. Time was money and the clock was ticking.

My next movie assignment was two days of off-camera recording in mid-July, while I was still at Chelsea. My father died in 2012, and when his estate was settled, I received a stack of *Feelin' Good* production stills, including these showing me performing some function at an orchestra session conducted by Arthur Korb. Could we have been recording Arthur's score so early in the process? I recognize ACE Recording Studios, and Arthur is definitely conducting, and I can think of no other recordings for *Feelin' Good* that required so large an orchestra.

1964-1974: A DECADE OF ODD TALES AND WONDERS

In this photo, Arthur is the confident bespectacled gentleman on the left. I'm the intense brute on the right.

These photos cannot accurately reveal the entire orchestra, each section properly miked and baffled, all seeing the music for the first time and nailing it in one rehearsal and a few takes. Yes, there were four-track Scully's, and some solos were recorded after the master, but to say the music in that room was brilliant is an understatement.

FORTY SONGS AND A MOVIE

I'm letting the photos tell their tale (since I'm fuzzy on the details, anyway), but to me, these pictures are worth thousands of words, (and judging by the size of the orchestra, thousands of dollars, too). Considering the evidence, I suggest the first of the two days in the studio was for the recording session, and the second was probably the mix.

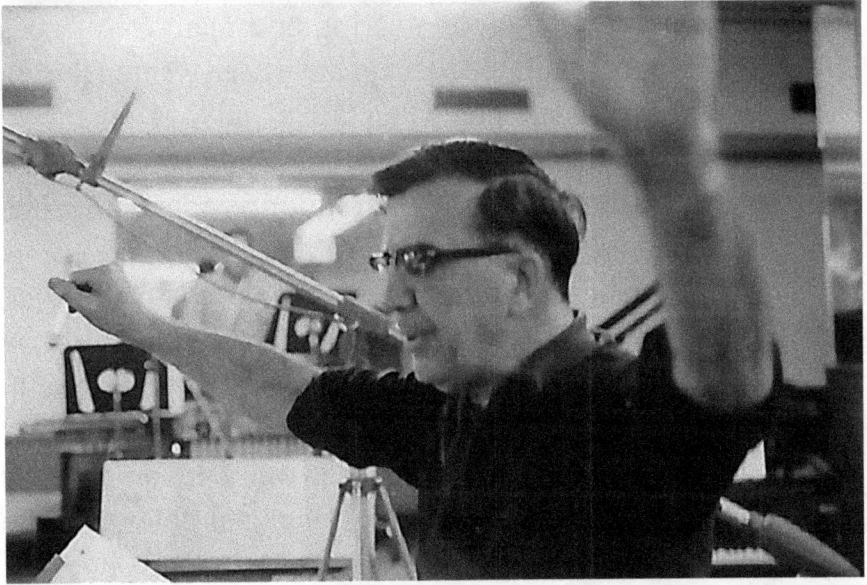

Online, you'll learn that Arthur Korb (June 21, 1909 – March 16, 2003) was an American songwriter of popular music, born in Boston, Massachusetts, attended Harvard University, earned his Bachelor of Arts and Master of Arts degrees there and joined ASCAP in 1953. But I had the joy of working with him, and I'd like to add that Arthur was also a wise, talented, gracious, and caring human being.

1964-1974: A DECADE OF ODD TALES AND WONDERS

From the Naval Station at Newport, Rhode Island, I'd have to allow an hour and a half to two hours to get up to Boston, and my shooting schedule was adjusted accordingly. Fortunately, my liberty weekends were unaffected.

When the Montclairs won the Battle of the Bands, my father asked me to compose two original songs for them, for the movie. I can't find a date for the 1965 Battle of the Bands, but I have a record of going up to Boston on a weekend toward the end of August to rehearse the Montclairs, and a week later, going back to supervise their recording session. I don't remember the session, but the names on the call sheet were Benny Melanson, Tom Cooley, Johnny Ferro, Stephen Cooper, Walter Cooper and Brian Houston.

I never saw a complete script, and many sequences shot when I was unavailable seem to have been written during the week, shot on weekends when talent and locations were available, and cobbled together in the editing room. Maybe shooting what's available, and then shooting connecting bits for continuity, is just another form of *cinéma vérité*.

I was on limited duty when I reported to the Flag Administrative Unit of the Commander-In Chief of the Atlantic Fleet in Norfolk, Virginia on September 12th. Thereafter, in September, October, and November, I was rarely flown up to Boston, and then only to do interior scenes as autumn set in, the leaves changed color and the days grew colder. Boston was outside the mileage allowed for weekend liberty, but with a round-trip airline ticket, it was allowed. Then, in January 1966, I stopped taking pain killers and was admitted to Portsmouth Naval Hospital, Virginia, for further evaluation.

In the hospital, I had a lot of time to myself between physical therapy sessions, so I wrote more songs and Red Cross volunteers soon had me entertaining the sick and wounded on the other wards. One dear lady asked me if I'd be willing to play on the locked psychiatric ward. She explained that they might not be demonstrative, but they would really appreciate it, and went on to say I'd be in no danger. The most dangerous patients in the ward were sedated and there was a corpsman on duty at all times. In gratitude for all the kindness the Red Cross had shown me, I said I'd be happy to do so.

I limped noticeably, but was otherwise ambulatory. The Red Cross lady introduced me to the 2nd Class Hospital Corpsman on duty, and he let me in. A chair had been placed in the middle of the room for me, but instead of sitting, I chose to rest my left knee on the seat, so I could turn from time to time to include all the patients in my presentation. I admit to being a bit startled when the Red Cross lady guide and hospital corpsman left and locked the door behind them, so I was delighted to see the corpsman reappear inside the caged-in area of the ward.

As for the patients, one wandered about, gesturing and making unintelligible noises, but most seemed catatonic as they lay in their racks, staring into space.

I must have played and sang for a half hour or more, much to the delight of the corpsman, but with little or no positive reinforcement from the patients. None at all, unless I count the wandering babbler, who continued to wander and babble throughout, louder when I sang, and softer when I stopped. That might count as a reaction.

1964-1974: A DECADE OF ODD TALES AND WONDERS

Bill Somers, the corpsman on duty was married and lived off-base, but had to stay in the barracks when he drew the duty. He asked me to come down to his barracks that evening, to play a few songs for the corpsmen, and promised to take me to his place for the weekend to meet his wife and daughter, and enjoy a home-cooked steak dinner. I wasn't flying to Boston, so I happily took him up on his offer.

His wife, Judy, was bright and welcoming, his daughter Lisa, was a well-behaved toddler. I played songs and told them stories, but the steak Judy served was so well-done it could have gone straight from her oven grill to a cobbler's shop. After dinner, ever so politely, I asked to return the favor, and cook dinner for them, some time. They said yes, and that was the beginning of a beautiful friendship.

This is probably a good place to make another hospital related observation. In order to return to limited duty, I had been prescribed a regimen of pain killers that were less effective in managing my pain than in interfering with the performance of my duties. I suspect they are also largely responsible for my uncharacteristic fuzzy-mindedness, revealed to some extent by my current inability to clearly remember much about the making of *Feelin' Good*.

I know I wasn't there when the Montclairs' "Battle of the Bands" sequence was recreated in the Pike Productions sound stage, but it would necessarily be after the songs were recorded. Their performance of "Feelin' Good," a song I wrote for them, combined with their exciting on-stage presentation, resulted in the working title, *Rock Around the Hub* being changed to *Feelin' Good*.

The Montclairs on the "Battle of the Bands" stage at Pike Productions.

1964-1974: A DECADE OF ODD TALES AND WONDERS

Cameraman Paul Holzwarth reads the light meter as James A. Pike, president of Pike Productions (and producer/director of *Feelin' Good*), sets up the closeup of the Montclairs' singers.

When I was overseas, Pike Productions had moved its facilities out of Lake Avenue and into a large, converted movie theater in Watertown Square. It's auditorium had been converted into a sound stage, and the main offices, animation stage, screening room, and editing facilities were located in the basement.

Shooting on sound stages allows a filmmaker to interrupt the action, move into the set for closeups, control ambient sound, and avoid the undependability of natural weather phenomena by substituting controlled special effects, as in the foggy nightmare sequence on the next page.

FORTY SONGS AND A MOVIE

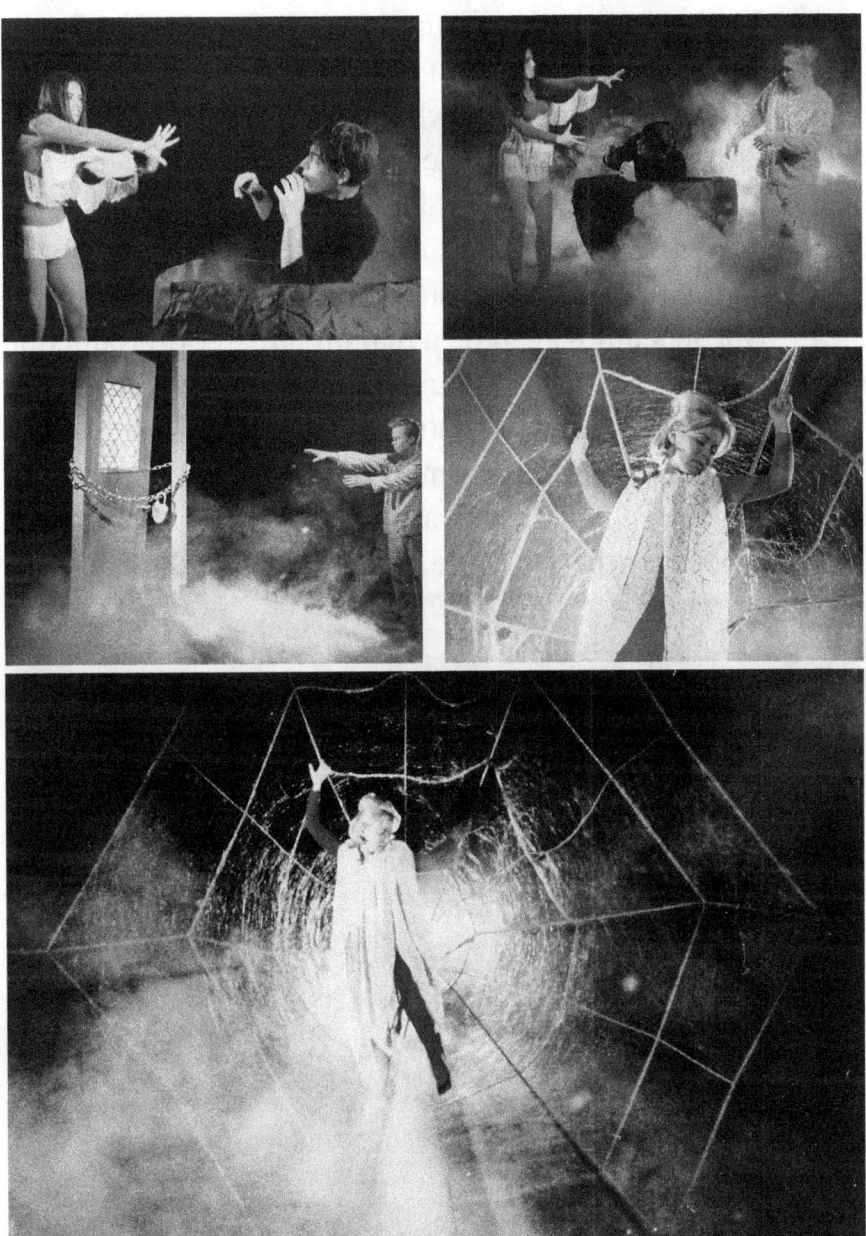

Bambi's bunny buddy, Thumper, said, "If you can't say something nice, don't say nothing at all." I've always considered that good advice, especially when asked about this nightmare sequence, shot on the sound stage at Pike Productions in Watertown Square.

1964-1974: A DECADE OF ODD TALES AND WONDERS

You've seen in the photos from the Battle of the Bands what can happen when you shoot in outdoor locations, especially in New England, where the weather is constantly subject to change, no matter what the forecasters may predict. Fortunately, those sudden changes sometimes work in your favor. At the Battle of the Bands, it did finally stop raining, and the show was able to go on.

But scheduling can be a real nightmare. If production is postponed by an act of nature, unless you have cover sets where you can continue shooting out of the weather, you're just out of luck. Location rentals, talent and crews are paid according to the call sheet, rain or shine. Fortunately, the weather held for these picture vehicle location shoots.

When, in the middle of nowhere, Danny (Ron Stafford), tries to put some moves on Elaine (Leslie Burnham), she furiously gets out of his car, preferring to walk rather than ride with him.

But it's a long way home from nowhere, so I have to rescue her, and would you believe, I run out of gas, and Danny finally rescues both of us? My girlfriend, Karen (Patricia Ewing), didn't believe it either.

1964-1974: A DECADE OF ODD TALES AND WONDERS

With a magnifying glass, see cameraman Ken MacAskill, on a pontoon forward of the bow rail, my father, just inside it, his right ear obscured by the camera lens, soundman Bob Smith back to the bow rail, and my mother, Elsie, hunkered down between the benches, operating the boom mike. Costar Patricia Ewing and I sit two benches forward of the swan, and the lad with the captain's hat, peddles the boat around the pond.

In the sequence shot in The Loft coffeehouse on Charles Street in Boston, my younger brother Gregory was the camera assistant (top center). My father, directing, crouches by the camera.

Filming interiors on location is difficult, too. All the gear, including costumes, makeup and hair stylists need space to do their jobs, and few locations have adequate electricity to power the lights, camera, and sound gear, so generators and generator operators may also be required. The Loft provided coffee and snacks, which saved the space normally set aside for a craft services table.

Jennie Rider (above), performs her original song, "Ride the Rainbow." In the coffeehouse crowd shot (below), the handsome guy all the way over on the right is my older brother Jimmy.

    I wasn't in town when this sequence was shot, so I didn't know my older brother (right), was in it until I saw this still. I don't remember seeing him in the movie, so maybe this shot ended up on the cutting room floor.

According to an article in the May 29th, 1966 *Boston Sunday Globe*, the English singer-songwriter's real name was Brenda Nockolds, so I assume Jennie Rider was the name of her character, created by Pike Productions for the role in *Feelin' Good*.

I'm going to guess that craft services were provided for the Montclairs' pizzeria sequence by the pizzeria, and just as well, because with all the equipment, cast, and crew, there would be little room for a snack table. In addition to prepping the location for shooting, the action has to be blocked and rehearsed before shooting begins. Typically, crews report to locations early in the morning, sometimes before dawn, but with all the prep required, few productions can start rolling sound and picture much before lunch time.

1964-1974: A DECADE OF ODD TALES AND WONDERS

In 1966, violent opposition to the Civil Rights Movement caused some Southern theater owners to refuse to book *Feelin' Good,* for fear they might be held liable for rioting incited by this scene.

The title made it imperative that the movie leave the audience *Feelin' Good,* so Ted (me), and my sweetheart, Karen (played by Patricia Ewing), are finally back together, and on our way to the final concert.

Paul Holzwarth operates one of the cameras for the grand finale exterior location sequence filmed on the Charles River Esplanade.

In this shot, I'm performing "Watch Out Woman" on stage with the Brattle Street East (left to right), Guitarist Dave Connor, Drummer Rob Cavicchio, Bass player Terry Ney, and Guitarist Frank Werner. The four other significant characters in the foreground are my screen girlfriend, Karen, dancing in front, one "row" back, Danny, dancing with Elaine, (in black, wearing a bandana), and between Karen and Elaine, Judi (played by Judi Reeve), hugging herself to stay warm. The blustery day was great for sailboats, but more than a little chilly for the cast.

The next time we were all together, was at the world premiere of *Feelin' Good* at *The Paramount Theater* in downtown Boston, with a marching band, searchlights, and motorcade complete with a motorcycle police escort.

1964-1974: A DECADE OF ODD TALES AND WONDERS

(above) Patricia Ewing, Judi Reeve and I arrive at the premiere. (below) My father ushers us through the crowd and into the theater.

Finally, on the big night, with all the excitement in the air, Filmmaker and Pike Productions president, James A. Pike, accompanied his stars, Patricia Ewing and me, on our way into the downtown Boston Paramount Theater for the 26 October 1966 world premiere of the first Boston-based, feature-length, widescreen, color, musically inspired, theatrical motion picture, *Feelin' Good*.

1964-1974: A DECADE OF ODD TALES AND WONDERS

I have no photos to prove it, but my corpsman friend, Bill Somers, upon being honorably discharged from the Navy, moved to Boston with his wife, Judy, and daughter, Lisa, and were here in time to settle in, get a babysitter for Lisa, and attend the World Premiere.

COFFEEHOUSES, CONCERTS, CAMPUSES, AND CLUBS

In June 1966, honorably discharged, I flew home to Boston, Massachusetts, a huge college town with a combined enrollment of over 150,000 students from Boston University, Harvard, Northeastern, Boston College, MIT, University of Massachusetts, Suffolk University, Tufts, and the Bunker Hill Community College. Depending on your preference, according to both the contemporary mainstream and underground press, that year, our "best and brightest" burned their draft cards, exploited draft deferments by milking four-year college degrees into six-year engagements, in spite of (or because of), the "enlightenment" achieved through liberal undergraduate use of "consciousness enhancing" drugs.

My own views were necessarily subjective, and I did my best to avoid the vilification disguised as political discourse, but I'm the guy who preferred pain to drug-induced relief. In "Sing a Song of Blues," a more recent effort recorded on the *Reconstructed Coffeehouse Blues* CD, I attempted to recapture and express my personal feelings of alienation, shared by so many returning veterans today. What the hell had happened to the America I served while I was in the Navy? Small wonder I preferred the company of Spooky and the ducks (not a rock ensemble, but my faithful English Setter and the ducks that followed my dinghy, hoping for bread crumbs as I rowed around the lake across the street from my father's house in Newton Centre).

I had put aside money earned from being in *Feelin' Good*, so I bought the tempera paint, brushes, and heavy paper I'd need to illustrate *The Red-backed, Scaly, Black-bellied, Tusked, Bat-winged Dragon*. I planned to complete a prose version to submit to book publishers, but work was going slowly, money was going fast, and time was running out. I'd been told that my years in the Navy entitled me to unemployment, but the Commonwealth of Massachusetts Division of Employment Security disagreed. I'd listed myself as a writer and illustrator in my application, and was informed that, as such, I was not unemployed, but self-employed and therefore, ineligible. If that was so, I countered, since I hadn't any income from it, why couldn't I just fire myself and collect on my Navy unemployment, but to no avail. I had been classified as self-employed, and the next in line had already been called.

I think I spent the rest of that day out on the lake, hostile thoughts fueling my sense of outrage at the perceived injustice, and only returned to shore when Spooky began shivering in the cold.

In September 1966, the city was bursting at the seams with college students, some holding anti-war rallies to indoctrinate the freshman class, spewing hatred of the military-industrial complex, the establishment, and proudly inciting everyone within earshot to join in civil disobedience. I was becoming withdrawn and increasingly hostile, angered by what I perceived to be anti-American rhetoric.

Then Ron Stafford ("Danny" in *Feelin' Good*), dropped by to ask if I had any news on when the movie would be released. I didn't. He'd spent the summer on Cape

Cod, and when he asked me what I'd been doing, I showed him some of my illustrations and told him about boating with the dog and the ducks.

He invited me to go with him to a Hoot Night. "Hoot," I learned, was short for "Hootenanny," a jam session for folksingers (and a TV variety show on ABC in 1963 and 1964, featuring popular folk music acts). I asked him what made him think I'd be interested in going to a Hoot Night.

Evil sorcerer, Akimera, and Gump-Gump, his dragon accomplice.

"Women," he said. "Bring your guitar."

That night, we went to The Loft, the tiny coffeehouse in downtown Boston that I later learned was also featured in *Feelin' Good.* Everywhere I looked there were young ladies in mohair sweaters, their long, straight hair in ponytails held in place with sticks and bits of leather, wearing heavy "Peace Symbol" medallions on chains hanging around their necks that effectively helped their sweaters hold their shape. They were packed in like sardines, all the way up the stairs, guitars in hand. I had no choice but to squeeze in among them. There were probably some guys there, too, but I really didn't notice.

When it was finally my turn to go on, I began by telling the crowd I didn't know where all the flowers went. I didn't take them. And I had no idea what was blowing in the wind, but I was pretty sure I was allergic to it. And as for Michael, I suggested we set up a fund to buy him an Evinrude outboard, because it was obvious he'd never get to shore by rowing. The crowd laughed. I played some original tunes, won the $15 prize, and was reintroduced to the world beyond the dinghy, the dog and the ducks.

I suspect all the rooms I played in the sixties are gone now, but back then, coffeehouses were all the rage with the college crowd, many of whom were too young to drink liquor. The Loft and The Turk's Head in the heart of Boston's fashionable Back Bay, and The Unicorn Coffee House on Boylston Street all flourished, as did King Arthur's in Boston's "Combat Zone," a saloon, styled "a coffeehouse with a liquor license" by its owner, Mark Edwards.

Boston is "The Hub" of New England, and a big-time liberty port. The Combat Zone is the name given to its entertainment district by the locals. In the sixties, it featured palatial theaters, bars, restaurants, and strip clubs that catered to the large numbers of uniformed servicemen, who prowled its streets, making it appear like a neon-lit combat staging area. Dope dealers, prostitutes, and pimps plied their trades in the side streets and alleys, requiring an enhanced presence of both military and local police.

Mark Edwards had difficulties booking talent for King Arthur's. Folk singers' repertoires generally featured a large number of protest songs, not likely to be popular with G.I.s. I had been entertaining troops since 1964, so when Mark heard me on that first night at The Loft, he suggested I could consider King Arthur's my homeroom. On weekends, if I wasn't booked elsewhere, he hoped I'd

The Knight's Marching Song, 1966, Watercolor, once displayed at The Sword in the Stone coffeehouse, now in my daughter, Lisa's collection.

consider hosting Hoot Nights for him, for which I'd be paid, (guest performers were not paid). I agonized for two, three, -- maybe even four seconds before I agreed, and in short order, Boston's Combat Zone became my "comfort zone."

It was a perfect arrangement. Working for Mark, I could continue to work on the illustrations for *The Redbacked, Scaly, Black-bellied, Tusked, Bat-winged Dragon* during the day, and earn money almost any night I needed money for art supplies.

My repertoire included my original songs "End of Summer," "Ali Baba Ben Jones," "Land of the Giant Bugs,"

"Till the End," two of the ten songs I wrote for *Feelin' Good*, "I Beg Your Pardon" and "Don't Hurt Me Again," and some popular folk songs, especially "The Cat Came Back," and The Kingston Trio's "Charlie on the MTA," which always went over big with Boston crowds.

One night, early on, Danny Gravas showed up with his guitar at King Arthur's, so I put him on. I don't remember what he played, but he was head and shoulders above all the others that night. His repertoire was unique, and he stayed around to hear me perform. My account of that first night is apocryphal. The incident I now describe may have come on a second or subsequent night, but it is absolutely true, and happened early in our on-stage musical collaborations, none of which were ever rehearsed.

I was on the podium, playing the intro to my version of "House of the Rising Sun," and as I did, Danny rose, held up his guitar and with a nod asked to join me. I'd heard him earlier, so with an answering nod, I bid him come on up. He did, guitar, chair and all, as I played a second intro, and before I'd completed it, he'd joined in, picking along, but with the addition of a descending bass line that introduced an element of spine-tingling suspense and passion to the piece. My version of "House of the Rising Sun" was mostly ad-lib, based on a pre-Animals folk version, the story of a young girl, ostensibly my sister, lured into drugs and degradation by the pimp owner of that notorious house of ill repute.

With Danny picking, I switched over to strumming, softly, then more loudly as my tale unfolded. Finally, as I was forcibly removing my drugged sister from the premises, the pimp owner confronted me and . . .

"I shot that no 'count bad man,
Shot him clean through the head,
And he lay there in a pool of bad man blood
Yeah, I left that bad man dead."

I've modified the lyrics I sang only slightly, but the verse above is from that night's ad-lib, captured on a mini reel-to-reel tape recorder running at ridiculously low speed.

At the end of the song, the stunned audience reaction was tremendous (as coffeehouses go), which is to say, most sat quietly and clapped, but a few actually rose to applaud, and I think we heard a few loud whistles, too. Of course, we were in the Combat Zone, in a venue with a liquor license, on a liberty weekend for military personnel assigned to ships or shore installations nearby, which may have contributed to that enthusiastic approval.

I was not the first to recognize Danny's talent. He was a professional, signed by a powerhouse New York agency with a contract to record an album with 20th Century Fox in 1964, when he was sidelined by an auto accident that prevented him from meeting his contractural obligation. When I met him, in 1966, he was pursuing an advanced degree in Education at Boston University.

Danny Gravas (1963)
General Artists Corporation
New York City, New York

Danny was ex-Navy. He'd enlisted in 1959 and was a coxswain on an Assault Boat

1964-1974: A DECADE OF ODD TALES AND WONDERS

in support of the SeaBees in Da Nang when he was badly shot up during a landing operation, air-lifted to Mannheim, Germany, for emergency treatment, stabilized, and further transferred to that same Portsmouth Naval Hospital in Virginia where I had been sent for physical therapy from Fleet Headquarters in Norfolk. Both Navy veterans, he and I were among the most prominent "folk artists" in Boston's Combat Zone until that day Mark Edwards called to say King Arthur's had lost its liquor license to urban renewal. Mark wanted me to know that he was buying the Turk's Head on Charles Street, planned to redecorate it and reopen as The Sword in the Stone, and hoped I'd continue to perform for him there.

And here's another revision to my life's story, based on my recent conversation with Danny. I'd never been to the Turk's Head. The only Charles Street coffeehouse I'd played until then, was The Loft, so when I next heard from Mark, telling me that he was open, and would love to display some of my *Red-backed, Scaly, Black-bellied, Tusked, Bat-winged Dragon* artwork on his walls, I packed up my watercolors and brought them with me to the new Sword in the Stone, believing it to be the redecorated Turk's Head.

But Danny assures me that although the Turk's Head was sold, it was not sold to Mark, and under its new ownership, continued as the Turk's Head for some time. And if anybody should know, it's Danny Gravas, First President of the Folk Guild of Boston, Massachusetts. His daughter, Natalie, sent me the inner page from *Broadside,* a Boston-published coffeehouse-oriented printout that took its name from the propaganda leaflets handed out by both sides during the American Revolution.

Sword in the Stone

May   523-9168

F	5	Bill Madison
Sa	6	Bill Schustik
Su	7	Closed
M	8	Hoot & Auditions w/ Dan Gravas
Tu	9	Best of hoot
W	10	Chris Wertenbaker & Felicity Johnson
Th	11	Paul McNeil
F	12	Jaime Brockett
Sa	13	Bill & Renee
Su	14	Closed
M	15	Hoot & Auditions w/ Dan Gravas
Tu	16	Best of hoot - special
W	17	Jim Dahme
Th	18	Paul Geremia
F	19	Dan Gravas
Sa	20	Bill & Renee
Su	21	Closed
M	22	Hoot & Auditions w/ Dan Gravas
Tu	23	Best of hoot
W	24	Marc Worthington

Turk's Head
227-9524

May

F	5	Nancy Michaels
Sa	6	Chris Smither
Su	7	Steve Koretz
M	8	Paul McNeil
Tu	9	Jim Dahme
W	10	Paul Geremia
Th	11	Dan Gravas
F	12	Nancy Michaels
Sa	13	Chris Smither
Su	14	Steve Koretz
M	15	Paul McNeil
Tu	16	Jim Dahme
W	17	Paul Geremia
Th	18	Dan Gravas
F	19	Nancy Michaels
Sa	20	Chris Smither
Su	21	Steve Koretz
M	22	Paul McNeil
Tu	23	Jim Dahme
W	24	Paul Geremia

From a May 1967 issue of *Broadside*.
(image courtesy of Natalie Gravas)

Clearly, Danny hosted Monday night Hoots at The Turk's Head, and regularly played The Sword and the Stone on Thursday evenings, which substantiates his claim that Mark's new coffeehouse was built on the bones of the Oriental.

Danny began telling me about when Dylan was a no-show at a concert he and Danny were booked for at Tufts University. Certain the tale would interest my readers, I asked him to write it down and send it to me. "Sure," he answered. "Would you like to see Bob's letter, too?"

Danny's story starts in spring 1963, when Bob Dylan was staying in a three-story apartment building on Putnam Avenue in Cambridge, Massachusetts, with Richard and Mimi Farina, Joan Baez (Mimi's sister), and Tom Rush. Eric von Schmidt was a mentor to both Danny and Bob, and so, when Danny dropped by to talk to Tom [Rush], he was surprised when Eric answered the door. He told Eric that Bob had been a no-show, and the next day Danny came home to find the

1964-1974: A DECADE OF ODD TALES AND WONDERS

I mix pour me another drink. the
chink falls all over my glass.
she starts tellin me about some
concert. I punch her out an yell
"I never heard a such a thing" the
clock strikes. a birdy pops out an
says "you gotta concert" I bullwhip
the bird an send him flyin out the
window. the bartenders roll out the
door. get run over by a milk truck.
the cops come. the chick shoots herself
they say "do you know anything about
this?" I say "no. I was at a concert.
I hear one tell the other t put a to
on me. I walk out the door whistlin.
draggin my tail. the milk driver is
answerin questions. I whistle louder.
he winks. he yells "hey, that was a good
concert" I say "gimme some milk"
he says the cops took it all. I walk
up the street. a jukebox is playin.
a few cars pass. kids cross the corner
dogs piss on the hydrant. an an ambulance
unfolds from out of the nite.)
         sickly tho. I did not know
of this concert you speak of. if I'd of
known, most likely I would've been there
but I will see you again. I'll see you
next time. there is no such word as a
long time (or far away). there is only
now. I'll see you in the next now.

                   an think of me as your
                                ringo star
                      reavishly
                        an unawake

note, typewritten on the outside of an old envelope, in his mailbox, signed by Dylan. Bob had an excellent relationship with Eric. In his first album, Bob sang Eric's "Baby Let Me Follow You Down," a song he'd learned from Eric in the green pastures of Harvard University. Dylan was also in good stead with Ramblin' Jack, who introduced Danny and Bob to Woody Guthrie, but as Bob grew famous, he withdrew, started a family, and Danny never saw Dylan after his motorcycle accident in 1966.

By late October 1966, when *Feelin' Good* premiered, I enjoyed widespread name recognition from radio ads and articles in all the Boston newspapers that helped put both me and the new Sword in the Stone on the map. And my illustrations on the walls at The Sword and the Stone led to requests for the story as well as the songs, so I recited *Princess Gwen's Satire, Merlin's Prophecies, The Evil Sorcerer's Spells,* and *King Galowyn's Creed,* bellowed by the king at the successful conclusion of a mighty battle.

"Come along, then! Back to Galwalk Castle! There'll be rivers of wine! Oceans of ale! Delights such as you've never dreamed of . . . Never let it be said that a man left my table hungry! Never let it be said that I denied a weary traveler shelter! Never let it be said that a man went thirsty under my roof! Never let it be said that a guest left my castle without a full purse, a fresh horse and a new cloak on his back! There are tales to tell and songs to sing! Eager young wenches with generous hearts and warm dispositions," (which led to some interesting conversations centering on comparisons of courtly customs of yesteryear and the sexual revolution we were witnessing in our present).

1964-1974: A DECADE OF ODD TALES AND WONDERS

I enjoyed doing the shows, but wasn't interested in pursuing a life playing in bars or coffeehouses. Recordings and concerts were my focus, and writing songs was to be my ticket. I reasoned that if people wanted to hear my songs live, concert promoters would have to book me and the rock band I was hoping to put together.

I thought I met Gordon Lightfoot (not the one you think), at The Loft, the first night I played there, but my recent research indicates it was in January 1967, at either King Arthur's or The Sword in the Stone. Gordon G. Lightfoot (no relation to folk-singer and recording artist Gordon M. Lightfoot), was a carpenter and folk music enthusiast with a small, well-equipped recording studio in Jamaica Plain. He couldn't afford a daytime studio manager, didn't want to leave the studio unattended, so if I'd answer the phones and book the night and weekend recording sessions, he'd let me use the studio for rehearsals during the day, and even record demos for me, free, and all I had to pay for was the recording tape.

Of course, I jumped at the chance to have a rehearsal hall in a recording studio where I could record demos. I'd have to put my illustrations on hold, but I could still earn money playing coffeehouses, and having a rehearsal studio put my plans to form a rock band on the fast track.

I began in January, about the same time Ray Fornier flew up from Nashville to record a series of live performances at a Boston nightclub. Ray was blind, and many believed that was his special advantage, especially in recording live performances. Not distracted by elements "in the show," he recorded exactly what he heard in his earphones, and noticed ambient audio interference sometimes missed by sighted engineers.

COFFEEHOUSES, CONCERTS, CAMPUSES, AND CLUBS

The widely used state-of-the-art, 4-track, sound-on-sound analog recorders were Scullys, but Gordon had installed two Ampex 4-track, sound-on-sound analog recorders, and while Ray was in town, he wanted to try them out. He'd be recording the live act at night, so Gordon arranged for him to come over during the day.

Ray asked me to play something to test the system, so while Gordon guided Ray around the control room, I set up in the "out-of-control room," and sang and played "Till the End" (my vampire song), "Don't Let Me Change Your Mind," "Grey Day Lady," and "Love Me Again," (now retitled and recorded as "Stay By Me" on my *Tea Party Snack Platter* album).

When I'd finished, Ray immediately called Roy Acuff of Acuff-Rose Music, who invited me to come to Nashville. It was an intriguing offer, but I wasn't a country-western singer, and I reasoned that if I was good enough to be invited to Nashville, I was probably good enough to be accepted in New York City, too, so I declined and continued to put together a band of my own.

It was still winter when I was introduced to Karl Garrett during his last semester at Boston's prestigious Berklee School of Music. With only one semester to go to earn his degree, he was planning to leave Berklee to study classical guitar with André Segovia in Spain. Karl had heard of me, and was impressed by the fact that I had access to a recording studio, but was unfamiliar with my work, so I brought him home and played him tapes of my songs from *Feelin' Good* and my solo demo recorded at Lightfoot. Those recordings of my original songs were enough to convince classical guitarist, Karl Garrett, to stay in Boston and help me put together a band.

1964-1974: A DECADE OF ODD TALES AND WONDERS

With my savings running out, I had been staying part time on Lake Avenue and part time with Bill, Judy, and Lisa, but, keeping strange hours, needed to find a place of my own. I remembered a small basement apartment in Brighton that had once been rented by a friend from South Africa, and knowing he'd moved on, I went to see if it was available -- and if I could afford it. It had been turned into a storage area, but the plumbing was still in place, and it looked to me like it could easily be restored. I contacted the building manager, told him I remembered when it was an apartment, and said I wanted to rent it. We settled on a most reasonable $65.00 a month and he cleaned it out and turned it back into the cozy bachelor pad I remembered.

Bill Somers had to go to Florida to see his folks, and asked me to keep an eye on Judy and Lisa. I assured him I would. When two weeks passed without hearing from Bill, I asked Judy if she'd heard anything. Had someone died?

She broke into tears. They hadn't fought. He'd just left her, saying he had to get away and he wanted to be with his parents. She was working at Honeywell, but didn't earn enough to cover car payments, rent, Lisa's babysitter, groceries, gas and utility bills . . .

Keeping an eye on them was one thing, and I was happy to do it, but I could hardly help Judy when my own finances were so meager and irregular. The toughest nut was her rent. My place was small, but Bill and Judy had taken me in, and my place would do until something better came along. I'd sleep on the couch, Lisa's crib could go in the hall, and Judy could have the bedroom and closet. It wasn't an ideal solution, but it saved her more than $200.00 a month. We'd share the grocery bill. Three could eat almost as cheaply as two. Their apartment had been furnished, so moving was

COFFEEHOUSES, CONCERTS, CAMPUSES, AND CLUBS

mostly a matter of packing. We'd get by. Besides, whatever Bill was going through, I thought I'd hear from him soon.

About then, Mikey Joe, bass player from The New Jesters, the band I'd sang with at the Natick High talent show in 1965, came on board. He found our rhythm guitarist, George Brox, and ex-Navy Band drummer, Phil Vitali, hereinafter Phil V, both out of work because they had lost their instruments when the club they played was firebombed and the club's insurance refused to pay the claim.

Phil V was wary of me, partly because of my name recognition. He'd played drums for Freddy Cannon, (famous for "Palisade Park" and "Tallahassee Lassie"), but when Freddy's career took off, Phil V and the rest of the original band had been left in the lurch. I had to swear an oath that I would not abandon him if I was offered an individual contract. I had no trouble swearing the oath, because I had once, thoughtlessly, been the cause of a similar unhappy situation, and remembered my remorse when I realized the consequences of breaking up The Nightstar's (sic) and The Vampiros to form The Five Beats.

We rehearsed nearly every day for three months, and by then, we had some 80 original songs, enough to start booking gigs as a band that played all-original material. Our plan was to avoid bars, develop new songs, and land a recording contract. We called ourselves Travis Pike and the Boston Massacre, featuring me, the singer-songwriter with a locally recognized name. The Boston Massacre linked us to our city's revolutionary history, set us apart from the anti-establishment, drug promoting subculture, and seemed fitting for a band with two literally "burned out" musicians (George and Phil V), a one-eyed lead guitarist (Karl), a kid (Mikey Joe), and me, a half-crippled singer-songwriter.

1964-1974: A DECADE OF ODD TALES AND WONDERS

One of the first songs the band learned was "A Red-backed, Scaly, Black-bellied, Tusked, Bat-winged Dragon." At first, the guys were skeptical, but it was a lot of fun to play and once we started playing gigs, it went over well everywhere, even in soul rooms and psychedelic venues where some people in the audience would inevitably jump up and start trying to dance the Charleston.

Richard Turner, a Boston-based PR man, became our manager, and in the summer of 1967, set us up in a week-long gig in a Cape Cod nightclub. About halfway through the week, the club owner said he wanted us to play Wilson Pickett's "Funky Broadway." I reminded him that we only played original material and said if he or his patrons wanted to hear "Funky Broadway," it was on his jukebox. The conversation ended with him shouting, "You play 'Funky Broadway,' or else!"

The following day, rehearsing our sets for that night, a club employee told me I had a phone call at the phone booth outside. Remembering that George and Phil V had been firebombed out of business, the club owner's "or else" was disturbing.

I opened the door and scanned the road for suspicious looking cars. The phone booth was by the side of the road, the receiver dangling by its cord -- waiting for me. Considering where I might dive for cover if someone suddenly drove by and opened fire, I steeled my nerves and went to the phone.

The caller identified himself as George Pincus, a music publisher in New York City. He had heard our demo and liked "End of Summer." He wanted to know how much I wanted for it. I said if he wanted it, the band came with it. He said he wasn't a record producer, he was a publisher with a German client who would make "End of Summer" a hit song in Germany. He then offered me a price, which he said was the most he had ever offered for a song, and said I was a jerk if I didn't take his offer. I said I guessed I was a jerk, and he hung up on me. Pincus George & Sons Music Corp. is still a major player in the music publishing business. They recently sold their publishing rights to six early Beatles songs for several millions of dollars. It was tough turning him down, but I had an oath to keep.

As for Travis Pike and the Boston Massacre's 1967 club date on Cape Cod, we played the gig without "Funky Broadway" and departed without incident.

In March 1967, Boston radio station WNAC changed its call letters to WRKO, its format to top 40 rock 'n roll, and began sponsoring "happenings" to attract listeners away from competitors, WBZ and WMEX. One such promotion was a *Harbor Happening*, offering 500 listeners a boat trip around Boston Harbor aboard the two Massachusetts Bay Lines cruise ships, featuring live music by Travis Pike and the Boston Massacre on one ship, and The Ramrods on the other. The *Harbor Happening* promotion meant both bands were touted over the airwaves for weeks.

On the 31st of July, RCA Records sponsored a bash at O'Dee's, a big soul room in Cambridge, Massachusetts, honoring one of their acts with ties to that city. The well-attended party ran from 5-7 p.m., but when the party ended, the crowd left and audiences for the rest of the week dropped off sharply. In a panic, the club manager contacted our manager, Dick Turner, about getting the widely-publicized Travis Pike and the Boston Massacre to finish the gig that weekend. If we took it, we could only play one night. We'd have to pack up and leave after Saturday night for the *Harbor Happening* on Sunday, August 6th. To our surprise,

1964-1974: A DECADE OF ODD TALES AND WONDERS

he booked us for the single night before the cruise, gambling on our name recognition from the ongoing radio promotion. His gamble paid off. That Saturday night, O'Dee's was packed solid and the crowd loved us.

In his 2018 interview for *It's Psychedelic Baby Magazine*, Lenny Helsing asked me about the most memorable gigs I'd had with the Boston Massacre and the

COFFEEHOUSES, CONCERTS, CAMPUSES, AND CLUBS

Tea Party. More memorable than the gig at O'Dee's and WRKO's harbor cruise was the Travis Pike and the Boston Massacre Labor Day Weekend gig at Gunstock Acres.

Gunstock Acres was a resort real estate development in New Hampshire ski country, more than a hundred miles north of Boston. On our way there, Mikey Joe's station wagon, carrying our instruments and amplifiers, collided with another vehicle. There were no injuries, but the car was disabled. A local repair shop gave us permission to push the car onto their lot, but there would be no one there to work on it over the long holiday weekend. When we were cleared to continue on by the authorities in Concord, New Hampshire, Gunstock Acres dispatched a courtesy van to fetch us and our equipment.

The lodge was a knockout, the food was excellent, our accommodations more than adequate, and our Friday evening concert was a hit with the sales force and their guests. On Saturday, Gunstock Acres' sales force and touring vans went to work showing properties. There weren't enough staff or vehicles to handle all the families at once, so we entertained families waiting for tours, too. Karl took a small crowd to one corner of the lodge and played classical guitar pieces, I took some youngsters to another corner and entertained them with my rhymes. I don't know how George, Phil V and Mikey Joe passed their time, but everyone seemed happy, and our afternoon concert literally rocked the mountainside, bringing people out of cabins on the adjacent mountainsides to dance to our music. I wouldn't be surprised if we entertained some of the boaters out on Lake Winnipesaukee too. After dinner, we played inside the lodge, and then I told stories to kids who'd been out looking at cabins earlier in the day, and wanted to hear my stories in rhyme.

1964-1974: A DECADE OF ODD TALES AND WONDERS

After breakfast Sunday morning, I was confronted by an angry mother and Gunstock Acres' Public Relations Director, Pat Granger. The mother claimed that the frightening stories I told her little boy had kept him and her, up most of the night. From what she said about the story, I recognized the piece as *The Twail's Tale*, and told it to them. They both enjoyed it, the mother graciously apologized, and we even received a lovely testimonial from Gunstock Acres.

GUNSTOCK ACRES Inc.

Executive Offices:
Statler Office Bldg. (Suite 814) Park Square, Boston, Mass.
617-542-0665

September 6, 1967

Mr. Travis Pike
97 Lake Street
Newton, Mass.

Dear Travis:

In behalf of Paul Thibert and the entire family of Gunstock Acres, may we thank and congratulate you for an outstanding performance at our Labor Day Open House party.

The cooperation from your entire group, not only in your musical endeavors but all around attitude and assistance in making this a memorable week end, is sincerely appreciated. We will look forward to the pleasure of your appearance in our future promotional endeavors.

Again, a warm thank you to you Travis, Carl, George, Mike and Phil.

Very truly yours,

GUNSTOCK ACRES INC.

Pat Granger
Patricia C. Granger
Public Relations Director

PCG;brd

Meanwhile, Dick Turner had been making the rounds in New York City with our demo album. He brought it to the owners of The Cheetah Lounge in downtown Manhattan. They liked it, but would never book a band calling itself the

COFFEEHOUSES, CONCERTS, CAMPUSES, AND CLUBS

Boston Massacre for fear of a riot. The Cheetah was too big to ignore. Most major record labels had offices in New York City. A showcase at The Cheetah would serve as an audition for us, so we renamed ourselves Travis Pike's Tea Party.

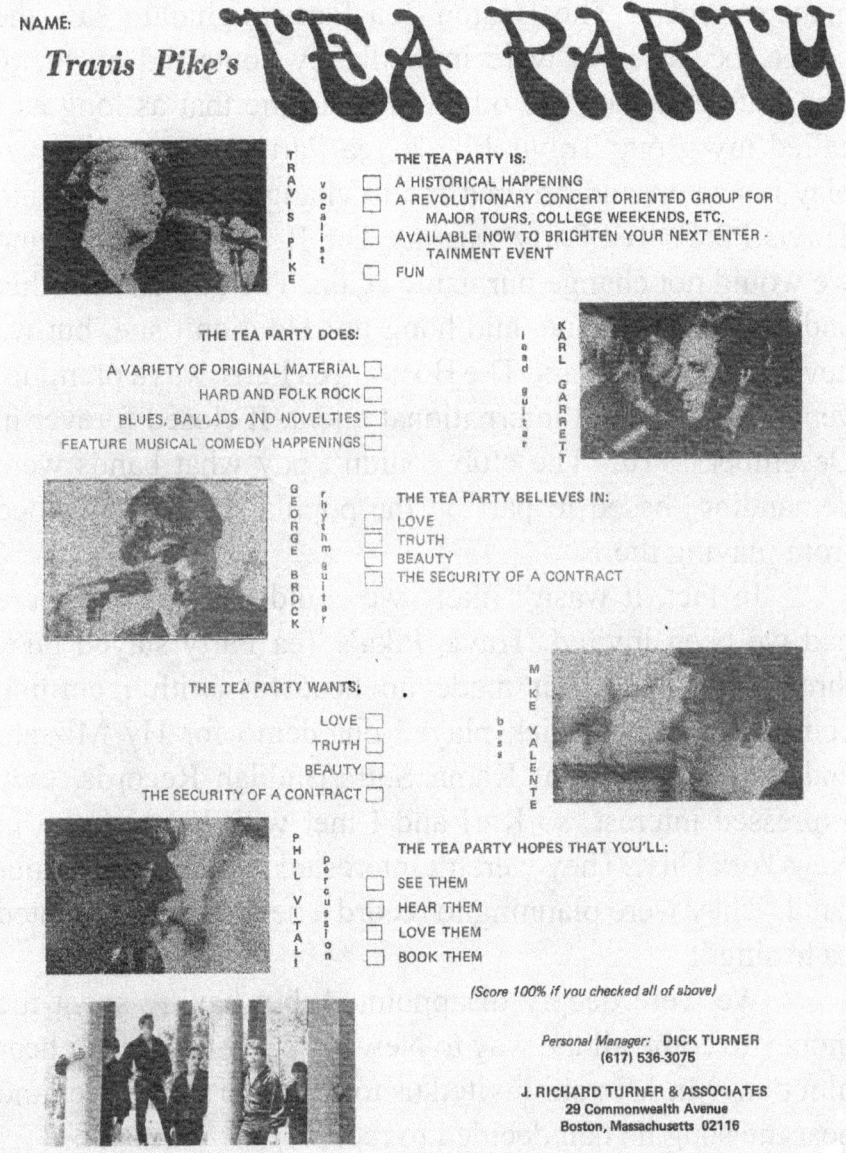

Our name change was reported in the *Boston Sunday Globe,* September 24, 1967 in *Record Time, Sound in the Round*: "Travis Pike and the Boston Massacre have changed their name to Travis Pike's Tea Party." Apparently, the management at The Boston Tea Party nightclub saw the notice, because we were immediately contacted by them. The irate caller on the other end told me that as long as I called my group Travis Pike's Tea Party, we would never play his room and ordered me to change our name. I said Travis Pike's Tea Party was not The Boston Tea Party and we would not change our name again. The guy on the other end threatened to sue, and hung up! He didn't sue, but we never played there, and The Boston Tea Party was a premium venue for local and international talent. It closed forever in December 1970. The club couldn't pay what bands were demanding, based in part on the popularity they'd gained from playing there.

In fact, it wasn't likely we could have played there had we been invited. Travis Pike's Tea Party stayed busy throughout 1967, but made no headway with recording companies. When Dick played our demo for Hy Mizrahi and Phil Steinberg at Kama Sutra/Buddah Records, they expressed interest, so Karl and I met with Kama Sutra in New York City. They weren't interested in our songs, or our band. They were planning to record a new song and wanted us to sing it.

We were deeply disappointed, but having spent the money to come all the way to New York, we decided to hear him out. Mr. Mizrahi invited us to meet the songwriter and hear the song he had decided to record.

In the next room, a young man sitting at a piano, played and sang the song for us. I thought it was awful.

Afterward, Mr. Mizrahi thanked the composer, and we went back to his office. I asked Karl if he thought we could do anything with it. Mr. Mizrahi told us not to worry about that; we wouldn't be playing it. They only used studio musicians for their recording sessions. "That song will go to number one," he said. We must have looked doubtful, because he asked, "Well, are you interested in singing it, or not?" "The only way that thing will get airplay is if you buy the time," I answered. He grinned, promised it would go to the top of the charts, and said goodbye.

Outside, I asked Karl if he thought I had mishandled the interview. He said he would not have been so polite. We returned to Boston, reported that we'd turned the offer down and why, and our decision was unanimously upheld.

About a month later, we began hearing The Lemon Pipers "Green Tambourine" on the radio. Judging by its commercial success, bubblegum pop was in -- and we were still outside looking in. My integrity was intact, but our prospects were no better than before.

In October, we played the opening two weeks of a new nightclub called Alexanders. At that time, everybody in Boston was excited that the Red Sox had made it to the World Series. Alexanders' owners insisted we perform "The Impossible Dream" from *Man of La Mancha*. We didn't sing it; but we did play it, leaving the singing to the club's patrons, whose enthusiasm made up for what they lacked in intonation. Sports history records that the Cardinals won, but in Boston, the report was that the Red Sox lost -- again.

1964-1974: A DECADE OF ODD TALES AND WONDERS

Toward Halloween, Dick Turner set up a showcase at The Black Russian, a downtown Boston nightclub. We performed our vampire blackout show, "Till the End," complete with coffin, cape and lovely female victim. Blackouts were popular in burlesque, where racy shows would end in a blackout on stage, keeping performances within local ordinances against lewd conduct in public. What audiences imagined happening when the lights went out was nobody's business.

I had played "Till the End" in coffeehouses. Even without the coffin and the girl in the nightie, it always went over well. Rock 'n' roll audiences expect loud music, costuming, exotic special effects, erotic posturing, leaping, strutting, head-bobbing, toe-tapping and finger-pointing. Unexpected and enthusiastically appreciated, was our full-blown stage show featuring a pretty girl who didn't sing, dance or play an instrument, but looked scrumptious in a diaphanous nightie -- screamed horror-show screams, and died on cue when I bit her neck.

A creaky effect, caused by dragging a guitar pick across the springs in the reverb unit, was my signal to get out of the coffin. The girl screamed again and backed away. I discovered the girl and said, "Listen to them -- the children of the night." As I continued the piece, I manipulated myself into her good graces, betrayed her with a bite on the neck and when she went limp, was supposed to return to my coffin, bemoaning my fate. "All these one night stands," I would say, "I wish I could find a steady girl." Then, laughing demonically, I would close the coffin lid, and the stage would go black.

That night, my "victim" died on my cape, making it impossible for me to rise until I shoved her out of the way. I had to sprint across the stage to get back into my coffin before the music cue shut the lid, leaving the club crowd screaming with delight.

1500 attend mixer Saturday night; Music provided by Tea Party

Photo by Steve Gretter

Travis Pike's Tea Party plays for a mixer Saturday night in the Student Center for one of the largest throngs ever to crowd the Sala de Puerto Rico. The mixer was sponsored by Burton House and BU's Charlesgate Hall.

November 11, 1967, I ushered for my brother Jimmy's wedding, but couldn't stay for the reception because I had the MIT Mixer that night. Halfway through the evening, my brother and his bride appeared. I hadn't been able to dance at their wedding, so they came and danced at my show.

1964-1974: A DECADE OF ODD TALES AND WONDERS

5:00- 5:15 Greetings
Awarding of Prizes
Announcements

5:15- 8:00 Community Singing in the Main Lobby
ALEX KING *at the Organ*

5:15- 9:00 Christmas Music in the Constitution Lounge
ESTELLE ESTES *at the Harp*

5:30- 8:00 Dinner in the 5th Floor Dining Rooms

6:30-10:30 Dancing in New England Life Hall
TRAVIS PIKE'S TEA PARTY

7:00-11:00 Dancing in the Charter Room
JEFF STOUGHTON *and his Orchestra*

7:30-11:00 Coffee & Conversation in the Snack Bar
Games & Cards in the Game Room

11:00 ... And to all a good night.

The page above is from the program for the New England Life Christmas Party. Our room filled up between 7:00 - 7:30 and rocked until 10:30. The first person to come up on stage and accurately say the entire title to the song, "A Red-backed, Scaly, Black-bellied, Tusked, Bat-winged Dragon," won a color TV set.

EVERYTHING CHANGED IN 1968

January was a good month for Travis Pike's Tea Party. George Popadopolis, who ran The Unicorn Coffee House, had made a deal with record promoters to provide a Boston showcase for new acts and new releases by established acts, in direct competition with The Boston Tea Party nightclub. He called his operation, set in the lower level of a concrete parking garage, The Psychedelic Supermarket, and Dick Turner was determined to get us booked there, if not as the headliners, as the opening act. Our first gig at The Psychedelic Supermarket was in early January 1968, when we opened for Moby Grape.

Mikey Joe had Moby Grape's album and said they were really good. I listened and agreed with him that they were good, but we were just as good. Still, I made sure that the songs I selected for our two sets were all showstoppers.

The Psychedelic Supermarket had a stage at one end. The acoustics were terrible, and there were no chairs for the audience, who were forced to sit on the frigid cement floor or stand all night. We set up as the crowd arrived. Moby Grape's equipment had arrived in big, metal touring trunks stenciled "MOB RAPE," with the "Y" of Moby and the "G" of grape wrapped around to the other sides of their shipping crates. Their flight in from New York City was later than expected, and when the band finally arrived at the Psychedelic Supermarket, they insisted on ordering take-out dinners and eating before they went on.

So we waited, and the crowd waited too, growing colder, more uncomfortable and losing patience. The show was already nearly an hour late when the club owner finally told us to go on, but to only play 20 minutes. Told to cut 25 minutes from our planned set left us with only four songs. Naturally, I chose the hottest four songs I had scheduled.

We went on and electrified the room. When, twenty minutes later, we played our break song, "A Very Merry Unbirthday," from Disney's *Alice in Wonderland,* and got off stage; the crowd began chanting "Tea Party."

Moby Grape kept the crowd waiting another 20 minutes before they came out to play. They looked great, sounded just like their album, and were tight and practiced in every detail, but that night, as Moby Grape finished their set and got off, the hostile Boston crowd began chanting "Tea Party" again.

Mr. Popadopolis had planned to sell tickets to a second show, but the people from the first show refused to leave. Finally, he sent us out to do another 20 minutes, leaving me no alternative but to cut the five "weakest" songs from our second set . . .

Dick Turner was there, and he went back to talk to Mr. Popadopolis during Moby Grape's flawless, but underappreciated performance. That night, after the show, Mr. Popadopolis told us to pack up our gear.

We weren't being fired. On the contrary. He was moving us over to his Unicorn Coffee House where we'd be the headliners, and bringing his current headliner, folksinger Tom Rush, over to the Psychedelic Supermarket to open for tomorrow night's Moby Grape performances.

And that's how Travis Pike's Tea Party first came to play The Unicorn Coffee House, which is an excellent place to introduce what I believe to be one of my most complicated, and slow-to-develop creative endeavors.

In my basement apartment on Commonwealth Avenue in Brighton, I awoke one morning, with an eerily beautiful song running through my head. No time for coffee, afraid of forgetting the unusual melody, I began seeking it out on my guitar. The melody was easy enough, but the harmonies were elusive. I kept striking false chords and progressions that failed to yield the desired result. It took me close to an hour to establish the patterns of melody and harmony I wanted. After playing it several times to be sure I wouldn't forget it, I fetched paper and pen to write the lyrics.

The specific haunting lyrical hook that awakened me was gone, so I thought a place-saver lyric following the melody line would work well enough, until I remembered the hook -- a single word that still rang in my head, but I couldn't remember what it was, only that it was "somethingstone." An hour later, the rest of the lyrics well-covered, I was still haunted by "somethingstone."

Even after a morning cup of coffee, I was no closer to discovering the mystery of "somethingstone" than before, but it was late enough now to wake up Mikey Joe and Karl in the top floor apartment. Karl had no trouble with the melody, but hadn't a clue as to what "somethingstone" might be, and teaching that day, he had to leave. I started pressuring Mikey Joe. Surely, between us we should be able to figure out a word to replace "somethingstone." "Yellowstone didn't work, and "silverstone" sounded like kitchenware.

1964-1974: A DECADE OF ODD TALES AND WONDERS

Nothing came to mind for him, either, and he hadn't eaten, so I told him to get dressed and I'd make breakfast. Then we could go over the song. A few hours later, we were playing it confidently, but still missing the hook, when George Brox arrived. Our bright, singing, guitar-strumming pal would surely have an answer to the mystery. He didn't. Around lunchtime, Mikey Joe came up with "Cherrystone." It fit the melody, so "Cherrystone" went into our repertoire.

"Cherrystone" had a haunting melody and interesting harmonies, but we almost never played it. None of us knew what it was about, but there were songs with nonsense lyrics coming out every day back then, so it just stayed "Cherrystone," until that first night at The Unicorn.

With our amplifiers, drums and P.A., we took up about a third of the room. If we played hard rock numbers, we would not only have deafened the audience, but probably brought the law down on us, so we played some of my ballads, folk-rock tunes, blues, and I decided to close one set with "Cherrystone."

Afterward, I was approached by a wild-eyed young man who assured me he was "cool." He just wanted to know if we dried them or smoked them?

I told him I didn't know what he was talking about and looked around for a bouncer. The wild-eyed one, maybe thinking I thought he was a narc, repeated how cool he was and promised not to tell. Would I tell him, at least, if it was smoked, sprinkled on food, snorted or baked in brownies? And did they have to be fresh or didn't that matter? At this point, George said the guy must think the song was about clams. We never played "Cherrystone" again. Hallucinogenic or not, Travis Pike's Tea Party was way too cool to sing an ode to a clam.

This photo of me, taken surreptitiously at The Unicorn Coffee House was taken by a fan on his "spy camera" in 1968, the first year Travis Pike's Tea Party appeared there. I have no photos of the rest of the band at the Unicorn, and whether this photo is from our first or second gig there is not known. What is known, from an article in the Friday, January 26, 1968 *Boston Herald Traveler* (q.v. on page 117), is that we were playing a return engagement at The Unicorn Coffee House that week. With so few photos of Travis Pike's Tea Party, this shot was chosen for the CD cover to my *Reconstructed Coffeehouse Blues* album.

Our manager introduced us to Squire Rushnell when we played at Alexanders, a genuine nightclub. Squire was a producer at Boston's WBZ-TV, who was looking for talent for his new variety show to be called *Here and Now*. Squire had said he'd be in touch when he was ready to go forward, and he'd come back around to say he wanted Travis Pike's Tea Party to be the new show's house band, and asked Karl and I to be the show's musical directors. Naturally, we agreed. It had taken a while, but it looked like we were finally on our way to fame and fortune.

We were booked for two more consecutive weekends at The Psychedelic Supermarket. The first with The Fugs, who by their own admission, were not musicians, but satirists. The Supermarket crowd found them hilarious. Spirit was next -- excellent musicians from Los Angeles. They rocked, but they were pretty jazzy. So much so that Karl and Phil V wanted to do a number in our Jazz Trio configuration, featuring Karl, Phil V and Mikey Joe, to show Spirit they were kindred spirits, but the audience reaction to our first show made me stick with plan A. There were five of us and Spirit, while obviously talented, didn't heat up the room the way we did.

That January 1968, *Boston Herald Traveler* article about the "Boston Sound" gave as much space to Travis Pike's Tea Party as it did to the Boston Sound, going into who we were, how and when we got together and our special skills. The reporter may have been a fan, but he was not clairvoyant. We never were signed by a major label.

EVERYTHING CHANGED IN 1968

Boston Herald Traveler, Friday, January 26, 1968

——— HUB-HUB ———

Boston Sound Stirs Interests

By JIM MORSE

The current Newsweek proclaims that the Boston Sound is "what's happening" in the music business today. Major recording companies have scouts here checking the sounds and musicians making them. What amazes insiders is not the sudden recognition, but the fact that the talent has been here for years with no recognition, not even locally.

The Beacon Street Union, The Phluph, Orpheus, and The Ultimate Spinach are the names of local groups whose albums are being released this week. The next combo to be snapped up by a big label will be Travis Pike's Tea Party. It took eight months to put this outfit together, and six months of rehearsals to learn the 80 original songs the group performs.

Karl Garrett, lead guitarist in the Tea Party, is considered one of the outstanding classical guitarists in New England. Pike, who is from Newton, starred in the movie, "Feelin' Good," which was filmed here two years ago. The group has been featured at the Psychedelic Supermarket in Kenmore Square and the Unicorn Coffee House, where it's making a repeat appearance this week.

1964-1974: A DECADE OF ODD TALES AND WONDERS

Back in January 1968, pundits were predicting the Boston Sound would eclipse the San Francisco Sound and the cold war between the mainstream and underground media began heating up. The Boston Sound was immediately labeled corporate hype - especially by fledgling, counter-culture, San Francisco-based *Rolling Stone Magazine.*

In fact, MGM record producer Alan Lorber's 1967 Boston Sound marketing plan was logical, but had little to do with sound in terms of intonation, instrumentation or style. His idea was to create a sort of "off-Broadway" clearing house for new talent spawned by Boston's coffeehouse scene, taking advantage of the city's quarter million college students as a proving ground. With the advantage of 20/20 hindsight, I think Boston was an excellent hub from which to launch an "American Musical Revolution," but I think the use of the word "sound" contributed to its collapse. Motown had a definitive sound. Nashville had one. San Francisco had one. Boston had many -- and because it had many, I don't think it ever had a single unique sound that could be specifically identified as a "Boston Sound."

Moreover, his marketing plan was anathema to Boston's Brahmins, the conservative upper crust of the East Coast establishment, who believed drugs, decadence and dissidence were promoted in pop music and lyrics. Their concerns were true enough, nationally and internationally, but less so in the Boston music scene.

We at ground zero, who believed we could identify a San Francisco Sound or a Liverpool Sound by listening to recordings originating in those markets, found no such unifying sound dominating our local music scene. The most popular sound in dance clubs was the Motown Sound. Folk music, much of it only "folk" in style, still drew young people to coffeehouses, but even Dylan went electric at the *Newport Folk Festival* back in 1965, and by 1968, Travis Pike's Tea Party, drums, electric bass, electric guitars and all, was playing in coffeehouses, in Boston and Providence, Rhode Island. Rock, blues, jazz and country all remained popular in their dedicated venues.

We finished January back at The Unicorn, our fourth weekend in a row for George Popadopolis, just before the start of the Tet Offensive in Vietnam. The effect of the Tet Offensive was indirect, but nations are made up of people, and people, whether engaged or detached from the events that shape their world, are nevertheless compelled to experience the effects of their nation's histories, economically, politically, psychologically, and spiritually, and the ramifications of events in 1968 still shape our lives.

Perhaps that's why I never knew, or maybe just forgot, that according to a notice I found online, the J. Geils Blues Band was to play a *Rock 'n' Roll Festival* at The Catacombs to benefit Project 50, a YMCA affiliated organization, on February 14th and 15th. The show, featuring Sky People, The Third World Raspberry, Cloud, Travis Pike's Tea Party, and The Colwell-Winfield Blues Band was cancelled when the venue lost its license after a police raid.

In April, Squire Rushnell launched his variety show *Here and Now.* For people unfamiliar with the pecking order among Boston's radio stations in the late sixties, WBZ radio was the powerhouse for Top 40 rock 'n' roll. Reasoning the TV show would finally get us a recording contract, we had signed on, and shortly thereafter, recorded "If I Didn't Love You Girl" and "The Likes of You" for Alma Records -- not the major label we'd hoped for, but Joe Saia's label, and Joe was the owner of the AAA Recording Studio where we pre-recorded the music for the TV show.

We'd been discovered by a group of students from the Rhode Island School of Design who owned The Rubicon Coffee House in Providence, a great venue with enthusiastic fans in a small but packed room. They began booking us regularly, one weekend a month. The morning after our April performance, Mikey Joe's station wagon was vandalized and some equipment, including his bass guitar, was stolen. The local authorities told us that on that Saturday night, April 13th, there had been a rash of crimes which they believed were in reaction to the assassination of Martin Luther King, Jr. We were simply a random target.

WBZ put *Here and Now* on hiatus to work out bugs in the show. It had been keeping us busy, but now we would be available to play at *The First Annual Boston Pop Festival* at The Psychedelic Supermarket on Friday, May 17th. It was fun to be back in front of a live Boston audience, and we shamelessly promoted our new recording, asking our fans to call in and request to get it played on the radio.

William Phillips, a critic covering the festival wrote, "Travis Pike's Tea Party performed in about every conceivable pop style from straight rock to psychedelic to folk to rinky-dinky ragtime. Aside from an excessive fondness for gimmickry and bad humor, they are pleasing and versatile entertainers."

I don't know William Phillips, but his review sounds accurate. With regard to our gimmickry, I think we did our vampire show there, coffin and all. It was the kind of thing we would do at a festival. And maybe the vampire's wish that he could find a steady girl could be considered bad humor, but ultimately, Travis Pike's Tea Party's material reflected all the current musical trends in Boston -- which brings me back to The Boston Sound.

To me, the Boston Sound was neither sound nor genre, but an eclectic and inclusive melange of sounds. I had been active in the coffeehouse scene, but my roots were even deeper in show tunes and rock 'n' roll, and I composed in "every conceivable pop style." We were a Boston Sound, but not part of that promotion. Lines I discovered in one of my notebooks summed it up. "Now let our course be set, and if the Muse sings true, when the dragon sails, there'll be a bench for you in my long ship." Originally about staying the course in my fantasy-adventure *Long-Grin*, to me, it applied to Travis Pike's Tea Party, as well.

Then, on June 6th, 1968, the night he won the Democratic Party's California Presidential Primary, Robert Kennedy was assassinated in the pantry of the Ambassador

1964-1974: A DECADE OF ODD TALES AND WONDERS

Hotel in Los Angeles. The war in Vietnam was not only ongoing, but escalating despite Walter Cronkite's editorial, and all around me, I saw the pernicious effect of the drug-culture mantra, "tune in, turn on, drop out," fueled in part, by much of the popular music and media pundits of the sixties, an ongoing assault on everything I believed about America.

We were officially "on hiatus" when we received the phone call saying the show had been cancelled.

WBZ-TV 4
1170 SOLDIERS FIELD ROAD BOSTON MASSACHUSETTS 02134 254-5670

WBZ - WBZ-TV BOSTON
WINS NEW YORK
KYW - KYW-TV PHILADELPHIA
WJZ-TV BALTIMORE
KDKA - KDKA-TV PITTSBURGH
WOWO FT WAYNE
WIND CHICAGO
KPIX SAN FRANCISCO
KFWB LOS ANGELES

GROUP W

WESTINGHOUSE BROADCASTING COMPANY INC

June 24, 1968

TO WHOM IT MAY CONCERN

This will inform you that Messrs. Travis Pike and Karl Garrett of "Travis Pike's Tea Party" served as music directors and arrangers for two television pilot programs here at WBZ-TV, Boston.

Their contributions were impressive. In addition to arranging and supervising the production of several "hit" songs performed on the programs, Travis Pike and Karl Garrett wrote and arranged theme music for instrumental bridges.

Should you require further information, please feel free to contact me at 617 254-5670.

Sincerely,

Squire D. Rushnell
Executive Producer

SDR:dz

Being on hiatus had inferred that they would be making adjustments to the format and we'd go on from there. Apparently, the "bugs" in the show (although not the giants of my song, "Land of the Giant Bugs"), were tough and tenacious -- and while still afloat, we were suddenly cut adrift, without a pilot. The lovely reference letter from WBZ arrived a few days later.

Worse than the cancelled TV show, as far as I was concerned, was that WBZ Radio switched format from Top 40 to adult contemporary, which meant they wouldn't play our record, and WRKO, now the dominant Top 40 station in Boston, refused to play our record despite frequent fan requests -- and angrily said as much to some of the callers.

It was time for me to re-examine our paradigm. Summer was upon us, and everything was booked. We were unlikely to land any significant new gigs until the colleges reopened in the fall. George was all for taking the summer off. Phil V was trying to line up a summer gig with a jazz combo. Karl had some guitar students, but they barely paid the rent -- and if Mikey Joe went home to stay with his parents for the summer, Karl wouldn't be able to make the rent at all. I could hold out, but I feared the band might fall apart if I couldn't get something going right away. Of course, if our record took off, we'd be fine, so I decided to focus my attention on that.

Recordings are the permanent record of who's who in music. We only had one 45 rpm single, although we had been featured in radio promotions and even, briefly, had a TV show, and radio and TV broadcasts, unless taped and re-released to the public, are gone when the show is over.

Generally, reviewers don't cover one night stands. Unless their readers can attend or avoid a performance, the review is meaningless. And if someone who did see us mentioned it, the conversation would likely begin, "You missed a great show last night!"

Our loyal fan base was numerically insignificant. Many of our gigs were private functions, like the *Harbor Happening, The New England Life Christmas Party* or the *Gunstock Acres Real Estate Weekend*. Others were sponsored by clubs, fraternities, or sororities for their members and guests. These events were not small -- 1500 students and their friends showed up at one MIT mixer -- but such events were not open to the general public, and usually featured ads specifically intended for their targeted audiences.

Thanks to our Rhode Island fans, we were the first rock band ever to perform at *The Providence Arts Festival*. Even so, I calculate the number of people who saw us and heard us perform between May 1967 and May 1968, when we were most active in the New England marketplace would come to somewhere between 45,000 - 60,000 persons. Overall attendance at our events might be almost double that, but fans are repeat customers, and I try to count fans only once, no matter how many performances they attend.

I went to WRKO to ask program director, Mel Phillips, why he refused to play our record. We met in the lobby of the building in Kenmore Square where my father had been a Vice-president of RKO, and where he worked at WNAC-TV, until he left to form Pike Productions.

Mel was shouting at me as he came down the stairs to the lobby that he didn't care who my father was. (I hadn't invoked my father's name. Perhaps the receptionist who announced me told him.) He raved on that by doing the TV show at WBZ, I had gone over to the enemy, and now that WRKO had emerged triumphant, he would see to it that Travis Pike's Tea Party would never be played in Boston. I was astonished by his tirade. We had worked on a short-lived TV show. He was programming music for radio.

By his raving and the zealot's gleam in his eyes, I saw that attempting to reason with him was a waste of time. Clearly, as long as he controlled the programming, Travis Pike's Tea Party would be "banned in Boston," which, historically speaking, put us into some rather interesting company. So, I grabbed Mel by his mutton-chop sideburns, kissed him goodbye, and bolstered by applause from the employees and visitors in the lobby, turned on my heel and "left the building."

What could I have done differently? I won't say I had remained cool, but I had overcome the impulse to strike him dead on the spot, so that was something. What would I tell the band? By the time I got to the street, I resolved to tell them exactly what had transpired, why I had behaved the way I did, and let the chips fall where they may.

School was out, the clubs in town and on Cape Cod were already booked for the summer, and we were not. Roger LaChance, one of my biker fans who had moved to California, called to say he was back in town for a few days, gathering up the last of his belongings, and wondered if he and a friend could stay with me. I said they could. He wanted to know where we were playing so he and his California friend could see us. When I told him we weren't

1964-1974: A DECADE OF ODD TALES AND WONDERS

playing anywhere and why, he offered to take the whole band back with him to check out the scene in Los Angeles. Phil and Karl had obligations in town, George had gone down to Cape Cod, but Mikey Joe and I were free to go. Roger rented a trailer, he and his friend helped load our gear, we climbed up into his pickup truck, and with Roger leading the way in his Austin-Healy 3000, set out for Los Angeles.

This August 1968 issue of *New England Scene* features the Travis Pike's Tea Party article, citing our enthusiastic reception at the *Providence Arts Festival*, but sadly fails to provide the date for it.

EVERYTHING CHANGED IN 1968

TRAVIS PIKE'S TEA PARTY

By BILL EDWARDS

There's a new power in Boston Music. As is often the case one good musician pulls together several mediocre talents, forms a group, and enters the commercial pop field. But now a group of career-minded professionals are finally beginning to appear on the Boston scene. One of the most notable of these is Travis Pike's Tea Party.

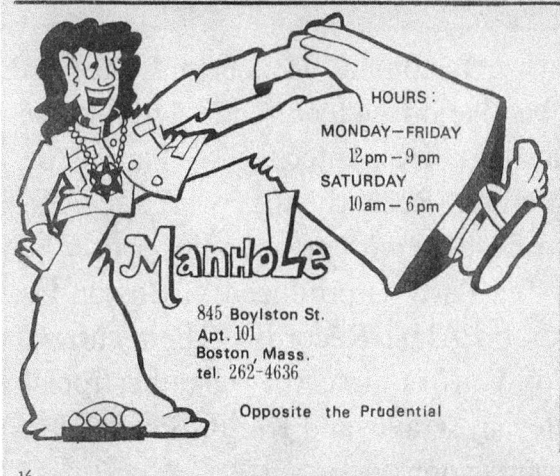

HOURS:
MONDAY—FRIDAY
12pm – 9pm
SATURDAY
10am – 6pm

Manhole
845 Boylston St.
Apt. 101
Boston, Mass.
tel. 262-4636
Opposite the Prudential

Karlo, the oldest member of the group, hails from Philadelphia, is head guitarist, third vocal and one of the principal arrangers. Uncle Phil is from Dedham, and one of the better percussionists in New England. Juris was born in Riga, Latvia, but raised in Boston. He's second guitar and second vocal and his background in folk music is extensive. Mikey Joe is the youngest member of the band. Since The Tea Party, he has become a competent bassist.

Travis is a native Bostonian. He's been front man for a German show band and was featured in a movie for which he wrote eight songs. He wanted the Tea Party to be a different sounding group. Recently they were received at the Providence Art Festival with great enthusiasm.

Travis Pike's Tea Party is produced in Boston by Joe Saia and records on Alma Records. Their current single, "The Likes Of You" is almost a "chamber rock" sound and was written by Travis and Karlo. Production on their first album starts soon.

16

Travis Pike's Tea Party fans might be able to make out the text on this reduced actual page with a magnifying glass, but readers without a magnifying glass will find the complete text copied on the next page.

TRAVIS PIKE'S TEA PARTY by Bill Edwards

There's a new power in Boston Music. As is often the case one good musician pulls together several mediocre talents, forms a group, and enters the commercial pop field. But now a group of career-minded professionals are finally beginning to appear on the Boston scene. One of the most notable of these is Travis Pike's Tea Party.

Karlo, the oldest member of the group, hails from Philadelphia, is head (sic) guitarist, third vocal and one of the principal arrangers. Uncle Phil is from Dedham, and one of the better percussionists in New England. Juris was born in Riga, Latvia, but raised in Boston. He's second guitar and second vocal and his background in folk music is extensive. Mikey Joe is the youngest member of the band. Since the Tea Party, he has become a competent bassist.

Travis is a native Bostonian. He's been front man for a German show band and was featured in a movie for which he wrote eight songs. He wanted the Tea Party to be a different sounding group. Recently, they were received at the Providence Art Festival with great enthusiasm.

Travis Pike's Tea Party is produced in Boston by Joe Saia and records on Alma Records. Their current single, "The Likes of You" is almost a "chamber rock" sound and was written by Travis and Karlo. Production on their first album starts soon.

In fact, when the August issue hit the news stands, Mikey Joe and I were already in California, and getting ready to bring everyone else to Los Angeles, never imagining that, as a group, we would never return to New England.

These contact sheet blowups above are the only remaining photographs I have from Travis Pike's Tea Party. The silhouette on the left is George Brox, who had gone to Cape Cod for the summer, leaving us with no contact information, so we could not find him when we moved to the West Coast. The center photo is our "jazz trio," Karl (left), Phil V, with the teacup on his head, (center) and Mikey Joe (right). We're all in the photo (right), Karl at the far end, Phi V, his face obscured by the teapot, Mikey Joe, probably complaining we're out of tea, me, listening to him complain, and George, probably looking for tea bags in his guitar case.

I wasn't in Southern California very long before, armed with our demo record, I visited the Whisky A Go Go on Sunset Strip. It was booked months ahead, but after listening to our demo album, the man-in-charge said if I would agree to let the Whisky introduce us on the West Coast, he had a group he could reschedule in late August, if I'd be ready by then. The Whisky A Go Go offer was better than I had dared hope. I alerted Karl and Phil V, but wasn't able to reach George on the phone.

I then called Judy. She and I and Lisa had been living together in that tiny bachelor pad for over a year, and they had become like family to me. I worried about how they were getting along without me, and I missed them.

Judy worked at Honeywell in Newton Highlands, and every weekday morning, she'd get up early, make breakfast for herself and Lisa, drop Lisa at the babysitter, put in a full day's work, pick Lisa up on her way home, make supper for all three of us, and then put Lisa to bed. Realistically, if I didn't see them in the morning before they left, I might not see them at all. On nights we ate together, I'd sometimes sing songs or tell stories, before they went to bed. Like any other mother holding down a full-time job, her weekends were devoted to laundry, shopping, and cleaning, leaving little time for recreation.

When I had gigs, I seldom got home before 2:00 a.m, and I'd frequently sleep in. They'd pussyfoot around the place until I woke up. Judy reminded me that she and Lisa actually came to a few rehearsals at Lightfoot, but about the only time we actually had together was on Friday or Saturday nights when I didn't have a gig, and we might go to a drive-in movie. The best thing about drive-ins was a babysitter wasn't needed. When it got late, Lisa just curled up and slept in the back seat. And every once in a while, on a Friday or Saturday afternoon, we'd all go to a Chinese restaurant for an early dinner, if I had a gig that night.

In 1968 they filmed *The Boston Strangler*. One of his earliest victims lived in an apartment building on Commonwealth Avenue, two doors from us, and whenever Judy gave out her address, she was reminded of that fact.

My opportunistic decision to pack up and go to California gnawed at me. The record companies were all leaving New York City and coming West too, so it looked like the move would be permanent. I'd been sending Judy and Lisa postcards from Hollywood, but now that I was planning to move the whole group out, I wanted to talk to Judy. I told her on the phone that she'd be amazed at how affordable rental housing was in La Puente, California, even houses with swimming pools and orange trees in their yards.

I told her how much I missed them both, and if she wanted to come to California, I'd be happy to fly back to get them. I could rent a bungalow and we'd all be together again. And knowing that this was a very big deal, and her family might not be happy about it, if she wanted to, we could even get married. Her answer was that she and Lisa missed me too, and she'd love to join me, but she wasn't so sure about getting married again. I've since learned that Southern California was at least as big a draw as I was, because Judy was always cold living in Massachusetts. (I remember that summers were hot and muggy, but Judy only remembers how cold Boston was all the rest of the year.)

Karl found a guitar teacher to take over his classes and would be flying out in a matter of days, so I asked him to buy a round-trip ticket, and I'd use the return portion to fly back to Boston to fetch George, Phil V and his wife, and now, Judy and Lisa, too. I planned to buy a station wagon for the drums and luggage, and with Judy's Volkswagen beetle, and whatever George had, we'd trade off the driving. Judy said she'd try to transfer from her job at Honeywell in Newton Highlands to the Honeywell in Los Angeles.

1964-1974: A DECADE OF ODD TALES AND WONDERS

One of the first things I did when I arrived in Boston was buy the Rambler wagon above. I turned it over to Phil V so he could start loading it for the trip. His drum set had to go in first, and it didn't leave room for much else, but they had about a week to sell, give away, or throw out whatever they couldn't bring.

I couldn't find George. Without his vocals and rhythm guitar parts, we couldn't play our songs the way they were on our demo and make the date at The Whisky, I had to act quickly. Karl and Mikey Joe were both staying with Roger, so I called them from Boston and told them to find a replacement and start teaching him our songs.

Judy and I had no furniture worth moving, so we'd be driving to California in the Volkswagen. We filled a few boxes with clothes and small household items and shipped them to Roger's house in La Puente. That night I called Roger to alert him to expect the boxes, and talked to Karl and Mikey Joe. Their news was good. They'd found a perfect replacement for George. I told them to start rehearsing and expect us to be there in about a week.

EVERYTHING CHANGED IN 1968

That first day, with loading and all, we only drove the 467 miles to Niagara Falls. That leg of the trip took eight hours, but the Falls weren't much out of our way, and now, at least, we'd be able to say we'd all seen Niagara Falls.

The following morning we drove southwest, stopping overnight in Vandalia, Illinois. According to my trip log, that nearly 700 miles took us 11 hours.

The next day, we drove through Stanton, Missouri, stealing time to visit the Meramec Caverns where Frank and Jesse James hid out from the law, but late that afternoon, in Tulsa, Oklahoma, 463 miles into the run, the rear axle on the Rambler gave out, costing us most of my ready cash to get it fixed. We all hunkered down in our motel rooms and only picked up the car just before closing time the next day.

1964-1974: A DECADE OF ODD TALES AND WONDERS

On day five, we set out early, drove 650 miles in eleven hours, checked into a motel in Albuquerque, New Mexico, had supper, and tried to get some sleep.

We drove straight through to Los Angeles the next day (nearly 800 miles), finally arriving at 3:30 a.m. at the Lucky Seven Motel in Baldwin Park, California, about 24 miles east of Hollywood. The following afternoon, we called to say we'd arrived, and we'd see everyone tomorrow.

Early the next morning, we joined Karl, Mikey Joe, and the new man, Lonnie, for breakfast at a Denny's restaurant in La Puente. I asked Lonnie how many of our songs he knew. Karl answered for him. "None. We decided to wait for you." I couldn't believe my ears. They did nothing the whole time I was gone but listen to the Top 40 songs Lonnie already knew. We had a gig coming up at the Whiskey, and they hadn't even started rehearsing. Phil V and I still needed to find places to live, so I told them to start working on our songs. Phil and I would be back when we were settled in.

A local realtor, Bob Winings, found a tiny bungalow for Phil V and his wife, and an apartment over his realty office for Judy, Lisa, and me that would do until we could get back to work. I explained our situation to Bob, and asked him if he knew of a rehearsal hall we could rent, cheap. He did better than that. He offered his own house in Covina, and offered to let Mikey Joe and Karl stay in his guest room - free room and board - although a cynic might argue that Karl paid for them both by playing impromptu classical guitar concerts for Bob, his family, and friends.

We barely had time to unpack before Judy started work at Honeywell in West Covina. Bob's house in Covina was further out, but soundproof, and he gave us permission to use his kitchen and bathrooms. There was even a swimming pool, if we needed to cool off. I might have thought the Fates hadn't abandoned us after all, but our rehearsals were lame. Lonnie was excruciatingly slow to learn parts. It soon became clear we wouldn't be ready in time to meet the scheduled gig at the Whisky, so I called and cancelled. It was a disaster. We were jobless and starting over in California. All our fans, friends and families who might have helped us through a rough patch were 3,000 miles away.

Bob Winings' Real Estate Office on Francisquito Avenue was practically under the 10 Freeway overpass, and the windows in the apartment above were louvered, so the noise was next to unbearable. I bought a new Curtis-Mathis color TV set on time, and we had to play it at full volume to hear the sound. We couldn't stay there long with the constant roar from the freeway. Bob said, being a veteran, I was eligible to buy a house, no money down, on the G.I. Bill, and he knew just the place for us. It was on a quiet cul-de-sac nearby, had two bedrooms and was listed for $18,800. The price was intimidating, but even with the taxes, the payment on a 30-year-loan was well within our budget, so we bought it, based mostly, I believe, on the fact that Judy could show steady income from her job at Honeywell.

We moved in while we waited for the paperwork, and having decided to get married, set out to find a preacher that would be acceptable to our absent families. I thought it was perfect that our Baptist minister was a recently converted Jew, and we'd be his first wedding, but we had to put the ceremony on hold until my mother could come out for the wedding.

1964-1974: A DECADE OF ODD TALES AND WONDERS

Phil and June were our Best Man and Bridesmaid. My mother and Adam flew out to be there to witness the occasion, Judy took a day off from work, and on that Monday morning in October, I thought we had everything under control.

As we were getting ready, my mother asked who was picking up the cake. I told her we weren't having cake: we were having ice cream. She replied, "I'm talking about the wedding cake."

After all the weddings in all the movies I'd seen over all those years, a wedding cake had slipped my mind, but I'd recently seen one in a bakery window, so I knew where to go to get one. If I hurried, I'd be back with the cake in plenty of time for us to make our appointment with the preacher.

I think I made it to the bakery in less than ten minutes, and the saleslady at the counter was thrilled when I said I needed a wedding cake. She wanted to know how many guest we were expecting so she could help me decide how many tiers it should have. I thought a moment and came up with thirteen. The saleslady said I should figure sixteen, to be on the safe side, and the bride would probably want to freeze a piece for next year. I figured she knew her business better than I did, so I agreed. Then she asked when I'd need it. Today, I told her. I was getting married in about an hour.

The saleslady was shocked when she realized this wasn't a bad joke and began trying to help me. She had a birthday cake from the day before that hadn't been picked up, if that would do. She thought she could change the frosting message from Happy Birthday to Happy Wedding, if that would work, but she had nothing for a second tier. I asked her if she could just stick a plastic bride and groom thingy in the middle of the cake, and she chose a small one that wouldn't overpower it. I thanked her profusely while she boxed it up, then paid for it, and hurried out to the car.

The ceremony was held in the office at the local Baptist church. In the photo of the wedding party, left to right, Phil's wife, June, Phil V, my mother, Adam, me, Lisa, and Judy.

On a final, nuptial note, Adam was not fooled at all by the transformation of the cake. When Judy began to cut it, he snuggled in next to her and began singing "Happy Birthday." The minister took this picture for us in the front yard of our house, with the neighbor's garage door in the background. I'm glad my mother and Adam came. This photo proves again that Adam really is my baby brother, about eighteen months younger than Lisa, the sweet little girl in the front row.

1964-1974: A DECADE OF ODD TALES AND WONDERS

Lonnie was married with a child and place of his own, but had quickly run out of money while we rehearsed. I subsidized him as best I could, but his bills kept mounting for all of September, October, and November, -- three months of rehearsals during which we tried to teach him our songs and his parts in them.

We were all getting short-tempered and recriminations began to fly. Bob Winings attended several sessions. One day, in the middle of an argument about Lonnie's slow progress and our desperate need to start earning money, Bob offered a solution. He was opening a beer and wine dance bar on Arrow Highway in nearby Glendora. If we wanted, his Guru-V could be our "home room" while we got up to speed. Lonnie and the rest of the band could play Top 40 stuff, then I could come on to do our original material. As for income, we'd all get a piece of the action from the bar.

We really had no choice. For the next two weeks, the band spent most of its time practicing pop tunes while I stewed, played tambourine or cowbell and learned harmony parts to Top 40 songs that could be played on any jukebox by the original artists for a dime. In week two, I insisted we work on at least two original songs a day. But that didn't mean we mastered them. I felt lucky if I added one or two original songs to the list by the end of any week.

Judy wrote my mother a letter on 29 November 1968, reporting things were looking up. We were still rehearsing night and day, but it would end when we started working in December at Guru-V in Glendora, California. Looking back now, I realize we'd been out of work for all of five months. No wonder nerves were frayed and tempers short.

We were working, but the money was terrible. We would have had to fill the room at least four out of six nights to get by, but only four slow nights and the weekend didn't cut it. We ate at the bar, each of us running a tab (deducted on payday), that left everyone but me owing the bar at the end of the week. The few customers we had liked us well enough, and our small crowds kept getting bigger, but much too slowly for anything more than subsistence.

Everyone knew I wasn't happy performing Top 40 tunes, but Bob wanted to keep us at Guru-V to build up his clientele, so he offered the full night's bar percentage if I'd perform my coffeehouse routines on Monday nights as a solo act. I needed the money, so I took him up on it. My Monday night crowds remained small, not atypical for coffeehouse venues, but I told my stories, sang my songs, and my "commissions" continued to trickle in until Chuck Monda, my first California friend and fan came along.

1964-1974: A DECADE OF ODD TALES AND WONDERS

A frequent Guru-V customer during the week, Chuck never showed up on weekends, but once I began doing my coffeehouse routines, I don't think he missed a single Monday night. I worked the room the same way I had worked the rooms in Boston, chatting with customers from the stage, before, during and after each set. Sometimes early, or late if business was particularly slow, I'd join them at their tables.

I think I may have had more people at my Monday night shows, than the whole band had on the other three weekdays, but in all fairness, there was no Monday Night Football in those days, and in the quiet bedroom community of Glendale, California, I suspect whatever nightlife there was during the week, was pretty much residential.

At one time or another, I think Chuck brought all of his friends from Mount San Antonio College (locally called Mount SAC) to hear our "East Coast band," but I never saw him on weekends. It turned out on weekends, he went to The Posh in Pomona, a beer and wine dance hall where there were plenty of girls with whom he could dance the night away.

Somehow, maybe through Chuck, The Posh's owners heard about the great "East Coast band" at the Guru-V and came to hear us. They liked what they heard and made an offer for five nights a week at The Posh, paid in real money! As a result, our Guru-V gig only lasted a few weeks, and was followed by a New Year's Eve gig at an American Legion Hall. The year 1968 had begun auspiciously for Travis Pike's Tea Party, then went all to hell. On our first California New Year's Eve, in 1969, things were finally looking up again.

KNOWING WHEN THE PARTY'S OVER

Chuck and his friends celebrated with us when we moved to The Posh. It was everything Chuck had said, a big beer and wine dance hall in Pomona, not far from the California State Polytechnic University, Pomona campus. By then, with about 30 of our original songs back on our list, we had agreed with the management to play half a set of Top 40 hits, and then I would come on and finish the set with our original songs.

On our first night on stage, a girl came up to me and asked if we were "straight." We couldn't be Travis Pike's Tea Party and not know that "tea" was a popular euphemism for marijuana, but our name came from our Boston heritage. I assured her we were straight. She leaned closer and warned me that someone nearby was a Narc. "That's okay," I said. "We're straight." She said something to the effect of never saying she didn't warn me, and disappeared into the crowd. What was that all about? In Boston, "straight" was like "Straight Arrow." It meant law-abiding, and by extension, that one did not do drugs. Was the reverse true in Southern California?

I didn't know The Posh held a dance contest every Saturday night. The owners moved through the crowd during the early sets, selecting ten couples to compete for a $100 prize. Our second Saturday night dance contest provided one of my best memories of those days.

1964-1974: A DECADE OF ODD TALES AND WONDERS

Couples were allowed to request the song they wanted played for their dance. For our first dance contest, the contestants put in eight requests for "Land of a Thousand Dances," which Lonnie sang while I bashed my thigh black and blue playing tambourine, one for Johnnie Taylor's "Who's Making Love?" which Lonnie sang while I switched over to cowbell, and wonder of wonders, a request for one of my original songs, "Oh Mama," for which I sang the lead and Karl and Lonnie sang harmonies.

I don't know who won the contest or which song was played for their dance, but the second week, there was one request for "Who's Making Love?" (same couple, I suspect), and then, nine requests for "Oh Mama." In a single week, "Oh Mama" blew "Land of a Thousand Dances" right out of the room! It was a glorious personal triumph, but after singing "Oh Mama" nine times in a matter of 30 minutes, I was more than ready to sing "A Very Merry Unbirthday."

At The Posh, the money was good, and we were allowed to showcase our original songs. The owners even tried to help us land a record deal and they actually came back with a tentative offer from Mike Curb's Sidewalk Records. Travis Pike's Tea Party turned it down. They insisted any deal we signed had to be with a major label. None of us knew that Capital Records distributed Sidewalk Records, or that Mike Curb had been at the reins of MGM during the Boston Sound fiasco, and that it was his negative comments in *Rolling Stone* Magazine in Spring 1968, condemning the Boston Sound, that contributed to the collapse of that marketing campaign. I wonder if he knew Travis Pike's Tea Party was a Boston group.

KNOWING WHEN THE PARTY'S OVER

Little changed at our next gig at Barnacle Bill's, a small, rowdy dance bar on Foothill Boulevard in Duarte, about a half hour from Hollywood. The pay was decent, and by then we had about 60 of our original songs in with the Top 40 tunes. No longer on life-support, we weren't exactly healthy, either. In New England, Travis Pike's Tea Party had played concerts and sets of nothing but original songs at special events or in special showcase venues.

Now, everything we had pledged to avoid when we became a band in Boston, had become our reality on the West Coast. No longer an all-original concert band, we played dance bars to survive. Instead of starring in weekend concerts, we worked as a house band, five or six nights a week, and even with 60 original songs back in our repertoire, because we were playing in dance bars, the patrons requested the same familiar songs, night after night -- and that went for ours too! Our original song list grew smaller and smaller as we played only the most requested of them, and the mix with the Top 40 material changed, but never went away.

We hung in for a while longer, but I found it depressing. I stopped writing new songs and had to force myself to go to work. It became clear to me and to Phil V, the drummer, that Travis Pike's Tea Party had run its course.

In March, the guys who owned The Posh drove me into Hollywood to meet Billy Sherman, a talent manager and cofounder of Valiant Records, who released two of my favorite "Sunshine Pop" hits by the Association, "Along Came Mary" and "Windy." It was a pleasant meeting that went nowhere, but we did share the elevator on the way down with Johnny Mathis.

1964-1974: A DECADE OF ODD TALES AND WONDERS

In April, to no one's surprise, Phil V and I quit. Mikey Joe asked me to help them come up with a new name for the group. I suggested *Quo Vadis*. The irony was lost on him. He didn't know that in Latin, it meant "Where are you going?" All three thought it sounded classy, so they adopted it. Six months later, they broke up. The sad answer to my Latin question was "Nowhere."

The night of our final group performance, the Rambler that brought us west gave out. I made it home, but the car was undriveable, so I sold it for its tires to a man who lived across the street, and walked to a local used car dealership. Old-timers may remember that TV commercial with the cute gal in the white cowgirl hat telling us all to "join the Dodge Rebellion." I certainly do, and it might have been running through my mind when I saw that turquoise 1964 Dodge Polara V-8 four-door sedan. Having just been paid, I had enough in my wallet to make the down payment, and Judy couldn't believe her eyes when I drove it into our driveway.

Phil V returned to Boston, but I stayed in California and took a steady job cleaning a dance bar. A lot of people might think that going from headliner to "head" cleaner, (nautical, remember?) would be a comedown, but in fact it suited me admirably. Remember, I started doing janitorial work with Fuzzy, cleaning the Newton Centre Market and Bonozoli's Beacon Restaurant when I was a teenager, so I knew what was required and had experience sweeping, scraping up gum, swabbing, waxing and buffing. Best of all, I'd only be working a few hours in the morning -- every morning -- but then I was free to come home to my writing, composing, illustrating, research, or whatever moved me.

KNOWING WHEN THE PARTY'S OVER

My schedule allowed some quality time with my new family -- except on Saturday and Sunday mornings, which isn't to say we didn't spend most of them together. They came with me to help clean the bar, but cleaning up toilets and urinals after wild and wooly Friday and Saturday nights, was pretty disgusting. Maybe that's why it paid better than playing rock 'n' roll.

In August, I wrote a jingle for a Pike Productions commercial for Almacs Stores. The extra income came in handy three months later, when the clutch on Judy's VW gave out. Thinking I might turn it into a Dune Buggy, I put the VW up on blocks, then bought a turquoise 1964 Dodge Dart Convertible for Judy that actually matched the Dodge Polara. It was amazing how good they looked when they were both parked in the driveway. People might even think we were wealthy back in 1964.

With my afternoons free, and an excellent library nearby, I pursued my independent studies. I don't remember what triggered my interest in the Czechoslovakian Spring of 1968, but in 1969, I read every book the library had on Dubcek's reforms and the subsequent Soviet invasion, which may have only numbered four books at the time. Was my interest reinforced by the fact that my father, while at WNAC-TV in Boston, was involved in bringing to television, *Suffer the Little Children* and *Weltschmertz*, two documentaries about the 1956 Soviet invasion of Hungary? I don't know.

The story I began writing in January 1970, was fiction, a suspense thriller intended for the big screen and based on the historical events of the summer of 1968, but featuring a secret policeman of my own invention, a Slovak known to the Soviets as "Novotny's Talons," and whose exploits were only mentioned in whispers, and attributed to *The Witch of Wenceslas Square.* I forgot about it until I began researching this book, but I still get the creepy-crawlies just thinking about it.

That summer of 1970, I sold the VW for parts to somebody who wanted to build a Dune Buggy more than I did. To celebrate (on a day when I obviously wasn't working on *The Witch of Wenceslas Square*), I visited with Chuck and his friends and the conversation drifted into a discussion of dream cars. Chuck had his Pontiac Gran Prix and Rich Stange had his Ford Model A. Others dreamed of Corvettes or T-Birds, but my dream car was a Mercedes Cabriolet. No one knew what it was or what it looked like, so I sketched one, calling attention to its baby carriage convertible roof trim, and a good time was had by all.

Apart from the angle of the trunk, which would have been correct for a pre-war Cabriolet with a continental kit, my sketch was fairly accurate.

In September, with a healthy down from the sale of the disassembled VW, I bought a 16' fixer-upper outboard Cabin Cruiser and trailer, and began contemplating nautical family adventures. I used to love rowing around the lake in Newton Centre, but although I was ex-Navy, and graduated from boot camp at the top of my class, I had no practical experience at sea. My new boat needed a lot of work, and would be dry-docked for some time before it could go back in the water. When I learned the US Coast Guard Auxiliary offered classes in boating safety, I decided some nautical instruction was in order.

In November 1970, I officially qualified in basic seamanship, and was invited to join the Coast Guard Auxiliary. By then, I'd learned a lot about their mission, described in those days as assisting in "non-law enforcement programs such as public education, vessel safety checks, safety patrols, search and rescue, and marine environmental protection." I'd have to buy a uniform before the next season got underway, but my little cruiser would never pass a CGA examination in its current state, and I hoped to get some first-hand experience in powerboat handling.

United States Coast Guard Auxiliary

MEMBERSHIP CERTIFICATE

THIS is to certify that ___TRAVIS EDWARD PIKE F-11-3___ has met the requirements of the regulations governing the membership of the United States Coast Guard Auxiliary, has been found BASICALLY QUALIFIED and has this _27th_ day of ___NOVEMBER___, 19_70_ been enrolled as a member.

C. F. GAILEY, JR., CDR, USCG, Director of Auxiliary
_11th_ Coast Guard District

1964-1974: A DECADE OF ODD TALES AND WONDERS

At our New Year's party, we toasted Chuck, for having escaped the draft in his last year of eligibility, but on January 2nd, his notice to report arrived, mailed in December 1970.

I was haunted by my 1968 song, "Don't You Care At All." The Tet Offensive was two years earlier and if anything, the war was escalating.

I stayed in the Coast Guard Auxiliary. The CGA is a volunteer organization providing experience, talent and resources for Maritime Safety Outreach, Search and Rescue, Security Patrols, Disaster Response, and Pollution Response. If a civilian vessel passes a free examination, a decal is issued, which in many cases reduces insurance costs for the boater. Should a vessel fail, the examiner gives the discrepancy report to the boater, showing what needs attention in order to pass a subsequent inspection.

Auxiliary members, and their thousands of boats, are frequently first responders in emergency search and rescue and resupply operations after floods or hurricanes, especially in inland waterways where the regular Coast Guard are unavailable or unable to navigate in the shallow waters -- and they do it all without compensation. What the organization chiefly needed at that time was more Courtesy Motorboat Examiners to inspect recreational power boats to assure they were in compliance with all Federal and State boating laws and promote safe boating to the public. I took the course and qualified as a Courtesy Motorboat Examiner in March 1971, but my personal interest was in Auxiliary Search and Rescue Patrol (AUXSARPAT), to which end I qualified as an AUXSARPAT Navigator in May 1971.

United States Coast Guard Auxiliary

CERTIFICATE OF ADVANCEMENT

THIS *is to certify that* _____TRAVIS E. PIKE III F 11-3_____ *has satisfactorily completed all requirements for* _____COURTESY MOTORBOAT EXAMINER_____

in the Coast Guard Auxiliary.

_____C. F. GAILEY, JR., CDR, USCG_____, Director of Auxiliary

ELEVENTH Coast Guard District

MARCH 17, 1971

Certificate of Advancement

United States Coast Guard Auxiliary

This certifies that _____Travis Edward Pike_____ has satisfactorily completed all requirements for and is hereby designated a

_____AUXSARPAT NAVIGATOR_____

in the Coast Guard Auxiliary

Certificate No. 439

Awarded this 20th day of May, 19 71

JOHN E. EPPINK, Rear Commodore
ELEVENTH COAST GUARD DISTRICT

1964-1974: A DECADE OF ODD TALES AND WONDERS

Certificate of Advancement

United States Coast Guard Auxiliary

This certifies that ___TRAVIS E. PIKE___ has satisfactorily completed all requirements for and is hereby designated a

___AUXSARPAT COMMUNICATOR___

in the Coast Guard Auxiliary

Certificate No. _698_

JOHN J. EPPINK, Rear Commodore

Awarded this _7th_ day of _September_, _1971_

ELEVENTH COAST GUARD DISTRICT

When I qualified as an AUXSARPAT Communicator, my excellent scores in every part of my training, convinced my Flotilla Commander that I could best serve the Auxiliary as an Instructor, training others in the various specialties required for Search and Rescue duties, and I made that my next goal.

In addition to trying to be a useful member of the community, I was writing screenplays and songs, auditioning musicians, and cleaning the bar, every day, ad infinitum, ad nauseum.

I'm a morning person (perhaps not my most endearing trait, or so I am given to understand by my beloved). Nevertheless, my brain cells are fully engaged as soon as I awaken, as if celebrating the fact that they made it through the night, full of exciting notions, all crying for attention. Alone, cleaning the bar, with wonderful insights and ideas coursing through my mind, I interfaced with my employer through notes, since I'd be gone before he ever arrived.

I naturally assumed that by the time he awoke, performed his morning ablutions, dressed, imbibed whatever stimulant he employed to kickstart his brain, and drove to work, he'd be awake enough to appreciate my observations, and often shared them with him in my notes, written as much to entertain as to inform. For example, when I saw a note from my employer asking me to be sure to hose down the area directly outside the back door, I was perfectly happy to oblige. And if it please the court, note that he left me a note, and I replied to his note with my own, taking the opportunity to inject a modicum of levity as I explained why I was unable to comply with his wishes. Confident that the following was one of my better efforts, I submitted . . .

"I don't suppose that anyone knows about the hose,
The hose that goes to the sink?
I've searched the highs. I've searched the lows.
I've looked all over, goodness knows.
I just don't know what to think!"

I never imagined a clever little rhyme could get me fired, but for some reason, it infuriated him. Why really doesn't matter. I'm not even certain that he did fire me. Maybe I quit. What matters is that in October 1971, I was out of a job, and had to find another, right away.

I put out feelers to all my local friends to be on the lookout for something I could handle. Fortunately, when my two former roadies, New England bikers Jon-Jon Hayes and Phil Cataldo, now living in Anaheim, California, heard I was looking for work, they offered me a job with them, installing awnings, building porches, and installing ramps and stairs on mobile homes. They were pulling jobs directly from a factory outlet in Fullerton, as often as desire or necessity required. Furthermore, the pay was excellent and the job would still leave me plenty of time for writing. I wasn't sure if my bad ankle could handle it, but I needed work, so I wrapped it in an Ace bandage and told them I'd give it a try.

I had to drive to Phil C's place in Anaheim, at least 60 miles a day and between 30-60 minutes each way, depending on traffic, just to get to work and back. Then I'd ride with Phil C over to Fullerton to load the truck, and then ride in the truck with Phil C and Jon-Jon to get to the job site.

The work was hard and the hours long, but it was not as relentless and often nasty as cleaning the bar every morning. With my bad ankle, I had to be particularly careful how I went up and down ladders to install awnings, but I worked okay on the scaffold. The hardest part of installing awnings was digging holes for the metal anchors that supported the columns, especially, in Orange and San Diego Counties, where you could be digging through decomposed granite. When mattocks weren't enough, we'd rent a jackhammer, which did the job, but cut into our profits.

Porches and stairs were heavy work. The porches were supported by 4x6 beams set on jacks we inserted into holes atop prefabricated concrete piers -- the higher and longer the porch, the taller, heavier, and more piers needed to support it. Porch floors were made of 4x8' sheets of $1\frac{1}{8}$" tongue and groove plywood, heavy, but usually carried by two of us at a time. Even so, loading and unloading the job on the truck was hazardous for me. I had to be sure of my footing, lest I slip or twist my ankle and fall under the heavy loads. My Latvian friends had taught me how to use a power saw, so trimming the edges of the porches and crawling around on my hands and knees to staple down the outdoor carpeting was a snap. Screwing in dozens of pickets and posts for stair and porch rails was simply a matter of making sure they were level and holding the drill properly, and it looked like I'd be making enough money to follow my dreams, if I ever could find the time.

Early one morning, I drove to Anaheim to get paid for the job we'd just completed, even though we didn't have another job until the following week. On the way home, as I came off the 5 Freeway North, on the on-ramp to the 10 Freeway East, I saw what appeared to be a long-haired hippy chick with an autoharp, hitchhiking up to the freeway. It's against the law to hitchhike on the Freeway, but as she was alone and carrying an autoharp, I pulled to the side of the on-ramp and told her to get in. I gave her my lecture about the dangers of hitchhiking, and the trouble she'd be in if she was picked up by the highway patrol, and told her that the only reason I stopped for her was because I was a musician and saw her autoharp.

She told me she sang and accompanied herself on the autoharp, had written music to go with all the Elven lyrics in Tolkien's *Lord of the Rings* and would like to audition for me. (I'd never read *Lord of the Rings*, so that was not a big attraction to me, but I was always on the look out for musicians.) She was on her way to Covina, just beyond West Covina, so I offered to take her all the way to her destination. It turned out the place was pretty swank, and she was house sitting for the owners while they were on vacation.

Inside, the first thing she did was pour us each a lemonade. I watched as she drank about half of hers before I drank any of mine. Better safe than sorry. Then we went out to the patio, and sat in the shade by the pool at the back of the house, while she played and sang her songs for me.

Her autoharp accompaniment, an attempt at dramatic strumming, but without any picking at all, frankly left me cold, but she had an angelic singing voice. However, everything she sang was in what she thought Elven should sound like, and I didn't understand a word.

Bored out of my skull and eager to get out of there, I thanked her for singing for me, told her, truthfully, that she had a lovely voice, and suggested her program was best suited to a coffeehouse scene with a college crowd, and she should probably advertise it as an artistic impression of Tolkien's Elven songs. I also suggested she'd do better if she had a guitarist accompany her, too.

I rose to leave and she asked me if I'd play some of my songs for her. I had no guitar with me, but there was a Martin in the living room, and eager as I was to get away, I played "Gray Day Lady" and "Shaggy, Shaggy Blues," which sound nothing like the songs she played for me.

She liked them, and had a record producer friend at Stormy Forest Records in Hollywood that she was sure would be interested in my songs, and offered to introduce me to him. I'd never heard of Stormy Forest Records, but she called her friend and made an appointment for the following week. We exchanged phone numbers and true to her word, she called,

KNOWING WHEN THE PARTY'S OVER

gave me directions back to her house to pick her up, and we drove to Mark Roth's home on Ogden Avenue in Hollywood.

He was pressed for time, but wanted to hear my songs. I suggested that I perform my short narrative rhyme, *The Lori,* with the songs I'd written to go with it. That sparked his interest enough that he listened to my entire performance, and immediately set up a recording session for the following week, at a small MGM recording studio on Fairfax Avenue.

The next day, out of a clear blue sky, Rich arrived at my house in his Model A. He'd seen my dream car, parked on a street in Pomona, with a "for sale" sign in the window, and offered to take me out to see it.

Rich was right! It was a rare 1954 Mercedes-Benz Cabriolet A, listed for $5,000. In 1968, the average price for a new car was $2,822, so this not-quite-yet-classic was not exactly inexpensive -- but if I ate a lot of peanut butter and jelly sandwiches, I might be able to afford it. Suddenly and unexpectedly, I had before me a rare opportunity to purchase my dream car. Being homeowners with good credit, it would have been no problem to get a loan on a new car, but we had to jump through hoops to get the bank to grant us a $5,000 loan to buy a classic automobile.

One such hoop was we had to pay 20% down. Rich had his eyes on Judy's Dodge Dart, so we agreed to sell it to him for half the down payment, but I was still afraid someone else might come along and snap up the classic before we could.

I had a recording session coming up, and I was trying to figure out a strategy to get the bank to finance a classic automobile, which to them was just an old car, and to finance it for more than the cost of a new car. Jon-Jon, Phil C, and I were in the middle of the pre-Christmas crush, with coaches competing for space in the most desirable mobile home parks, and all of them clamoring to have their porches, stairs and awnings installed before the holidays. It was an awful time to have to take a day off, because it was a wonderful time to make a lot of money -- enough in a single week to come up with the rest of the down payment on the Mercedes.

Stormy Forest Records was paying for the recording session, the date had been set, I was fully prepared as far as both the rhyme and the music were concerned, and I didn't dare suggest a postponement. In fact, the session was a snap. It took more time to set up for the recording than it did for me to sing, play the songs, and tell the tale, because the studio was experimenting with a new stereo microphone that, placed between the vocal and the musical instrument, allowed the engineer to set different levels and equalization on either side of the mike, and adjust them, as if they were two separate microphones during recording. Why that would be superior to using two mikes and recording the vocal on one and the guitar on the other, still escapes me.

I have good mike technique, developed from working live, so I knew enough to lean in on soft passages and back off on the howlers, but Mark was in the booth with the engineer, and they had me run through parts of each song so the engineer could get the right balance of level and equalization for each. When they were finally ready to go, Mark told me to just play and sing it the way I did at his house, and I recorded the entire piece in a single pass. Then I sat quietly as Mark and the engineer talked about the result. I interrupted once to ask if I could hear a playback, and Mark hit the talkback and asked me to stand by a minute. A short time later, the engineer came on the talkback and asked me if I'd play a bit of "Oh Mama" for him. I did until he said it was enough, and asked me to play the whole song for him, one more time.

Maybe my mike technique was not quite as good as I thought, or maybe, caught up in the moment, I had really gone for broke and overmodulated. For whatever reason, I re-recorded that song in its entirety, and when it was done, Mark came on the talkback and announced happily, we were out of there. As I drove him back to his house, he said I was fantastic, and he'd call me when he had a mix.

When Judy asked me how it went, I told her I hadn't heard the recording yet, but Mark said I was fantastic and we'd have to wait for the mix -- a story I must have repeated more than a dozen times over the next day or so, to Jon-Jon, Phil C, Phil C's wife, a guy at the awning warehouse, and friends who called to ask how the session went.

I didn't have an answering machine, so Mark must have left his message on someone else's machine when he called to say he was submitting *The Lori* to Universal Studios for a TV Special. The first I heard of it was when I called him a few days later to ask if he had the mix yet. He said he'd played it for the creative types at Universal and they loved it! (He actually said their names, but they meant nothing to me, so I don't remember them.) Excited by the prospect, I asked what came next, and he said "patience." About a week later he called to say their marketing department had shot it down, saying it wasn't commercial and they wouldn't be able to get sponsors for it, but he was already working on another deal . . . and he'd be in touch.

Suddenly, just about a week before Christmas, my friends and I were out of work. All the jobs orders had been filled or pulled, and we might as well take a few weeks off to enjoy the holidays. Having brought in more than $700, I went to the bank and made the deposit to secure the $4,000 car loan (collateral for the bank, should I fail to make the payments and they had to repossess and sell the car), and dedicated the rest of my windfall to making the holidays merry and bright. Had I been at the installation business longer, I'd have put it aside, but unaware of the doldrums between the holidays and the end of February, I didn't.

We took possession of that incredible Mercedes Benz 220 Cabriolet A in January 1972. The lovely, barefoot girl with one foot inside the chrome edged suicide door is my darling Judy. If you can take your eyes off her, you may notice the fog lights and one half of the set of German police horns on the front bumper. And if you're wondering why, in January, there's no snow on the ground, you haven't been paying attention. We left Boston, Massachusetts (and its winters) in 1968, and moved to Los Angeles County, California. To put it in an even better perspective, if you're one of the millions of viewers, worldwide, who've ever watched the New Year's Day Pasadena Rose Parade on television, we're just a few miles south of Pasadena.

After the holidays, Phil C and Jon-Jon called or went by the warehouse daily, hoping to pull some work. After about three weeks of haunting the warehouse foreman, he promised to call Phil C as soon as a job came in, but told him that work wouldn't really pick up until the end of February or early March. I had already made the first car payment out of the generous holiday gift checks we'd received from our families back east, and had set aside enough for a second car payment, if I didn't get work before March.

Helpless is one thing. Hopeless is another, and I refused to go there. I decided this prolonged hiatus was an excellent time to explore other options and submitted my screenplay to

1964-1974: A DECADE OF ODD TALES AND WONDERS

The Red-backed, Scaly, Black-bellied, Tusked, Bat-winged Dragon to Walt Disney Studios. Then I called Hanna-Barbera, and their man in charge of acquisitions scheduled a meeting with me. That meeting was encouraging in terms of my work, but their production pipeline was already going full steam with half-hour TV shows, and he wasn't really in the market for a feature. Ultimately, Disney passed, too.

With three of us working on porches and awnings, any of us could take a day off whenever needed. I subscribed to *Variety, The Hollywood Reporter,* and various musicians' contact services, and took days off whenever I had to follow up leads in Hollywood.

One such lead produced a meeting with Raoul Alteresco, aka Ray Arco, a working member of the Hollywood Foreign Press and president of Beaux Arts Productions. We had lunch at the Formosa restaurant in Hollywood, where the walls were covered with signed headshots of many of Hollywood's most famous movie stars.

I presented him with the screenplay for *The Red-backed, Scaly, Black-bellied, Tusked, Bat-winged Dragon*, which he promised to read and get back to me. Beaux Arts Productions had previously imported Romanian animated short subjects, compiled them into what he called a "roadshow," and successfully marketed them in the States. The meeting went well, and he paid for lunch.

Judy didn't like to drive the Dodge Polara, and refused to drive the Mercedes Cabriolet to work at Honeywell, so in March, we traded in the Polara, and bought a 1966 VW Bus for her on credit. Installations were picking up, and I drove to Phil C's house every morning, and parked the Mercedes in his driveway. Then we'd both get in the truck, meet Jon-Jon at the warehouse, and load up a job. By July, we were back in full swing again, with as much work as we could handle, when we hit a figurative bump in the road that threatened to put us all out of work.

A new State regulation to protect consumers from unscrupulous installers required one of us to become a licensed C-61 contractor, to legally keep our lucrative business going. One of the prerequisites for applying for the license was at least four years in the business. None of us qualified.

Jon-Jon quit and moved up north, but Phil C had a family and all the obligations that come with that, so we made a deal with the owner of Aluma-Craft Awnings, a licensed contractor, to continue installing on his payroll. The immediate result was that our incomes fell by approximately 40%, partly because of the contractor's fees, and partly because working for one of the several contractors who sold product out of that Fullerton warehouse, rather than any of them at any time, we didn't have as much work, but that left me more time to pursue my personal goals.

I completed all the requirements to become an official United States Coast Guard Auxiliary Instructor on 24 October 1972, and then, so that I could teach all the specialties required, qualified as an AUXSARPAT Crewman-Towmaster on November 1972.

Although I was a member of the Coast Guard Auxiliary for two years, I never got to inspect a motorboat or participate in a search and rescue operation, but I learned enough to realize my little cruiser was only fit to be a lawn ornament.

1964-1974: A DECADE OF ODD TALES AND WONDERS

D U P L I C A T E

United States Coast Guard Auxiliary

CERTIFICATE OF ADVANCEMENT

This is to certify that ___TRAVIS E. PIKE F 11-3___ *has satisfactorily completed all requirements for* ___INSTRUCTOR___ *in the Coast Guard Auxiliary.*

___R. E. DILLER, LCDR, USCG___, Director of Auxiliary

ELEVENTH Coast Guard District

___24 OCTOBER___, 19 72

Certificate of Advancement

United States Coast Guard Auxiliary

This certifies that ___Travis E. Pike___ has satisfactorily completed all requirements for and is hereby designated a

___AUXSARPAT CREWMAN-TOWMASTER___

in the Coast Guard Auxiliary

Certificate No. ___1391___

___JOHN J. EPPINK___, Rear Commodore

Awarded this ___20th___ day of ___November___, 19 ___72___   ELEVENTH COAST GUARD DISTRICT

162

KNOWING WHEN THE PARTY'S OVER

In the picture, I'm not saluting. I'm preparing to remove my "cover," as I enter the house. The image was captured from an old VHS recording made by my older brother, Jimmy, when he visited me in California more than a decade after I left the Coast Guard Auxiliary. He wanted a picture of me in my foul weather jacket and cap, to show to our brother, Gregory, an enthusiastic sailor moored in Newport, Rhode Island, who regularly sailed the waters of Rhode Island Sound and Buzzard's Bay. I love the image, but I'm not in uniform; I'm in costume.

However, I'm glad to have been a useful member of the United States Coast Guard Auxiliary, and proudly take my cap off to all the CGA, past and present, for their contributions to boating safety, disaster relief, and now, to our nation's security.

1964-1974: A DECADE OF ODD TALES AND WONDERS

In November, Raoul called to say he'd read *The Redbacked, Scaly, Black-bellied, Tusked, Bat-winged Dragon*, loved it, had spoken to one of his Romanian animation contacts about it, and wanted me to come in so we could discuss the possibility of a Romanian-American co-venture. This time we had lunch at the Astro-Burger on the corner of Santa Monica Boulevard and North Gardner Street, just south of his apartment, and I paid for lunch.

To understand Raoul, you should know that he was an Eastern European member of the Hollywood Foreign Press, loudly conversant in several languages and, as every Romanian would know by virtue of his surname Alteresco, rather than Alterescu, a Romanian Jew, considered a Gypsy in his homeland. High volume was his natural voice, often shrill, and almost always excited about whatever he had to say, and prone to shout over you if you spoke before he was finished. His Talmudic attitudes were moderated to the degree that he extended their provenance to select non-Jews, of which group, I had become a prominent member.

Raoul told me his Romanian contacts would only be interested in participating in a co-venture, if at least half of the budget came from the U.S. He volunteered to translate the screenplay into Romanian, and pursue the deal for me, but he'd want a piece of the action, and a co-producer credit if a deal came of it.

I asked how much he figured the budget would be and where we would get the money? He said he couldn't give me any figures until the Romanians had read the script and detailed their participation, but the animation would not only be superb, but cost much less than anything we could do over here. To come to a figure, they'd have to do a detailed breakdown of all the elements they were expected to provide. Of course, the voice actors would be part of the above the line, and we'd be responsible for providing the dialog tracks, but we could save a fortune if the Romanians supplied the effects tracks, and a Romanian orchestra played the score. I said I'd need to think it over, and he hugged me and joyfully screamed in my ear that he knew we'd be working together the first time we'd met!

He then invited me to a very special Christmas holiday party at a house on top of Nichols Canyon, with several members of the Hollywood Foreign Press that he'd like me to meet. He'd been able to wrangle me an invitation, and told me I absolutely had to come. I don't remember if it was the Saturday or the Sunday night immediately before Christmas Eve, but I said I didn't know if Judy had anything planned and I'd have to check with her. "Of course," he shrieked, "Bring your wife, too." I told him I'd invite her and get back to him. "Marvelous!" He shouted. "I can't wait to meet her!"

In fact, so close to the holidays, all the guns had fallen silent. Phil C and I would likely be out of work at least until the end of February, so I had no excuse not to go. When I returned home, I told Judy about the meeting, what we'd discussed, and that we'd been invited to a party at the top of the Hollywood Hills. Judy didn't want to go, and immediately began reciting a verbal list in support of her decision. It would be impossible to get a babysitter at such short notice, she still had so much to do to get ready for Christmas and really couldn't spare the time. She stopped short of nothing to wear, and told me I should go, if I wanted.

I was still thinking it over when the phone rang. It was Raoul, calling to see if Judy and I were going to come to the party. I told him Judy was too busy getting ready for the holidays and couldn't make it. "But you're coming, aren't you?" he wailed.

"Yes. I'll be there," I answered.

"Excellent!" He shrieked, then told me to be sure to bring my guitar, pick him up at his house, and we'd go together in the Mercedes. I'd never find the place without him.

The big night came, and with a sigh, I left the comfort of my house to venture into the unknown. Raoul guided me to the beginning of Nichols Canyon Drive off Hollywood Boulevard. At first, it was straightforward enough, but then it became like a large, skinny snake dropped on a hot griddle, twisting, writhing and turning back on itself, and all the way, climbing ever higher, with ever more precipitous drops to the canyon floor below, barely enough room to squeeze past parked cars hugging the side of the road, and terrifying when a car approached on its way downhill. As I white-knuckled my way up the hill, Raoul recited the guest list, telling me all the people I would meet, what they did, and why they were important, none of which I retained.

I'm happy to say, there really was a small plateau at the top of the hill, with a sprinkling of houses all perched on the hillside, some on stilts, or so it seemed, jutting far out over the canyon. Our host's house was small, but spectacularly situated, with a pool that seemed to protrude out into space, ready to detach itself from the patio at the first rumble of an earthquake. Inside, the din was almost unbearable, many different conversations and a number of different languages, some I recognized and some I did not, each competing to be heard over the others. As Raoul guided me around the room, introducing me to one and all, everyone I met was happy to greet me in English.

I was not particularly uncomfortable. In fact, I enjoyed being an observer, rather than the center of attention. The host and hostess were Jack and Ellen Hibler, and when I spoke to them in German, they were delighted. The snacks were excellent, the wine as well. I only had one glass, remembering that I still had to make it down that awful, unlit, narrow winding road later on.

In the course of time, as expected, Raoul and the host and hostess asked me to play for them. I grabbed everybody's attention by performing my short narrative rhyme, *The Peerless Goth*, in which I differentiate the characters by using distinct and separate voices for each, starting with the Drang's whiny, "Why me?" I think I followed with an exciting, quick-time finger-picking rendition of "God Rest Ye Merry Gentlemen" that satisfied seasonal expectations, then sang a clever, humorous German Drinking song, *"Es gibt kein Bier auf Hawaii,"* and concluded with my original ballad in German and English, "End of Summer."

As I returned my guitar to its case, an intense Frenchman approached, telling me that "End of Summer" was the exact *"zeitgeist"* he needed for the documentary film he was making called, *The Second Gun*, about the assassination of Robert Kennedy, and he absolutely had to have it for his main title theme.

The filmmaker was Gerard Alcan, and his selection of my song was widely and spontaneously endorsed by the

1964-1974: A DECADE OF ODD TALES AND WONDERS

Hollywood Foreign Press correspondents present, none of whom had ever heard me or my song before. In different circumstances, I would have been thrilled, but that night, I found it uncanny. I had met and spoken briefly with John F. Kennedy in my father's house, when he was being filmed for the political documentary that helped him win the Democratic nomination for president of the United States, and now I was being asked to provide the theme to a movie about the assassination of his brother, shot down in the pantry of the Ambassador Hotel in Los Angeles, immediately after he won the California Democratic Party's nomination for the same office. That night, I only promised to consider it, and as it was getting quite late, I had a long way to go, and hoped to make it alive down Nichols Canyon Road, I bid everyone goodnight. I left alone. Raoul was among friends and could easily get a ride home.

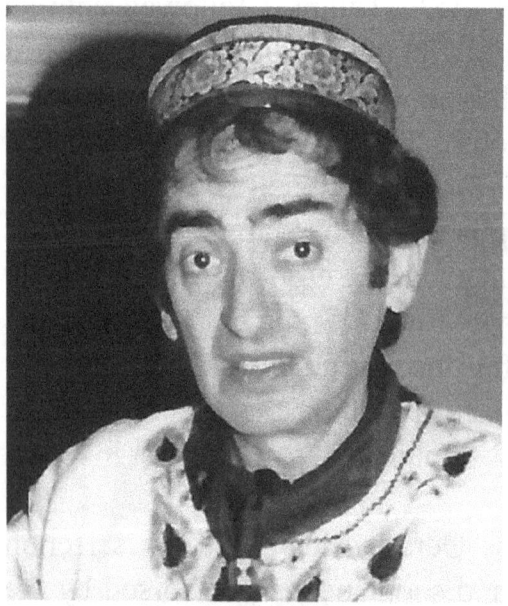

The fellow on the left is Raoul Alteresco, also known as Ray Arco, member of the Hollywood Foreign Press Corps, loud and personable founder and sole owner of Beaux Arts Films, and a most colorful and entertaining Hollywood character, who took an early interest in my rhymes, songs and stories.

FROM THE VALLEY TO THE BASIN

Today's air quality is much improved over that of the late sixties and early seventies. When Judy, Lisa, and I came west in 1968, we settled in West Covina, in the San Gabriel Valley, for two reasons. First, because Judy had transferred from her job at Honeywell in Newton Highlands, Massachusetts, to the Honeywell in West Covina, and second, because of Los Angeles' notorious reputation for smog.

I bought a house before I learned that most of the smog generated in L.A., flowed inland and wound up, concentrated, in the San Gabriel Valley. When we first moved in, I had never seen, and therefore had no idea we were so close to the San Gabriel mountains, until one fine, clear day, I was astonished to see the local foothills in daylight, looming over us, only minutes away by automobile. And I never saw the higher elevation peaks behind the foothills until their ridges were brilliantly illuminated against the night skies by raging wildfires. Many-a-day I watched in dread as the smog rolled toward us, and our early morning blue skies turned brownish-yellow. Those were the "stay indoors" days, and there were many of them. But it came as a complete surprise when I learned that, on average, the air quality was much better in the Los Angeles Basin, than in the San Gabriel Valley.

In early January, the mobile home doldrums were in effect, and ever since that memorable Hollywood Hills party, as Ron Moody's Fagin sang in *Oliver*, I'd been "Reviewing the

Situation," and exploring various options with Judy. I was an unemployed singer, songwriter, graphic artist, screenwriter, and poet, employed as an installer in the mobile home industry, and out of work until late February or early March. I'd looked in the want ads and there was no call for my skills anywhere in the San Gabriel Valley, but we were only about an hour away from Hollywood, where, as Eliza Doolittle's father, Alfred P. Doolittle (played by Stanley Holloway), sang in *My Fair Lady*, "With a Little Bit of Luck," in Hollywood my skills might lead to fame and fortune beyond imagining.

More a state of mind than a geographical location, "Hollywood" easily encompassed the Los Angeles neighborhoods of Laurel Canyon, Universal City, Studio City, and North Hollywood, as well as sections of the cities of Burbank, Culver City, and Santa Monica, and judging by the real estate ads, there were houses for sale or rent in some of those areas that we might afford. It was obvious to both of us that I'd have a better chance of furthering my career in "Greater Hollywood," but I feared I might be asking Judy to give up too much. That's when she told me, in no uncertain terms, that she'd married me, not the house or the appliances, and if I was moving to Hollywood, she was coming with me, for better or for worse. And then, as if to seal the deal, I received a call from Raoul.

Apparently, one of the Hollywood Foreign Press partygoers imported German films and was having them dubbed into English at MGM Studios. I suspect my multi-voiced performance of *The Peerless Goth* triggered the importer's interest. He spoke to Raoul and Raoul's call was to give me the date, time and location at MGM studios where the dubbing director was auditioning voice actors. I jumped at the opportunity, and wrote down the information I was to give the gate guard when I arrived at the studio. As I drove up in the Mercedes Cabriolet, he lifted the gate and waved me through. I had to stop to ask where the audition soundstage was, and where to park, but judging by the number of "sirs' in his directions, the Mercedes Cabriolet must have convinced him I was a VIP.

The auditions were on film loops, which meant that my scenes were spliced together on a roll of film, and marked with a red stripe that moved diagonally across the picture to signal when to say my line or lines. Having been practicing different character voices for years, and having been a musician, the combination of my multiple voices and timing knocked them over. Depending on the film, I could easily do double and even triple character parts, especially the silly ones, and my audition placed me at the top of the dubbing cast list.

Before I left I was given a list of dates and times when they wanted me back. The work was non-union, but my SAG (Screen Actors Guild), card from 1966 had expired at the end of that year and I'd never renewed my membership, so that was no problem for me. It was easy work, and if I could get enough hours, I could make more in a few days than I did in a week of doing porches and awnings.

The movies turned out to be soft-core comedies. I did three sessions, two or three characters in each, and had lunch once in the MGM commissary where real movie stars dined. I can't remember who any of the stars were that I saw that day, but I remember that the Curried Chicken was superb, although the Chutney was a bit too spicy for my taste.

1964-1974: A DECADE OF ODD TALES AND WONDERS

When I drove in for my fourth waved-through-the-gate dubbing session, I learned the session had been cancelled. Having braved morning rush hour traffic all the way from West Covina to Culver City, I was annoyed that I hadn't been notified of the cancellation. I submitted a trip charge for the gas and inconvenience. Not only was my trip charge ignored, I was stricken from the dubbing director's cast list, too.

No matter. We'd set our course. Judy stayed on at Honeywell, but applied for an opening at UCLA. I had set aside enough to see us through the new year doldrums, and earned some extra money dubbing, so feeling well-fixed, we allowed ourselves to spend some of our Christmas money on gifts we could report back to our families. And as January came to an end, we listed our house for sale.

Gerard called to invite me to dinner at his house, in the flat land at the bottom of Nichols Canyon Road. The lamb chops were perfectly prepared and the wine was superb. Of course, he wanted to convince me to let him use "End of Summer" for his film. I had already decided, when I accepted his dinner invitation, that I would, with the caveat that I was only granting him synchronization rights for the music on the film and not for the lyrics or any vocals. He said he'd have the paperwork drawn up right away. It couldn't have been more than a week later that I met him and his partner, Ted Charach in Al (Abraham) Kaplan's office at ABC Circle Films. In addition to being the president of ABC Circle Films, Al was a practicing entertainment attorney, and had drawn up the papers for the synchronization rights. It was my kind of meeting. All the paperwork was in order, I signed, received a check and we set a date for the recording.

Not long after closing the deal with Gerard, I received a call from Mark Roth, inviting me to a record industry soiree at his home in Hollywood. He warned me that the most important guests would be arriving late, due to previous commitments, which meant a late night and a long drive back to the valley for me. Judy didn't want to go, for any number of reasons, so I invited Rich to come with me, meet some celebrities, and make sure I stayed awake on the drive home.

Based on the Rolls Royce Corniche parked at the curb in front of Mark's house, at least one major celebrity was already there, and another must have left just before we arrived, because there was a parking space directly behind the Rolls. We'd been there about an hour when Mark approached, laughing. He told me everyone who arrived after I did, was asking him who owned the gorgeous Mercedes parked behind the Rolls. He hadn't known, and just realized it was me!

I acted shocked, and asked who had dared suggest that the host should park cars? He froze and looked strangely past me, as if in deep thought, or perhaps turning his ear to better hear me. Before I began to repeat myself to explain my witticism, he burst out laughing, louder than before, and told me the guy with the Corniche had just stormed out. I turned too late to see who it was, and probably wouldn't have recognized him, had I seen him. When I turned back, Mark had already returned to his other guests. Did he get my joke, or was he laughing at the man who left in a huff?

People always ask who else was at the party, and the truth is, I don't know. I'm pretty sure Richie Havens and Kathy Smith weren't there, or Mark would have introduced me to them. I heard Kenny Rankin's name mentioned, but

I don't know if he was there, coming later, already left, or just mentioned in unrelated conversation. Likewise, Frank Zappa. It's not that I was forgotten by my host. Mark dragged me through the crowd to introduce me to any number of important cogs in the music industry's ever-turning wheels, but imagine being dragged through a noisy crowd two arms' lengths behind your host, and arriving just in time to hear, "this is Travis Pike." But I shook a lot of hands, smiled a great deal, and told a lot of strangers I was glad to meet them.

In March, Phil C called to say Aluma Craft had laid me off, apparently because the contractor resented having an employee show up for work in a more elegant car than he did. What galled him most was that whenever it was parked outside his warehouse, everyone asked whose car it was, and it embarrassed him to say it belonged to one of his installers. I protested that the only time I ever parked the car outside the warehouse was when I went by to pick up our checks, and I hadn't been to Anaheim since before Christmas.

Phil C said there was no reasoning with the man, and offered to quit. I told him not to quit on my account. I was thinking of moving on, anyway, and suddenly realized as I said it, that it was true. If things went as I hoped and planned, I'd have had to quit soon.

There were few good jobs in the want ads, and most of the ones that were good, required college degrees. At first, I skipped over them, but then realized that the same G.I. Bill that let me buy a house with no down payment, might pay some or all of my college tuition. A fact-finding mission was in order. If I earned credentials in support of my skills, I might be eligible for some of those high-paying jobs.

That same day, I drove over the hill to the Pomona campus of the California State Polytechnic University to learn what the requirements for admission were, and whether the G.I. Bill would cover my tuition. In those days, I still believed that universities were where the best and brightest congregated to accrue wisdom, learn specialized skills, discover new areas of interest, exchange inspiring ideas, and establish lifelong bonds with classmates similarly inclined.

When my brother, Jimmy, returned to Boston University to complete his studies for his degree in Economics, he'd received credit for his time in the Army, so I brought a copy of my Honorable Discharge, and a printout of my College Level General Educational Development scores, hoping that, combined with my Navy service, they would lead to advanced placement that could allow me to enroll as a sophomore, or possibly even a junior.

I was shocked when the Admissions clerk who interviewed me said CalPoly did not give credit for military service (they do now), and did not offer advanced placement based on College level G.E.D. scores (they still do not). In 1963, my Navy College Level G.E.D. scores made me eligible for duty with the Navy's Nuclear Power Squadron, Officer Candidate School, and the Annapolis Naval Academy!

Meanwhile, I had a stack of forms to fill out, allowing the university to request my high school transcripts, S.A.T. scores, and verify my G.I. Bill eligibility, citizenship and residency. When I turned in the paperwork, the clerk questioned whether I really wanted to proceed, saying at nearly 30-years-old, I wouldn't be able to keep up with the younger students, and being married with a wife and child,

1964-1974: A DECADE OF ODD TALES AND WONDERS

suggested I would likely drop out by the end of the quarter. I insisted, the clerk take my non-refundable registration fee, so I was handed a catalog and told to select a major.

I chose Communication Arts, and then had to choose my classes for the spring quarter. The clerk strongly recommended I take no more than 12 units and suggested remedial courses in English should be my priority. By then seething, I said I'd take a chance that my English was sufficient to see me through, and signed up for 19 units, to wit; General Psychology, Introduction to Mass

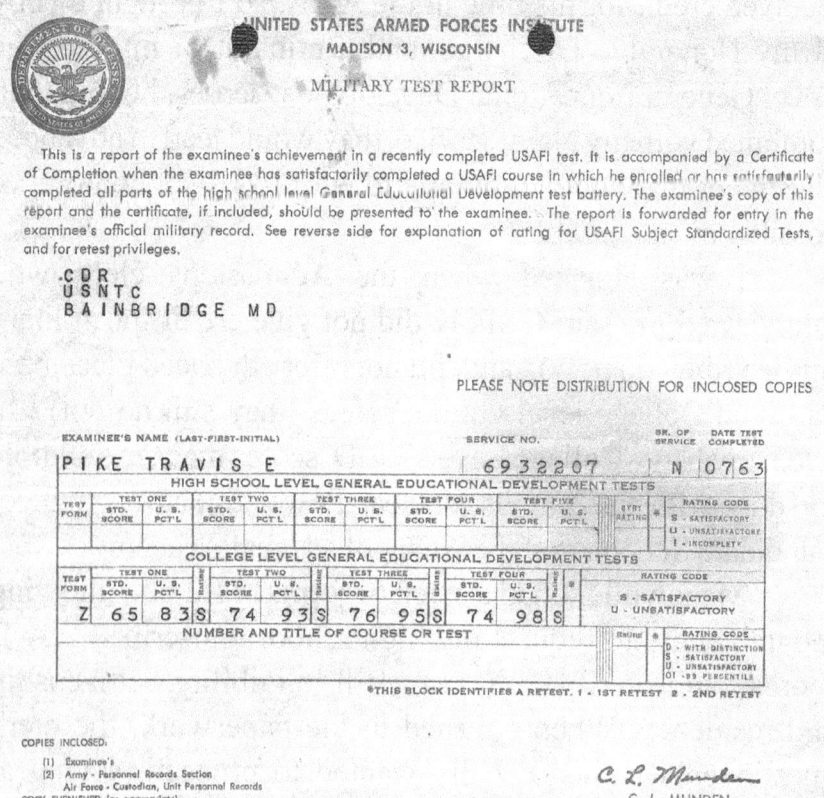

Communications, Reporting, Political Geography and Life Science. The clerk sighed, but took my check, and I left.

Someone told me that there was a difference between being laid off and being fired, and since I had been laid off, I'd be eligible for unemployment, but after the infuriating experience at CalPoly, I needed to cool off, and stopped for lunch before I went to the nearest California Unemployment Office. I'd accrued unemployment compensation credit at Aluma-Craft, but I was declared ineligible, because I'd enrolled as a full time student. Twice applied, twice denied, and facing financial hardship without the benefit of unemployment compensation, I vowed I would never apply for unemployment again . . . *and never have.*

When I told Judy my unemployment compensation had been denied, she never suggested I quit. She said we'd have to rework our budget, started going through our check register, and began itemizing our expenditures. We toiled late, but by morning, we'd figured out ways to meet all our financial obligations and still allow me to attend CalPoly. She even managed to add an occasional macaroni and cheese dinner to my proposed peanut butter and jelly sandwich diet.

Our house sold quicker than we'd imagined. We'd planned to move in summer, so Lisa wouldn't miss any school, but escrow closed in May. We made our final payment on the Mercedes, rented a two bedroom bungalow, and moved into Hollywood. The house on Curson was between Sunset Boulevard and Fountain Avenue, a few blocks east of Fairfax Avenue, and southeast of Mark Roth's house on Ogdon, and Raoul's apartment on Gardner, just north of Santa Monica Boulevard.

1964-1974: A DECADE OF ODD TALES AND WONDERS

We drove around the neighborhood to locate Lisa's new elementary school, grocery stores, gas stations, etc., and just a bit further east, came to La Brea Avenue. I had seen photos in National Geographic and read books featuring photos and reconstructions of exotic Pleistocene creatures in magazines ever since I first visited the Boston Children's Museum when I was in elementary school, most based on fossils collected at the world famous La Brea Tar Pits.

I asked Raoul if the street name had anything to do with them. It did, but the tar pits weren't on La Brea. They were bounded on the west by Fairfax Avenue, on the south by Wilshire Boulevard, and on the east by Curson Avenue. Bounded on the east by my new street? They were, but three miles south of our bungalow, not within walking distance for me, especially since I'd have to walk back, so Judy, Lisa and I drove down to see them on the weekend.

Today, entering at the corner of Curson Avenue and Wilshire Boulevard, you'll see a fenced area where a pond covered tar pit, methane gas bubbling to the surface, contains a life size reconstruction of a mammoth family, watching helplessly as the mother, caught in the tar, is losing her struggle to escape -- a thought-provoking feature then and now, and a must photo for visiting shutterbugs.

The George C. Page Museum of La Brea Discoveries, is one of my favorite places to bring out-of-town visitors. It's a wonder-filled showcase displaying Pleistocene period fossil skeletons of American Mastadons, Smilodons (in Boston, aka Saber-tooth Tigers), California Lions, Dire Wolves, Giant Sloths, ancient Bison, and even extinct indigenous species of the North American Horse. (The familiar horses we know today were introduced to the Americas by Spanish Conquistadors.)

1964-1974: A DECADE OF ODD TALES AND WONDERS

Our revised plan had Judy working at UCLA, and me attending CalPoly, just over the hill from our house, but our move, accelerated by the quick sale of our house, required us both to commute from Hollywood to the San Gabriel and Pomona valleys, with all the attendent woes of conflicting class hours, work hours, and babysitter schedules.

That April, I enjoyed all the attention the Mercedes Cabriolet received in the CalPoly parking lot, proudly inviting onlookers a peek at the gold medal on the dash signifying it had been named Best Car of the Year in 1955.

The bright spot on the far left of the dashboard, is the Gold Medal awarded the Mercedes Benz Cabriolet A for 1955 Car of the Year.

My joy was short-lived. Before the car warmed up, it smoked a little, and early one morning, starting out on my way to CalPoly, as I turned onto Santa Monica Boulevard, I was pulled over and cited for smoke by the Highway Patrol. I wasn't to drive the car until the 220 aluminum engine was serviced by a Mercedes dealership. A ring job, with all the peripheral costs involved in parts and labor was more than my peanut butter and jelly budget could manage. I owned a magnificent classic car, but couldn't afford its upkeep.

When Judy came home from Honeywell, I told her what had happened, and what I intended. Few people would ever own such an incredible car, and we were among them. We had many happy memories associated with our Mercedes Cabriolet A, but it was worth a small fortune (a larger fortune today), and I needed a car to get to and from school. I planned to trade it straight across for another car, and all we'd have to pay would be the license and registration fees. It was a sad, but necessary solution.

We'd just received our "pink" in the mail, signifying that we owned the car outright, so I walked down to the used car lot on Santa Monica Boulevard, near Raoul's apartment, and talked to the owner. He drove me back to the bungalow, checked the car inside and out, listened to the motor when I fired it up, and then drove me back to his lot. He invited me to look around, but the best he could do was a straight swap for a huge, white 1968 Cadillac Convertible. And so I swapped him, pink for pink.

That monster Caddy barely fit under our carport (and one time, with Judy driving, didn't quite fit), but the top went up and down smoothly at the touch of a button, it started immediately, and its enormous V8 engine had a lovely purr. I don't regret doing it, but sometimes wish I could have kept the Mercedes, especially when I see one listed now for sale at $168,500.

At CalPoly, I exceeded everybody's expectations, including my own. I aced all my classes, made the

1964-1974: A DECADE OF ODD TALES AND WONDERS

Departmental Honors List with a perfect 4.0 average, and had two short narrative poems posted in CalPoly's quarterly magazine *OPUS 17,* Spring Quarter 1973, Vol. 9 no. 2. One was *The Peerless Goth* and the other was the same *Lori*

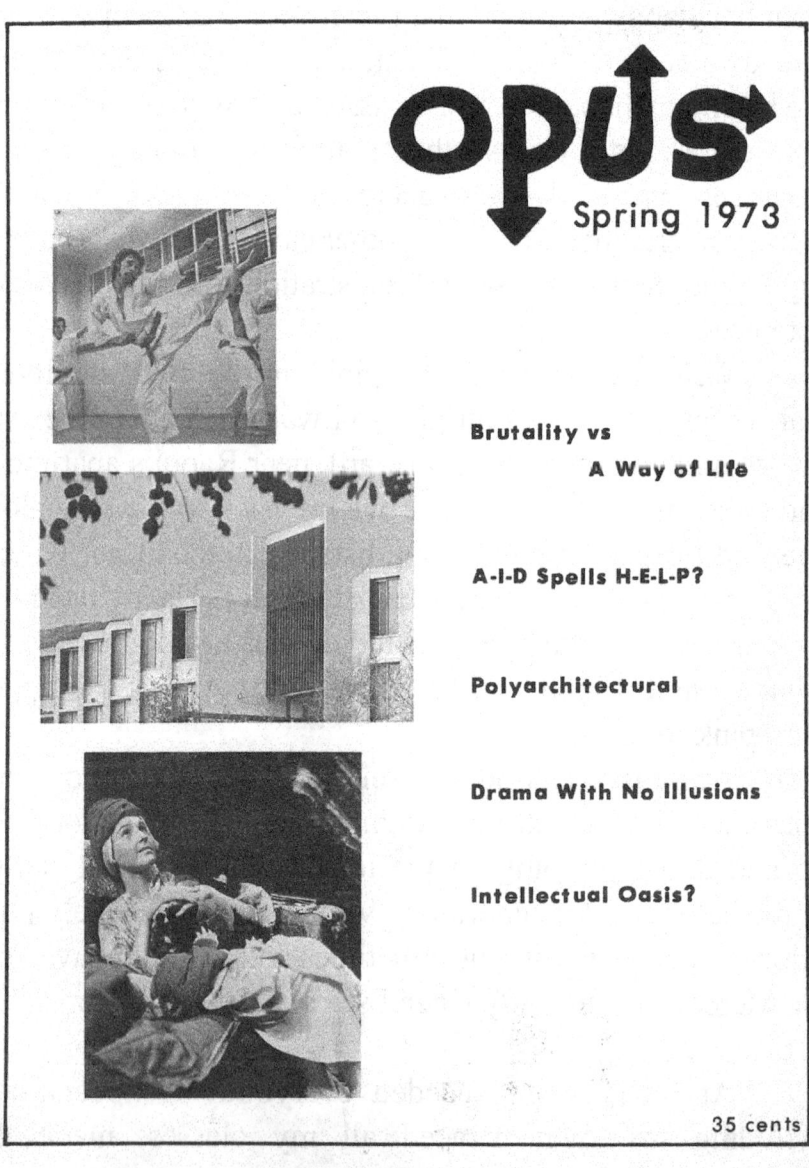

that Stormy Forest Records had previously optioned for the TV Special to be performed by me and animated under my supervision at Universal Studios. When the option lapsed, I offered *The Lori* and *The Peerless Goth* to the CalPoly quarterly, which published them with the caveat that the only rights granted were for the single publication, and that all other rights, including the copyright, remained the property of Travis Edward Pike. It was an unusual agreement, but I was an unusual scholar. Both *The Lori* and *The Peerless Goth* are included in this book's *Liner Notes, Lyrics and Rhymes*.

My grades were outstanding, especially since I'd been admitted on trial, and I'd had some unexpected insights from some of my courses that should prove useful in future projects. For example, some of the more Machiavellian applications of Political Geography that had come to my attention could easily be used in political thrillers and war stories of any historical period.

Judy was still at Honeywell, waiting to hear back from UCLA, so for my Summer Quarter, with Lisa home on vacation, we decided to save money on gasoline, books, and a babysitter, by limiting my course selection to 12 units available on Mondays, Wednesdays, and Fridays. After my first quarter, I chose courses that would fit my dates and times without conflicts, significantly narrowing my options. I found nothing exciting listed in my declared major, so I chose Modern Theatrical Practice, offered by the Drama Department, Visual Arts (an introductory art course) and U.S. History, a subject I'd somewhat neglected because of my abiding special interest in ancient civilizations.

CYCLOPS

The one eye shifts from side to side, sweeping all its field relentlessly in pursuit of what it may not see.

More times than once, that baleful gaze, in casting back and forth has paused to rest on me.

Behind that morbid eye, what thought, what discourse convolutes within what sort of brain?

The eye, it rests on me, and my two eyes are made to stare it down.

Does it wonder, now, if I possess two brains? I am of two minds, the one to flee, the other to inquire.

Perhaps the loathsome creature has but half a brain and cannot perceive what its one eye reveals.

Can some strange trick of depth perception, me motionless, disallow its ability to discern me from my surroundings?

I see the great shade flutter briefly, and then the eye comes back to stare.

What hostility lies just without its tortured gaze, that keeps it ever peering, ever alert, purges sleep, and causes that most singular eye to sweep and sweep and sweep.

It knows I'm here and now it closes its one terrible window on the world: is it a trick?

Would it have me move, prepare to flee and while I busy myself all unawares, then peek? Shall I be so easily played with?

Stupid Cyclops! I dare not take the risk. I'll not be first to move, though the heavens split asunder, though the land sink beneath the sea, though my flesh rot from my mortal frame.

Motionless and sightless, rest your eye. As for myself, I am the better equipped. I'll rest first one, and then the other.

The Visual Arts course required its students to submit an original work of art, based on a cube. At first, I had no idea what I could do that might be considered artistic, original and exciting, until I started thinking "inside the box." I made a cube with parallel interior walls, a large hole on one side, and a series of increasingly smaller holes all the way through to the opposite interior wall, where I pasted a cutout of a human eye staring back at the viewer. To add interest, I used Lisa's crayons to color the interior walls in the colors of the rainbow, and named my work, "Cyclops." Then, because *Cyclops* was "conceptual art," I wrote the text on the previous page and submitted it along with my cube. I received an "A+" for *Cyclops* in that CalPoly's Visual Arts project. The cube is gone, but the text remains.

I called Phil C to see how he was doing, give him our new address, and bring him up to date on all our news. He had news, too. He'd quit Aluma-Craft right after I'd been laid off, and was now working as a diesel mechanic. Happy for each other, we promised to stay in touch.

In 1973, when you were introduced, you were often asked for your astrological sign, and if a stranger wanted to start a conversation with you without introduction, a useful variant was to state, as an opener, what they thought (or pretended to think) was your sign. If they were right, they continued to regale you with their knowledge of the occult arts. On the other hand, if they were wrong, they feigned surprise, and said how unusual it was to meet someone like you, not born under whatever star sign they had originally proposed. If you answered either way -- and most did, if only not to be rude -- they'd accomplished their mission to engage you in conversation. As ridiculously dated as it sounds today, it was considered hip in the Age of Aquarius.

Our Hollywood neighborhood was fun to explore. Just southwest of us on Santa Monica Boulevard was The Sorcerer's Shop, where you could buy occult literature, scented oils, and colored candles in various shapes and sizes purported to aid a spell or protect one from a spell. I drove by recently, and it's no longer there.

A bit further south and west, on Melrose Avenue, was the Bodhi Tree Bookstore, a joy to browse, filled with books of mystical teachings, philosophies, theologies, and spiritual practices from cultures all around the world, and it featured colorful posters and trinkets not found anywhere else in such abundance. The physical store is no longer there, but The Bodhi Tree still exists, not in another dimension, but online at *bodhitree.com*.

Another esoteric resource was Manly P. Hall's Philosophical Research Society's Bookstore in Los Feliz. There, more than in any of the others, I found reprints of texts from earlier ages, discussing artifacts and layouts of spiritually charged locations now lost to us, but preserved in their illustrations. One such treasure in my collection is a photoprint of *The Celtic Druids* by Godfrey Higgins, Esq., originally published in 1829, in a Limited Edition, Copyright © 1977, published by the Philosophical Research Society, Inc., with an Introductory Preface by Manly P. Hall, founder of the Society, and author of several occult books, including *The Secret Teachings of All Ages.*

I had long been an independent scholar, necessary because many of the disciplines I explored and information

I sought were not part of mainstream curricula, and I needed to be aware of the influences, good, bad, and silly, that were shaping my world.

That spring I wrote the songs "Witchy Stew" and "The Stranger" for Majick, a new group I hoped to form with the help of the musician's contact services in my new neighborhood. Jack Hibler, who had hosted the party at the top of Nichols Canyon, was a partner in a Volkswagen repair shop, and when I was having trouble with the emissions system in the Volkswagen bus, Raoul told me to take it to Jack. It was good to see Jack again, especially in his work-a-day habitat.

Another revelation, first called to my attention by Andy Pearson when he interviewed me in 2017 for his *Fear and Loathing Fanzine*, was how much automobiles seemed to play a part in my career. I've given that some thought, and I think Andy was only half-right. It was the mechanics I met through my various automobiles, both here and abroad, that kept the ball rolling.

Jack was certainly the most financially successful of all my mechanical friends, and a good conversationalist, too. I hadn't seen him since the party, and we chatted while he had the bus fixed. Of course, he'd met me when I performed at his house, so to him, I was a singer-songwriter, first and foremost, and he and his wife, Ellen, both loved "End of Summer" every bit as much as Gerard. He wanted to know how my music career was going, so I told him about my aspirations to start a new group I was calling Majick. It was an innocent conversation, with no hidden agenda, but the result was that Jack offered to help underwrite my efforts, and as if to demonstrate his desire to be helpful, charged me nothing for having the smog device fixed.

A moment's digression is required to understand the hierarchy of German trades. Right out of what would be junior high school here, youngsters not going on to higher education (determined by test scores), choose a trade, and enter it as an apprentice. When they've learned their craft, they became journeymen, like my German mechanic friend Frank. Within any trade, advancement came with age and experience, and the most highly skilled in any profession would become masters. And the best and brightest of the masters might go on to become a *"Chef,"* which translates as boss, manager, employer, or owner. Jack was a Chef, co-owner of the VW repair shop, and clearly the most successful auto mechanic I ever knew personally, which goes a long way to explaining his house at the top of Nichols Canyon.

When I was leaving, he asked me to let him know what I needed to get started. We never mentioned a contract or a percentage. In fact, there was nothing in our conversation about anything other than what I'd need, and how he could help. I promised to crunch the numbers and let him know.

Our Hollywood bungalow was smaller than our house in the valley, so I disassembled our dining room table to make a new one, keeping only the legs and sliding structure to support a 24" wide leaf for larger dinners. The leaf doubled as the top of my new coffee table. Our three big dogs had ruined our sofa, so I replaced it with two 6' benches made from 1⅛" plywood with a fabric-covered 4" thick foam rubber cushion, providing seating for holiday dinners, and when pushed together, a guest bed.

Will lunch get by Lisa's three "tasters." Hard to see in this dark photo are Tim Tam (front left), Trax, (above him), and Tashia, at Lisa's side.

    I made "H-shaped" chairs of the same 1⅛" plywood, with finished 2"x2" tops and bottoms on both sides, patches of faux animal hide on the outsides, and seats of the same fabric-covered 4" foam, which, when lined up, served as a single, high-sided bed for visiting youngsters, and was far too small to accommodate any of our three huge pooches!

    Lisa's schoolmate, Dino Rico, lived just a few doors north of us on Curson Avenue. His father was Don Rico, an

1964-1974: A DECADE OF ODD TALES AND WONDERS

American paperback novelist, screenwriter, and comic book writer-artist for Marvel Comics. Some of his Depression-era works for the W.P.A. Federal Art Project in the mid to late 1930s became part of the permanent collections of the Metropolitan Museum of Fine Art, the Library of Congress, and the New York Public Library. I enjoyed his company and conversation when, from time to time, we'd walk around the block, discussing our on-going projects and past adventures. His wife, actress and choreographer Michele Hart, was the live, rotoscoped model for Hanna-Barbera's animated *Jana of the Jungle*, and remains our friend to this day.

    That summer quarter, I was also trying to assemble the group I was calling Majick. At first, it seemed promising. Now that I was living in Hollywood, I could take advantage of the musicians contact services to which I subscribed, and was talking to some serious contenders, auditioning and even holding some rehearsals at rehearsal halls Jack rented for me. It soon became clear that Jack wanted to be a player, too. I wanted a synthesizer to create musical effects for my songs, and chose a mini-Korg for the purpose. Jack bought it, and since it only played one note at a time, wanted to see if he could play it in the group. Although a distant relative of Richard Strauss, it didn't come naturally to him, but he persevered, and learned to play the parts I assigned him.

    I learned, at the start of CalPoly's fall quarter, that my G.I. Bill would run out at the end of next year's spring quarter. I never knew the G.I. Bill had an expiration date, a restriction only now, in 2018, removed from the program by an Act of Congress. I decided from then on, I would only take courses that furthered my professional ambitions and signed up for the Communications Arts Introduction to Film course, a Drama Department course on Directing, and two music courses, Fundamentals and Structure of Music 1.

I was interested to learn what academia taught with regard to motion pictures and learning what major differences one might encounter when switching from directing movies to directing stage productions. The Fundamentals of Music course taught notation, and the Structure of Music course was a first step toward learning orchestration, and provided me with instruction and experience toward credentials for what was, at that time, still my principal pursuit. At the end of the quarter, I was confident that I'd aced all my classes again, until my grades appeared and I discovered I had a "B" in Directing.

I'd done all the work, knew the subject matter, and scored highly on the tests. Along with a small group of fellow students, we'd submitted a Monty Pythonesque short, featuring skits performed by classmates and a complete short subject featuring my three enormous dogs as avengers for all the indignities suffered by dogdom, all synced to an audiotape soundtrack. Frankly, had I a copy today, I would proudly post it on Youtube. Unfortunately, we shot it all on Super 8 reversal film which leaves no negative from which to strike a print, and the original was retained by the CalPoly Drama Department. When we submitted it as our group project, the entire class enjoyed it tremendously, and the professor used it as the focus for his discussion of Theater of the Absurd.

Having unexpectedly lost my perfect 4.0 record, I went to see the professor to find out where and why I had missed the mark. He said he only gave "A"s to deserving Drama majors. It was the first I heard of it, and when I told him his unannounced policy had cost me my perfect 4.0 average, he was embarrassed, and offered to change it to a deserved A. I replied that to do so would be unfair to the others who had suffered my same disappointment, and not to bother. I wasn't going to finish college, so my scores only mattered to me, and it was enough that he told me my work merited an A.

At the end of November, Raoul came by the bungalow to tell me that he wanted me to write the screenplay for his "presold" American-Romanian co-production, *Caesar, the Sometimes Telepathic Lion*. I'd seen him excited before, and he was always excited about something, but this time, he was really over the top. He eagerly showed me photos from Disney's *Napoleon and Samantha*, and supported his presold pitch with a letter from its writer, Stewart Raffill, who wanted to direct it.

He also had a TV Special in the works -- *Halloween from the Castle of Dracula* centering on the historical Vlad Tsepesh (Vlad III, Prince of Vallachia, 1431-1476), aka Vlad the Impaler, upon whom the *Dracula* character is based.

I already knew who Vlad Tsepesh was, and played my vampire song, "Till the End" for Raoul.

It's hard to imagine that Raoul could possibly get more excited, but he did. His volume level rose at least ten decibels. He loved "Till the End," and Raoul claimed that his Romanian connections would be able to get us permission to shoot the special at the real "Dracula's" castle. If I'd write the Halloween Special treatment, I could easily feature my vampire song in it, and the song would be sure to help attract sponsors for the show, which would make it an easy sell to both investors and TV broadcasters. One thing Raoul had in abundance was enthusiasm, and since nothing else had yet materialized, I said I'd set aside some time to do both.

SAFARI FILMS, INC.

November 26, 1973

STEWART RAFFILL
President

JOSEPH C. RAFFILL
Vice - President

Mr. Raoul Arco
Ray Arco Productions
1114 Gardner
Hollywood, California

Dear Raoul:

I was delighted to hear that the people you met in Romania are interested in co-producing "THE CASE OF THE MISSING LION" and other similar films. As you know, I have been very excited about the possibility of doing a film with the lion in Eastern Europe. I feel the project exploits the lion's great potential as a character.

If the film is made in Romania I will be taking two lions, one of them to be used as a double and to perform some of the more physical activities. Upon arrival in Bucharest we will need two enclosed trucks/vans to transport the lions separately. For their permanent housing, the best thing would be a stable with two separate enclosures for the lions in an area where they will not be disturbed by people. As you know, the lions are extremely tame and neither the trucks nor stable will require the traditional heavy steel bars. Both lions eat approximately ten pounds of meat each per day, six days a week. I anticipate bringing with me two other trainers besides myself.

As you are aware, the lions are kept quite busy here with various productions so it will be important to establish a definite schedule for filming. Spring and summer would be best, climatically.

The prospects of acting the part of the animal trainer in the film pleases me very much and I have several young girls that have worked in various Disney films who, I believe, would be excellent to play my daughter in the film. However, using professionally trained actors, as you know, is not inexpensive even if they are children. Because the film should have a universal appeal and transcend the limitations of languages I feel the acting should have a "Chapliness" quality, where the actions and motivations of the characters are universally understood.

I would like to take this opportunity to also let you know that we have a great variety of other trained wild animals which have appeared in countless American film productions. In the very near future, now that our schedules are clearing, you and I should get together and finalize the screenplay. I look forward with great expectations to this fascinating and exciting project.

Yours sincerely,

Stewart Raffill

SR:br

P.O. Box 117 • Tarzana, California 91356 • (213) 342-7933

1964-1974: A DECADE OF ODD TALES AND WONDERS

1973 Golden Globe
Best Documentary
Nominee

The Second Gun

who really killed Bobby Kennedy?
the Ted Charach RFK Assassination Probe

"The Second Gun," a shocking new film makes the statement that the bullets in the gun of Sirhan did not kill Senator Kennedy, but another gun 'a second gun' fired at point blank range behind Kennedy in the Ambassador Hotel Pantry -- did! "The Second Gun" stars real life people who acted and reacted in this shocking episode of history.

CREDITS

Adapted and directed by...GERARD ALCAN
Based on the probe by...THEODORE CHARACH
Produced by ....THEODORE CHARACH and GERARD ALCAN
Original music theme "The End of Summer"
composed and performed by...TRAVIS E. PIKE
Art work...BILLY RASH
                                                                                                                   MARK JOHNSON
Prologue voice..T. MIRATTI
Narrator...DEAN RANDALL
Re-enactments........................RON GUIER and ROBERT MULLEN
Photographed and edited by..GERARD ALCAN
Additional Photography..STEWART RAFFILL
Assistant director...ELLEN HIBLER
Location sound...GEORGE EDDY
                                                                                                                    ZVI BOKER

Color by TECHNICOLOR
Titles and Opticals CINEMA RESEARCH
"THE SECOND GUN" -- All rights reserved
Copyright ©1973 by Theodore Charach and Gerard Alcan
AN AMERICAN FILMS, LTD. Release

GETTING INTO HOLLYWOOD

In December, when the Golden Globes announced their nominees for Best Documentary, Gerard sent me the blurb on the previous page. It was definitely a thrill to see my credit in print, among all the other contributors to the film's notoriety.

And Judy finally received a call from UCLA, telling her she'd landed a job in the School of Engineering, and she'd start work the following Monday.

Ellen Hibler, the hostess at the party on top of Nichols Canyon, had been the Assistant Director on Gerard's film, and was tied up with its promotion, but her husband Jack, to celebrate the movie's nomination, and Judy's new job, took Judy and me to the Moody Blues concert at the Los Angeles Forum. We were in the rafters, so far above the stage, that we could barely see the group, but we could hear them, and as the smoke from below began to collect under the roof, we closed our burning eyes, laid back and enjoyed the music.

I can't pinpoint the exact date, but it was early in the year when Mark Roth called to say that George Harrison was in town and coming over to talk to Mark about launching a new label George was calling Dark Horse Records. "Great!" I exclaimed, expecting further elucidation, but Mark just wanted to borrow our vacuum cleaner, and could I bring it right over? I loaded our Kirby in the Cadillac and drove to Mark's house, less than five minutes away, thinking he'd fill me in when I saw him. An attractive young woman, wearing absolutely nothing but a fishnet smock, answered the door, and seeing me holding the vacuum cleaner said, "You must be Travis," then took the vacuum cleaner, said thank you, and shut the door in my face.

> And as in uffish thought I stood,
> Outside Mark Roth's door,
> I decided Mark was stressed,
> Or else, he would have told me more.
> No excuse to ring the doorbell,
> I decided on the spot,
> Got in my car, and drove away,
> And gave it no more thought.

Well, no more thought than it deserved, which is to say a smidgen less than my complete and undivided attention.

It was nearly a week later when Mark called, and Judy answered the phone. "He's right here," I heard her say as she handed me the receiver, mouthing Mark's name.

When I said hello, Mark volunteered that the meeting hadn't gone the way he'd hoped, but he needed the vacuum cleaner for another week, if that was all right with me. I said he could hold onto it, but I'd need it back then.

When I hung up, Judy wanted to know what Mark said. I told her Mark needed the vacuum for another week. Judy waited for the other shoe to drop, but there was no other shoe. I reminded her that Mark had two huge German Shepherds that shed like crazy, but she would have none of it, and told me to tell Mark Roth we had three huge hunting dogs and she needed her vacuum cleaner herself!

The following week, when I picked up the Kirby, a different woman, fully dressed, answered the door. "You must be Travis," she said.

"I've come for the vacuum cleaner."

It was just inside the door and she stepped away so I could get to it. I quickly looked it over to be sure all the attachments were there, and they were, so I smiled, picked it up and left. As I was loading it into the back seat, she called from the doorway, "Mark said to tell you thank you!"

I smiled, waved, got in the car and drove away.

Researching for this book, I came up with two interesting facts. First, with regard to the meeting with George Harrison, Mark never told me any more about it, but in trying to fix the date of the events described, I discovered that in early 1974, George was in L.A., contacting people he knew with independent labels, to determine what would be the best way to launch his new venture. He spoke to Leon Russell, co-founder of Shelter Records, who had worked with George on the Concert for Bangledesh, and spoke to Mark Roth, because Stormy Forest's indy release of Richie Havens' version of George's "Here Comes the Sun," distributed through MGM Records, had been a big hit. I suspect George was doing some tactical research to determine the best way to launch his new Dark Horse Records company. What Mark had in mind, I don't know, but at the end of the day, George finally arranged to have A&M distribute Dark Horse Records, and never having heard Mark's side of the story, that's the best I can offer about the "other shoe" that never fell.

I saw Richie Havens once, in Mark's office, when I stopped by on business. Richie was there, but I was there to look over a contract, mostly boilerplate. I flipped through it quickly and left, so Mark and Richie could get back to whatever they were doing when I arrived. We nodded to each other to acknowledge each other's presence, but I don't think we ever spoke a word.

Kind of sad, really, because I now know that Richie was into environmental awareness, and had set up a fund to educate kids about the many environmental crises facing our planet, and environmental issues have motivated me ever since I first read Rachel Carson's *The Sea Around Us* when I was a seventh grader in Boston Latin School, in 1956-57.

I was extraordinarily busy when this all happened. At the close of CalPoly's Fall Quarter, I'd gone to the student book store and bought all the advanced music courses they offered that I thought I'd need to complete my music library.

For the Winter Quarter, I went back to three day weeks and only signed up for Documentary Film, Survey of Music, and Western Art. In addition to my official studies, I made time to write Raoul's screenplay, the treatment for his TV special, and a title theme for *Caesar, the Sometime's Telepathic Lion*. And I composed three new musical numbers for *The Red-backed, Scaly, Black-bellied, Tusked, Bat-winged Dragon:* an instrumental that sprung from the mind of the inebriated Mastersinger of Westles, who, upon hearing a maid complain that she had five things to do and only time for four, composed a ballet in 5/4 time; "Love Is," a musical conversation between my heroine, Princess Gwyn and my hero's half-sister, Aver, revealing their differing perceptions of love; and most outstanding of them all, "The Sorcerer's Waltz," intended to be sung by Akimera, my evil sorcerer, to his enslaved dragon, Long-Grin.

Influenced by Ron Moody's "Fagin," in the 1968 film *Oliver*, I laid out its melody, lyrics and orchestration, but my evil sorcerer would never serenade his dragon, so I set it aside -- until my wonderful brother Adam suggested we record it for my *Odd Tales and Wonders: Stories in Song* CD.

Now that we were officially colleagues, Raoul began inviting me to accompany him to screenings of soon-to-be-released major Hollywood productions that he'd be reviewing for foreign publications. It was a little like viewing movies in my father's screening room in Roxbury before they appeared on television, but in larger screening rooms, widescreen, in stereo, and in color! Alas, none of Raoul's "presold" projects ever made it into production, but my 1974 *Caesar the Lion Theme* became the theme for my production of *Grumpuss* in 1997.

In my spare time, with Jack Hibler's help, I kept looking for musicians to form the new band, Majick. In fact, Jack and I auditioned many and found several willing and capable, but the best being the best, when paying gigs came along, they had to take them. My proposal demanded a long-term commitment they couldn't make, without an income to provide "The Bear Necessities" of life.

1964-1974: A DECADE OF ODD TALES AND WONDERS

The 1974 Spring Quarter was my last. I continued my schedule of writing, composing and orchestrating on Tuesdays, Thursdays, Saturdays and Sundays, sparing just enough time to ace my selected Monday, Wednesday and Friday courses: 20th Century Art; History of Civilization; and an experimental multi-disciplinary program.

I took the Modern Art course for personal enrichment, and was particularly moved by the cubist sculpture by Raymond Duchamp-Villon, *Horse*, then on exhibit in the Los Angeles County Museum of Art's Sculpture Garden. It's a stylistic, contorted rendering of a horse's head, neck, and front torso, connected by a drivewheel, rod, and a great gear. To me, it conveys "horsepower" driving the machinery of the industrial revolution, and at the same time, replacing the tormented horse in our modern world.

The History of Civilization was necessarily abbreviated in order to present so much in a single course, but I was interested in the art of the ancient middle east, especially the Babylonian and Egyptian art of the ancient world, and thoroughly enjoyed the exploration of the classical art of Greece and Rome, all of which enhanced my perception and understanding of those periods dearest to me.

In the experimental, multi-disciplinary environmental studies group, I rediscovered both the themes and purpose that ultimately drive one of my most creative works, transforming my occult, contemporary, Faustian rock opera from that 1974 property, to *Changeling's Return,* the latest version of my musical fantasy adventure to address the evermore desperate ongoing environmental crises facing our planet and civilization in this 21st century.

GETTING INTO HOLLYWOOD

Toward the end of the spring quarter, with a much reduced 12 unit schedule at CalPoly, and time at home to rehearse with the musicians, I accepted an invitation to host the First Los Angeles Festival of Music and Mime for Lord Neptune and Lady Alice Productions.

1964-1974: A DECADE OF ODD TALES AND WONDERS

1st LA FESTIVAL OF
MUSIC & MIME

JUNE 9, 1974   2:10 P.M.

AMERICAN LEGION HALL, HOLLYWOOD, CALIFORNIA

PRESENTED BY **LORD NEPTUNE & LADY ALICE PRODUCTIONS**

Festival Host: MR. TRAVIS PIKE
FESTIVAL LIGHTING: LUISA VICTORIA PUIG

2:00   **THE FESTIVAL RAGTIME BAND**
       conductor: Don Peake
         1. SUN FLOWER SLOW DRAG . . . . Scott Joplin
         2. Sugar Cane . . . . Scott Joplin
         3. Pool Parlour Rag . . . . Don Peake
         4. The Cascades . . . . Scott Joplin
           featuring: "les Petits Mimes"

2:30   **THE RICHMOND SHEPARD MIME THEATER**
         "THE BIG TOP" . . . . By Ruth Saturensky
       adapted and directed by Mr. Shepard
       musical director: Jackie Lustgarten

INTERMISSION

4:00   **QUARTET IN D, K. 285 . . . . MOZART**
       Joseph Soldo: Flute.   Linda Rose: violin
       Pamela Goldsmith: viola   Jackie Lustgarten: cello

4:20   **MIME: ANTONIN HODEK**

4:40   **PIANIST: ROGER KELLAWAY**

INTERMISSION

6:00   **MIME: DORETTE EGILSSON**

15   **COMPANION PIECE . . . . DAVID ANGEL**

6:15	**INTRODUCTION AND ALLEGRO** . . . . **MAURICE RAVEL** Verlye Mills: harp Joseph Soldo: flute John Neifeld: clarinet Murray Adler: violin Ronald Folsom: violin Patricia Matthews,: viola Frederick Seykora: cello
6:40	**MIME: Young -- EVANS**
7:00	**"UNTITLED TWO" FOR CHAMBER ENSEMBLE AND TAPE** premier performance of this work written especially for this festival by Los Angeles composer: JOHN NEUFELD
7:10	**MIME: WHITNEY RYDBECK**
	INTERMISSION
7:50	**THE IMPROVISATIONAL QUARTET** Michelle Mention David Angel Frederick Seykora Arni Egilsson
8:25	**THE L.A. MIME COMPANY** Tommy McLoughlin Katee McClure Jan Munroe Whitney Rydbeck Tina Lenert Young-Evans
9:15	**THE LOS ANGELES FESTIVAL CHAMBER ORCHESTRA** "THE SEASONS" . . . . Vivaldi La Primavera (Spring) L' Estate (Summer) L' Autumno (Fall) L' Invemo (Winter) Murray Adler: violin soloist Ami Egilsson: conductor this performance is dedicated to Anthony Zungolo

In addition to enjoying the performances by the excellent mimes in the program, it was inspiring to work with talented professional musicians playing everything from jazz, to ragtime, improv, new age, and classical compositions. The show was not as well-attended as the producers and I desired, but those who came, stayed and enjoyed a magnificent show.

1964-1974: A DECADE OF ODD TALES AND WONDERS

Despite my off-campus activities, when I received my final grades from CalPoly, I had aced all my courses again, and was on both the Department's Honors List and the President's Honors List, too.

CALIFORNIA STATE POLYTECHNIC UNIVERSITY, POMONA

3801 West Temple Avenue   *Pomona, California 91768*

July 17, 1974

Mr. Travis E. Pike
1322 North Curson Avenue
Hollywood, California 90046

Dear Travis,

On behalf of the faculty of the Communication Arts Department, I congratulate you for being on the Dean's Honors List in Spring Quarter, 1974. As you have been on the list each quarter this year, you have earned the additional recognition of being on the President's Honors List. This represents an important academic achievement of which you justifiably should be proud.

We wish you continued success at Cal Poly and in all of your future endeavors.

Cordially,

[signature]

Gary D. Keele, Chairman
Communication Arts Department

GDK:cr

The California State University and Colleges

The CalPoly Communication Arts Department offered me a full scholarship, effective as soon as I'd earned enough credits to qualify as a Junior, but I needed one more quarter to do so, and without the support of the G.I. Bill, I couldn't do it. Had military service been credited at CalPoly then as it is now, I would have already been eligible, but in the event, Hollywood beckoned, and I was eager to consider whatever offers came my way, and get back to work on my original properties in development.

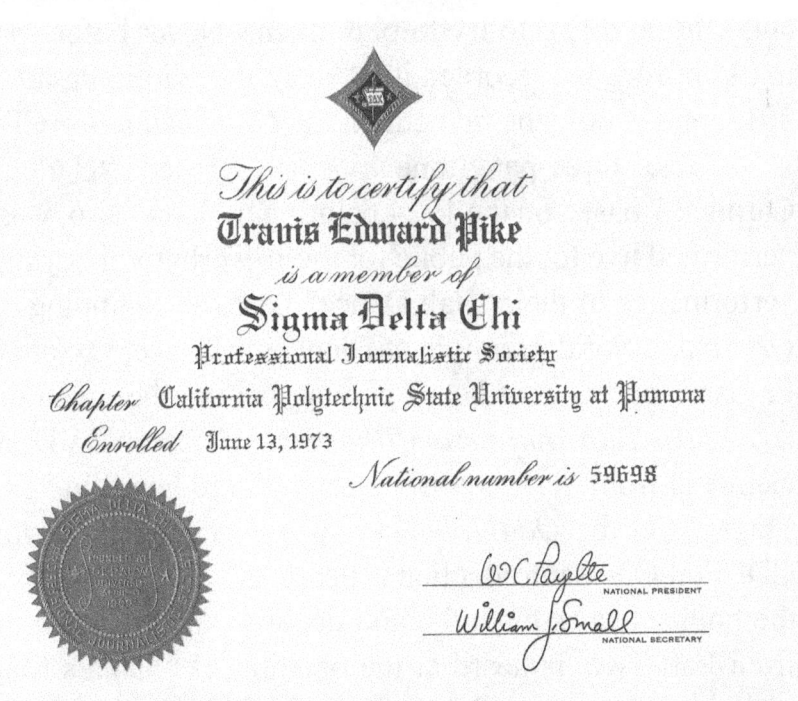

I was especially honored when the Dean of the Communication Arts Department handed me this membership in Sigma Delta Chi, the professional Journalistic Society as a parting gift to a colleague, but other than warmest regards, it changed nothing. Mentally, I had already moved on.

1964-1974: A DECADE OF ODD TALES AND WONDERS

Inspired by the music and musicians from the Festival of Music and Mime, and frustrated in my efforts to form a new group, my exposure to Modern Art combined with my independent study of music, and yielded "Passage of the Virgin to the Bride" a 1974 tone poem inspired by a painting by Marcel Duchamp, July-August, 1912. It evolved musically and with the addition of lyrics, became "The Andalusian Bride Suite," rescued from oblivion when my brother Adam, pulled a stack of notation from the bottom of my box of song lyrics, and said he'd like to try to play them. Never before played in its entirety, we recorded it in Adam's studio in Pasadena in 2015, and is now the first cut on the *Outside the Box* CD.

The three-part tone poem I called "Harlequin's Carnival," based on the 1924 painting by Joan Miro, was first performed live for the public for the 1997 rhythmic gymnasts' performance of their "Ball Dance" near the beginning of my *Grumpuss* world premiere at Blenheim Palace, Oxfordshire, England, and is now heard playing behind the menu on the *Grumpuss 20th Anniversary Platinum Edition* on DVD. More elements from "Harlequin's Carnival" are heard in "Santa's Magic," on the *Odd Tales and Wonders: Stories in Rhyme* CD. Part One's introduction is heard as Santa sneaks through the house, leaves his gifts, and departs; and the main theme from Part Two, is heard at the opening of "Santa's Magic," and a later section of Part Two provides the happy music heard at the end of the story.

"Five Things to Do, and Only Time for Four," composed in 5/4 time, is the music performed for the rhythmic gymnasts' "Hoop Dance" in *Grumpuss*.

As I pursued this fresh musical course, I began losing interest in Majick, and with so much time at home in Hollywood, I was available to my friends in the Hollywood Foreign Press, music producers, filmmakers, and an ever increasing number of artists in the associated industries.

Hollywood, California, Spring Quarter 1974, Travis displays his work score for "The Passage of the Virgin to the Bride," now "The Andalusian Bride Suite" on the *Outside the Box* CD.

I don't remember who introduced us to bright, aspiring clothing designer Cathy Palmer, but it had something to do with the Renaissance Fair, and I suspect that's why I played her the music I'd been writing for my medieval fantasy adventure, *The Red-backed, Scaly, Black-bellied, Tusked, Bat-winged Dragon*. She was impressed, but said she'd been told I had a costume book that I might let her see. I knew immediately what she wanted and pulled out my copy of the 1963 paperback edition of Carl Kohler's *History of Costume*. I left her alone to pore through it, and when she was finished taking notes, she asked if it would be possible for her to borrow it for a few days. The book was the costume reference I used regularly for my medieval fantasy, and I rarely lend books, even to close friends, but I acquiesced, after she promised to return it as soon as she finished with it.

Happily, Cathy was not only bright, but honest, and returned my book no more than a week later. By then, I had moved on to writing music for my contemporary fantasy. I had been working on "The Fool," and with her interest in the Medieval Period, I thought she might enjoy it. I already had the concept, melody and most of the words to it and was eager to try it out on her.

Clearly taken by the lyrics, she said I must have read Robert Graves' *White Goddess*. In fact, I'd never heard of it. That astonished her even more, and she said she'd bring me a copy. Thinking she meant to lend me her book, or possibly pick one up at the library, I told her I didn't know when I'd be able to make time to read it. Undaunted, she said when I did read it, I'd understand why she knew I'd love it, and promised to bring it by the next time she was in the neighborhood.

In fact, she bought a paperback edition of that *Historical Grammar of Poetic Myth* and gave it to me the very next day, calling my attention to passages she knew would be of interest to me, especially, Gwion's Riddle. I was hooked. I thanked her for the book, and she said she'd want to talk with me about it when I'd read it. As she left, her eyes seemed to sparkle, whether with joy or amusement, I really can't say, but she'd manipulated me into a position where I'd have to read the book in a timely fashion, and then get back to her with my reactions.

I have a good grasp of ancient history, mythology, and various arcane arts, and I'm a fast reader, but this book was heavy going, even for me. I read it through quickly, probably in less than three days, but with everything else I was doing, that qualifies as quickly. That first reading taught me what to expect, and I immediately began to read it again, this time pausing to contemplate what I read to tie all the threads together. It was almost as if I was holding up a mirror to my own work, and seeing it more clearly for the first time, reshaping some of what I'd already done, and opening new frontiers for exploration.

All the disparate elements of history, mythology, occult literature, and science that had always fascinated me, suddenly combined with insights gained from my participation in the CalPoly Interdisciplinary Studies group, and began blending into a cohesive musical fantasy adventure addressing the critical environmental issues civilization confronts today, through the lens of our unique and varied cultural heritages.

I didn't see Cathy Palmer often. She had many friends and was involved in many of their projects (including the Renaissance Fair), but one day she did stop by to pick my brain. She'd been invited to a costume party, hadn't either the time or money to create something stunning, and was desperate to attend. Could I help?

I think it was the first time I ever really looked at her with my artistic eye, studying the planes of her face, the set of her eyes, and her hair. Suddenly I knew what to do, if she was willing to go along with it. I stood her in front of a mirror and showed her the color print in one of my art books of the Matisse painting *Green Stripe*. I told her to look at her face, and imagine herself as the lady in that painting. If she could put her hair up the way it was there, and brought the makeup we'd need, I'd do her face for her. At first she balked, not believing her friends would know who she was supposed to be. I said she'd know, and could tell them if need be.

She was nervous when she came by on the evening of her party, but her hair was perfect and her clothes were appropriate, so with Judy's help, we did her makeup and the result was astonishing. She seemed more resigned than ecstatic, but thanked us and went on her way.

Cathy came by a few days later, clearly happy and excited, and told us that when the party hostess answered the door, she immediately welcomed her by saying, "Madame Matisse. Won't you come in?" I think Judy and I were almost as delighted as Cathy obviously was.

I no longer needed a car to go back and forth between the city and the valley, and when I did need a car for meetings or errands, I'd drive Judy to work at UCLA, do whatever I had to do during the day, and pick her up after work.

From the start, Jack Hibler had supported my efforts to form the new group we called Majick. Jack bought a Peavey P.A 120 Mixer - Amplifier, microphones, paid our Hollywood rehearsal studio rentals, and played the Mini Korg synthesizer he'd bought for the group, but Majick hadn't worked out, and my music courses at CalPoly freed me from the tyranny of groups and individual musicians. What I needed to proceed with my musical properties was a program that would appeal to potential musicians and provide me with the recordings I needed to interest filmmakers, stage producers and/or record companies, to put my work before the public.

But Jack was out serious bucks for his efforts on my behalf. No longer trying to form a group, and without any personal income to repay him, I gave him the Cadillac in settlement of my indebtedness, and was finally free to follow my dreams as I saw fit.

I abandoned the concept of a group I'd call Majick, and dedicated whatever personal magic I possessed to the fledgling rock opera I called *Changeling,* which, as *Morningstone,* I finally recorded with David Pinto in 1987, and mixed with Adam in his first 8 track studio in Pasadena. It has evolved again, and is now *Changeling's Return,* but that's the story for a book of its own.

Although as a singer-songwriter with an all-original band I hadn't achieved the success I'd sought, I wasn't a total failure. George Pincus once offered me a tidy sum for one of my songs. Hy Mizrahi and Phil Steinberg liked our voices enough to offer us a contract, Squire Rushnell hired us as his "house band" for his TV show, and we turned down a tentative offer from Mike Curb's Sidewalk Records. That being the case, I prefer to think of this period of my life as a success story, still searching for a happy ending.

Harvey Kubernik has authored 14 books, including heralded titles on Leonard Cohen and Neil Young. His acclaimed *1967 A Complete Rock History of the Summer of Love* was published in 2017 by Sterling/Barnes and Noble.

Inside Cave Hollywood: The Harvey Kubernik Music InnerViews and InterViews Collection, Vol. 1 was published in December 2017, by Cave Hollywood and Kubernik's *The Doors Summer's Gone* was published by Otherworld Cottage Industries in March 2018.

In November 2018, Sterling/Barnes and Noble will publish Harvey's book, *The Story of The Band From Pig Pink to The Last Waltz*, written with brother Kenneth Kubernik.

Over his 45 year music and pop culture journalism endeavors, Harvey has been published domestically and internationally in *The Hollywood Press, The Los Angeles Free Press, Melody Maker, Crawdaddy, Variety, The Hollywood Reporter, MOJO, Shindig!, HITS, The Los Angeles Times, Ugly Things, Record Collector News* and on *cavehollywood.com*.

In 2013, Kubernik penned the introduction to Pike's original *Odd Tales and Wonders,* and has since interviewed Pike several times over the last five years, making him something of an expert on this uniquely talented entrepreneur and Hollywood multi-hyphenate.

AFTERWORD: AN INTERVIEW WITH HARVEY KUBERNIK

HARVEY KUBERNIK
photo by Heather Harris

TRAVIS EDWARD PIKE
photo by Judy Pike

HK: I guess the first question has to be why did you decide to expand and revise your original book, *Travis Edward Pike's Odd Tales and Wonders, 1964-1974: A Decade of Performance*?

TP: In the five years of interviews since I published that book, I've released four more albums and I think I've learned what most interests my readers. In this book, I address those interests in much more detail than I did in the first book, or ever could in an interview. For example, U.K. based Lenny Helsing, in his long-form interview for *It's Psychedelic Baby Magazine* <psychedelicbabymag.com/2018/02/the-travis-edward-pike-story.html>, asked me what my most memorable performances were, and I realized that my most vivid memories of gigs were of those in which I had overcome adversity. And not just that. I also realized that what Lenny wanted, wasn't dates and places, but stories about those gigs and what made them memorable.

1964-1974: A DECADE OF ODD TALES AND WONDERS

In Andy Pearson's long-form interview for his U.K. *Fear and Loathing Fanzine* <fearandloathingfanzine.com/travis-pike.html>, he observed that much of my rock and roll history appeared to revolve around automobiles – and given that my first published song was the theme I composed for *Demo Derby* (performed by the Rondels), and that 28-minute b/w action featurette played on thousands of screens across the country with the Beatles, *Hard Day's Night*, he had a point. But for all my adventures and misadventures involving automobiles, it was the auto mechanics who maintained and rebuilt those automobiles who were largely responsible for keeping me and my name in front of the public.

AFTERWORD: AN INTERVIEW WITH HARVEY KUBERNIK

Today, I'm generally accepted as a Hollywood multi-hyphenate, filmmaker, screenwriter, and in this book about my early career, as a singer-songwriter, but I am now, and always was a storyteller, too. When I realized that was what the reading public wanted I found myself in one of my comfort zones. In the earlier book, I was trying to write in a genre I'd never explored before. I was writing a personal memoir but trying to remain objective, so I adopted what I considered a journalistic style, not of a news reporter, but what I thought was an appropriate style for a feature article about an interesting, but little-known character.

I was also writing mostly from memory of the life I lived a half century ago, and what I found in the newspaper clippings in my wife, Judy's, scrapbooks. This time around, she and I went beyond her scrapbook, doing forensic research in old check registers, and poring through old letters from family and friends in which the events described flowed more generically from one to another, revealing a more accurate chronology, and tracing the influences, impulses, and reasoning that governed my early choices and provide direction to the narrative.

HK: In some ways it's like *Godfather 2* after *Godfather 1*. It carries the initial text but it's much more vivid and expansive. I penned the Foreword for the original text, but after reading this significantly longer edition, and viewing all the new photos and documentation, I wonder what you will do with the initial publication? It still exists.

TP: It won't for long. I published it through Otherworld Cottage Industries, so when I release this more accurate and

215

more complete, 374 page book, *1964 – 1974: A Decade of Odd Tales and Wonders*, I'll take the 2013 edition out-of-print. This new book will cost more, due to the increased costs of publishing, and because there are many more pages of information, but I believe the public will find it more accurate and more importantly, more entertaining than the original.

HK: I know you didn't have a lot of the visuals when you wrote the first one, and many more pictures and documents have been found and included in the new printing. I personally think you have also become a better writer. Is it experience? Is it the result of the time and energy you spent to revise and add memories, new data, and facts you forgot or discovered through your research?

TP: I don't know that I'm a better writer. I've been writing and mentoring writers for years, in forms, formats and genres familiar to me, but I had never undertaken a memoir before. I was exploring a new genre for me, and writing about myself, rather than an historical figure or character of my own creation. I found that awkward, especially in trying to view my exploits without providing the rationale behind them. In a screenplay, you normally do not include a character's thoughts. The character's motivations must be made manifest through their actions and the reactions of the characters around them.

A memoir, as the name of the genre implies, is made up of memories shared by the subject, and the subject's point-of-view should illuminate those memories. A subject's unique point-of-view supplies the underpinnings of the tale being told, which is precisely the storyteller's art, but not the art of news reporters or screenwriters. Storytelling is what makes this book more engaging than the one before.

HK; You are writing about yourself. Do you censor or edit more in the upcoming volume or is your process and style pretty much the same?

TP: The only difference in writing this memoir and discussing my life with a friend is that I tend toward a more civil tone in my writing, which is not to say that I avoid an occasional rant, but if something or someone particularly galled me, I do tend to temper my commentary.

HK: I know a couple of musicians from back in the day emerged during the summer of 2018, and their contributions inform this book. Do you consider them research tools or people who verify or reinforce the facts within the journey?

TP: They're never tools. They're friends and colleagues, who not only validate and reinforce the facts, but in particular, Danny Gravas, who is not only still alive, but in possession of all his faculties, including a prodigious memory, and a wider circle of music industry colleagues than I ever realized, has much improved the section on the coffeehouses in Boston and vicinity – which is to be expected inasmuch as he was the first President of the Boston Folk Guild, now one of the founding organizations that make up *Americana*, a category of music including folk, country, blues, rhythm and blues, rock and roll, and would nowadays probably include my music, too, since it evolved primarily from those influences.

1964-1974: A DECADE OF ODD TALES AND WONDERS

I feature Danny in these pages because, while I was doing a solo act at King Arthur's, very similar to what I had done on the wards of the Naval Hospitals, Danny walked in, guitar in hand, to play a few songs. It was immediately clear that Danny was an excellent performer with a winning personality, and totally at ease on that stage, avoided by most folk singers of the day, whose anti-military repertoires disparaged and marginalized G.I.s. We were never booked on the same bill, but when one of us dropped in on the other's show, we would always find an excuse to play a few songs together. I don't know if I ever made him sound any better, but I know he made me sound great, and I suspect we both enjoyed it as much as our audiences did.

And now I know that Danny was ex-Navy, too, which helps explain why he was as comfortable as I was, performing at King Arthur's. Furthermore, his history of recording contracts and accidents preventing him from reaching his goals, rivals my own, and he only narrowly missed the brass ring we both sought in those days.

With his intimate knowledge of the New England folk scene, he corrected my error about the Turk's Head being converted to The Sword in the Stone.

Based on when I started as the daytime manager at Lightfoot Recording Studio in Jamaica Plain in January 1967, I now believe that offer came at The Sword in the Stone, or possibly King Arthur's. Either validates Mark's presence in my memory, and neither changes the facts that I became the daytime manager for Lightfoot Recording Studio, or that I rehearsed my new rock band, and recorded our demos there for the price of the recording tape. However, my stories

AFTERWORD: AN INTERVIEW WITH HARVEY KUBERNIK

are colorful enough without embellishment, and especially without erroneous data that might call them into question.

HK: You have many more visuals and photos. Did the inclusion of these new images dramatically alter the revised book?

TP: Without a doubt. When my father's estate was settled, I came into possession of photos, newspaper clippings, and graphics that I never had access to until now.

It is also true that writing this book, unlike in an interview where I must trust to memories of events, some more than a half a century in the rearview mirror, with Judy's help, I was able to establish more accurate dates and eliminate some errors in my earlier recollections.

HK: Sometimes book re-dos, or autobiographies, add a new chapter at the end of the original printing. But this is a whole lot larger, re-written text with some earlier text incorporated. What is the process of integrating new writing and data to existing text? Was it adding paragraphs? Was it making chapters longer?

TP: All that and whole new chapters as well. The most obvious is that in the original book, I mentioned I starred in the movie, *Feelin' Good,* and wrote ten songs for it. I dealt with it in less than two pages. In this new version, it rates 29 pages, and many production stills from the first rock musical ever made in Boston and vicinity.

HK: I know by comparing both books you have much additional narrative. For example you really took us into the 1969 Posh nightclub world of Pomona. Did you feel the impulse to further detail your live music career?

TP: A tip of the hat to Lenny Helsing for that. He's the one who asked me for stories about my most memorable performances. The Posh in Pomona was the biggest and best-paying dance bar in the area, and our first genuine paying gig in Southern California. But in detailing it, I also discovered that the "new" Travis Pike's Tea Party was a major setback for all of the remaining original players, and it all came crashing down far sooner than I remembered. Jim Morse's piece in the *Boston Herald-Traveler* on Friday, January 26, 1968, in HUB-HUB, about the Boston Sound, accurately reports that it took eight months to put this outfit [Travis Pike's Tea

AFTERWORD: AN INTERVIEW WITH HARVEY KUBERNIK

Party] together -- six months learning the 80 original songs the group performs. We arrived in California in August 1968, and crippled by the loss of our rhythm guitarist and second vocalist, George Brox, could not be ready on time for our introduction to the West Coast at the Whisky A Go Go.

We were back to square one, having to break in a new rhythm guitarist and vocalist, and trying to get him up-to-speed, taking us all of four months to get about 30 of our songs ready for performance. Our survival depended on the rest of the band playing top 40 hits, which negatively impacted our rehearsal time and further arrested development of the new man's mastering of our original repertoire.

HK: When you relocated to SoCal and the Inland Empire, the San Gabriel Valley, why did you feel the need or desire to keep singing and performing? You were a rocker and crooner in a world around you in L.A. and Hollywood pretty much defined by singer/songwriters with pianos or guitars, disco, glitter and glam rock.

TP: I think I arrived before disco, but to answer your question, having uprooted the three remaining original members of the band, I had an obligation to get them back to work at a performance level, as much for my sake as for theirs. I had a fully developed repertoire, arranged and polished in our particular configuration. Alone, all I could have done is demo the songs. Without the impact of the group's powerful presentation, I could not do them justice. I was vulnerable, the prisoner of my own success, confined by the real world performance skills of the band. At first, I doggedly tried to restructure the group in its original mold, but over time, I realized I was chasing a ghost. What had been, was no more, what might have been, would never be, and what was yet to come, no longer held my interest. During our last few months, I stopped writing songs.

HK: The discovery of new papers, documents and photos, not available the first time around, really enhance the new edition. Somewhere in the work did it feel like this had become an entirely new book, owing less to the first published one?

TP: It was a completely new work from the get-go, inspired by all the new documentation and the many interviews I'd had since 2013, not a few of which were with you.

HK: I really dug the chapter of your encounters with Richie Havens and his manager/friend, Mark Roth. Discuss this time period with me. You were almost signed to a real record deal.

TP: First, let me clarify. I once saw Richie Havens in Mark's office, but they were busy and although we nodded to acknowledge each other, we never spoke. That's especially sad because I understand we had a number of important interests in common.

In researching this book, I was surprised to discover that I met Mark in late 1971 and we met several times more between then and our final meeting in early 1974. We'd been discussing musical projects and strategies for more than two years. One day, early in our discussions, I was at his house for lunch, and his bright, sweet, and charming lady friend, Nancy Friedman, invited me to join them for a luncheon of

Sushi, which, by now, as I'm sure everyone knows, is fresh, raw fish. I once became quite ill on some kind of fish dish, and I had ever since avoided fish in all its forms, no matter if it was deep fat fried, broiled, boiled, cooked in stews, smoked on a stick, or impaled stem to stern and roasted over an open fire, but darling Nancy promised me that the hot mustard "cooked" it as you ate it, and she was so convincing that I forced myself to try it – and survived.

When Judy read this, she reminded me that it was Nancy who encouraged her to apply for the job at UCLA, and that Judy had given Nancy the exquisite cigarette case and lighter I'd given Judy, years earlier. Nancy smoked, but Judy had quit, and when Judy told me she'd given it to Nancy, I remember thinking what a fine thing that was for Judy to do.

HK: And, I learned a lot more about this real life character Raoul. I actually kept being more involved in your book when people like him came on your scene. Run him down.

TP: Raoul was a colorful member of the Hollywood Foreign Press Association, an outgoing irrepressible force of nature, for whom all rules of etiquette, assuming he had ever been exposed to them, had no effect on his personality or behavior. He spoke too loudly, laughed too loudly, and when he lamented, lamented too loudly and too long, but he was funny and engaging and I liked him very much.

I was his discovery, and he shared me with everyone he knew, and was always surprised if anyone he spoke to hadn't heard of me by then. He was definitely a Travis Edward Pike booster. I met Jack Hibler, Ellen Hibler and Gerard Alcan

1964-1974: A DECADE OF ODD TALES AND WONDERS

through Raoul, and I am sure it was Raoul who also kept me in touch with Al Kaplan, and introduced me to Igo Kantor. Through Igo, I met J. Bond Johnson, and through Bond, I met Frank Capra, Jr., and through Frank, I met Carl Pingatore, and the list goes on and on, but that has already taken us beyond the parameters of this book. Suffice it to say that Raoul was a mensch, flawed as we all are, but sincere, even when he exaggerated wildly, a genuine ally.

HK: Why did you feel you had to let us know about all the close calls, or movie studio visits, or deals that didn't happen or list some producers and directors or film and TV folks in this book? Do you think getting meetings at MGM and generating some options on your work is relevant? Do you think including these pit stops further illustrate your journey?

TP: Of course they do. My works represent my credentials in ways no diploma ever could. I earned them as I explored the different avenues that opened up before me. As for introducing readers to the producers and directors that were part of my journey, you just asked me to tell you more about Raoul, so you definitely found him interesting. This book is a memoir of my past, but it also marks the beginning of my journey into the world of the Hollywood multi-hyphenate I am today.

HK: Tell me about editing this book. A different set of skills from the first go round? I mean, how do you do it? Do you put it all out there on computer, review, edit, and re-arrange sections, and add more as things trigger more memories?

AFTERWORD: AN INTERVIEW WITH HARVEY KUBERNIK

TP: I generally start at the beginning, and when I come to the end, I stop. Arguably, my first book did that for this second book, dealing with the same period and subject matter, but as you point out, there is always more to tell. Revisiting the earlier book, with the insights I've gained from all the intervening interviews, and the advantage of 20/20 hindsight, I've made this one more accurate, more informative, and hopefully more entertaining than the first.

When I wrote and published the first book, I had only recorded two CDs—*Stories in Rhyme* and *Stories in Song* – but since then, I've released *Reconstructed Coffeehouse Blues, The Tea Party Snack Platter, Feelin' Better,* and *Outside the Box,* most of which derive from materials I developed during this period.

And yes, perhaps the most exasperating part of doing a memoir, is that there are always things overlooked, new wrinkles that appear, and you must constantly be on the lookout for errors that need to be addressed. There are always people and things that might have played a small, seemingly insignificant part during the first run through, until you come to the section where they rise to a level of importance in the narrative that requires their earlier introduction. Then, you must go back and insert that introduction where it fits most appropriately, and that throws off all the pagination and placement of illustrations, so that you have to plod back through the entire book to make sure all the text remains intact, the illustrations properly placed, and all the other minutiae that plague a self-published author. And publisher, as you well know, is just the latest hyphenate to be added to my collection.

1964-1974: A DECADE OF ODD TALES AND WONDERS

HK: There would be no book without your wife. She has been with you every step of the way. Did she serve as a consultant on the new version? Do you bounce things to her for review or feedback? Did she share memories of events to you that ended up augmenting your writing?

TP: She has been with me ever since 1966, first as a friend, and later as my wife, so she has lived most of this history with me, and tells me when her view of events differs from mine. She also kept the records that made our forensic research possible, and she was the one who tracked down the dates and periods of this or that event to bring order to my sometimes chaotic memories of the period. But most of all, she continues to support me in all my endeavors, even those she finds of dubious merit, and for that, I am forever grateful. And yes, she adds bits to the stories, especially where she interfaced with some of the people mentioned in this book.

HK: You've woven more of your family into this new edition. Pictures and reflections of your childhood, and some items that you didn't have a few years ago.

TP: That's true, and I've put those items to good use. I was especially impressed by the careful preservation of some of the newspaper and *TV Week* articles on my father, when he first brought feature films to television. They were in my mother's scrapbooks and I'd never seen them before, but when Judy helped my mother go through her boxes of memorabilia to determine what to discard, donate to charity, or keep for posterity, she found them and my mother let me have any I

AFTERWORD: AN INTERVIEW WITH HARVEY KUBERNIK

thought would be appropriate for inclusion in this book. One photo from a feature article in a contemporary newspaper is of the family, in my father's screening room in Roxbury in late 1954. If the date is correct, I am only ten years old, but if I am eleven, then the photo must date from 1955. Either way, that photo clearly sets the scene for our family at that time.

Judy, "The Lovely Girl I Married," is more than a song to me.

HK: You were the antithesis of the "turn on, tune in, drop out" counter-culture espoused by Timothy Leary and often depicted in articles, books, films and documentaries. You shared some of the same venues, but you offered rock 'n' roll that the new FM radio world didn't program or broadcast.

1964-1974: A DECADE OF ODD TALES AND WONDERS

TP: Neither the AM or FM radio world programmed or broadcast us, although as recently as the April 2018 issue of *Goldmine Magazine*, Lee Zimmerman's four reviews for his Quick Picks list, were all from my current releases on CDs. Of *Travis Edward Pike's Tea Party Snack Platter* CD, Zimmerman wrote, "All the songs included herein are radio worthy and hold up surprisingly well, even some 50 years past their prime. Timeless and tuneful, these re-recordings compare favorably with anything offered up by The Monkees, The Raiders, The McCoys, The Standells and others of that ilk."

HK: And here we are, 50 years later, and some of the same rejected or ill-fated songs have now achieved a second life on the internet and are being re-released or reissued in England.

TP: Since you bring it up, Travis Pike's Tea Party's 1967 Alma Records original recording of "If I Didn't Love You Girl" began appearing on compilation albums in 1994, when the song was included on the German compilation album

AFTERWORD: AN INTERVIEW WITH HARVEY KUBERNIK

Sixties Rebellion, The Backyard Patio. The following year, it was on the *London Records* compilation, *Tougher Than Stains*, and in January 2017, appeared on the new untouchables *le beat bespoké 7*, album released by Detour Records.

But the breakthrough, if that's what it is, came when my brother Gregory sent me salvaged reels of 35mm film that had been in my father's vault in Rhode Island, and damaged in the great flood of 2010. The cans were rusted shut, so I took them to Deluxe Labs to see if any of the film within could be restored. The film was warped, which made perfect color restoration impossible, but the mono optical soundtrack sounded great, so I color-corrected the film as best I could and posted them on Youtube in 2016. My Charles River Esplanade performance with the Brattle Street East, of "Watch Out Woman" was singled out that November in Tim Perlich's blog, *The Perlich Post*, when he wrote "The best music video of 2016, was actually shot in 1966."

Then, for the Winter Issue of *Ugly Things* magazine, Mike Stax wrote an excellent review of *Travis Edward Pike's Odd Tales and Wonders, 1964-1974: A Decade of Performance*,

1964-1974: A DECADE OF ODD TALES AND WONDERS

(Otherworld Cottage Industries, 2013), and published your six-page pictorial interview with me in that same issue.

Mole and Lois, over at State Records in the U.K., read *Ugly Things*, and between the book review, your interview, and the video clips posted on Youtube, decided to contact me about releasing a single of the two songs I performed on the Charles River Esplanade with the Brattle Street East, both of which had never before been released.

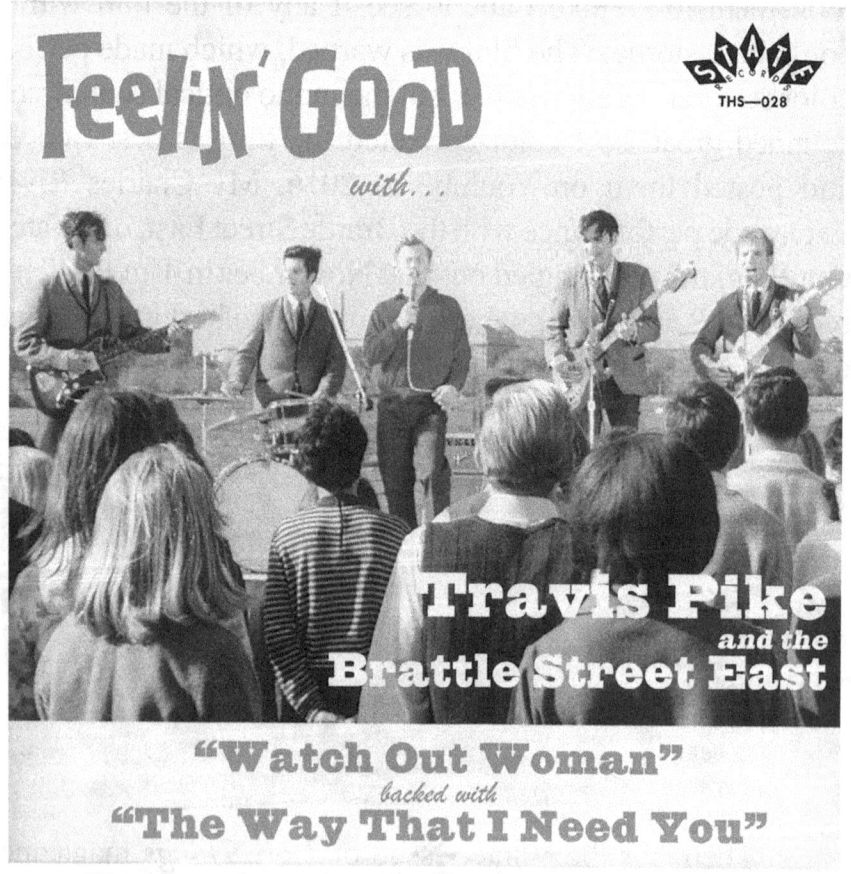

The record received great reviews in *Shindig!* and *Record Collector* magazine in the U.K., and in *Ugly Things*, and *Goldmine* magazine in the U.S., and began getting radio play in the U.K., several European countries, and wound up in *Shindig's* Best of 2017 issue as the third best single release of the year! And that all led to two monster reviews: Lenny Helsing's review in *It's Psychedelic Baby* and Andy Pearson's review in his *Fear and Loathing Fanzine*.

Best of all, those last two interviews addressed my current recordings of my original, never previously released songs from the sixties and early seventies, as did Lee Zimmerman in his *Quick Picks* column in the April 2018 Rock and Roll Hall of Fame Issue of *Goldmine* magazine in which he wrote, "the songs are of a vintage variety, but the arrangements meld both classic and contemporary elements. Pike may not have gotten his due early on, but this belated return makes the wait worthwhile."

HK: Now that I think about it, your saga maybe should have not been titled Odd Tales. What is so odd about your tale?

TP: You've already said it. If Travis Pike's Tea Party, and my original songs, were, in fact, the antithesis to the counter-culture revolution of the sixties and seventies, by all accounts that makes my story a very odd tale indeed, especially when considered within, or in counterpoint to, that period's pop music milieu, which makes it a wonder we worked at all – and drew crowds and loyal fans to our performances.

HK: Since your earlier book, over the last few years your catalog has grown and reached new eyes and ears. Many terrific reviews and some multi-page stories have been published chronicling your life and your music in your early twenties, and you and they are now coming to the attention of audiences here and abroad.

TP: I'm not sure there's a question in that statement, but all this contemporary attention certainly is a "wonder," is it not?

HK: Definitely a wonder . . . or as some might suggest, possibly a phenomenon whose time has finally come.

INDEX OF LINER NOTES, LYRICS, AND RHYMES

235   About the Music

239   *Feelin' Better*
      Seven Songs from the 1966 Movie *Feelin, Good* Revisited
      (and four more that weren't in that movie).

254   *Odd Tales and Wonders: Stories in Song*
      Seven Mid-Sixties Novelty Songs Revisited
      (and three that are only "novelties" on this CD).

268   *Reconstructed Coffeehouse Blues*
      Ten Coffeehouse Songs from the Mid-Sixties Revisited
      (and a new one in sixties coffeehouse style).

283   *Travis Edward Pike's Tea Party Snack Platter*
      Fresh Recordings of Eleven of Travis Pike's Original Songs
      Once Performed Live By Travis Pike's Tea Party, Revisited.

297   *Outside the Box*
      Some began as tone poems, others grew from seeds planted
      in the mid-sixties, and only now sprouted, and some were
      rescued by Adam Pike, whose curiosity about their
      scores finally brought them into the world *Outside the Box.*

315   *Odd Tales and Wonders: Stories in Rhyme*
      A 1964-1974 collection of short narrative rhymes
      performed in coffeehouses and concert halls.

353   *The Twaddle and the Gurck: An Interpretation*

LINER NOTES, LYRICS, AND RHYMES

There's more...

ABOUT THE MUSIC

This next section features lyrics to most of the songs I composed between 1964-1974 that survived and evolved over the ensuing years. Where two pages are required for lyrics, I tried to print them side by side, to facilitate singing along with the recording (which is how I learned to sing).

I am often asked where and how I get ideas for songs. A memorable experience -- good or bad -- may inspire a song. Quite often, a title or catchy lyric line will come to mind, and before long, the rest of that song's lyrics fall into place. Other times, a rhythm and melody will emerge as I work on lyrics. Then, I hurry to a guitar or piano to find those melodies and harmonies that seem best suited to the song.

What I am suggesting, when I speak of harmonies and melodies that suit the lyrics, or lyrics that flow from the melodies and harmonies, is that certain diatonic, pentatonic and chromatic scales, certain words, even musical phrases trigger positive or negative reactions in listeners. Whether these triggers are innate or learned is not clear, but certainly, enculturation plays a role. This becomes most obvious when one's musical experience includes Asian and African music. To Western ears, accustomed to diatonic scales, Asian and African harmonies may be dissonant and disturbing, even cacophonous. However, Westerners exposed to musical diversity may discover a transcendental harmony that is as engaging and moving as any offered by their own cultures.

LINER NOTES, LYRICS, AND RHYMES

An in-depth discussion of Asian and African music is beyond the scope of this book and the expertise of this author. My focus will be on Western music and on the instruments, rhythms and scales from other lands that to Western ears suggest adventure, mystery, exotic cultures and locations or, when heard in a familiar environment, evoke strange, supernatural, cheerful or disturbing emotions in the listener.

Today's proliferation of devices and media provide access to music from around the world, but until the advent of audio recorders, all musical experience came from live performances of secular or sacred music. Sacred music is generally intended to evoke an otherworldly sense of wonder, a sensation of being in the presence of God (or the gods), inspiring spirituality and the enlightened aspirations of its audiences. However, in ancient times, some gods and goddesses required blood sacrifices. Mars, the Roman god of war, still lends his name to "Martial Music" -- those marches, heroic themes, and calls to arms heard in military parades, international competitions and football games.

Secular music is worldly by definition and sometimes attacked by religious communities for the materialistic, irreverent, sacrilegious, carnal, and/or profane influences it may have on its audiences. Secular music includes pop, traditional or contemporary folk, or any music associated with periods or movements within the art music category. The court music of the Renaissance that conveyed the grandeur, power and sometimes the frivolity of the state and privileged classes, tone poems, baroque, classical, romantic, impressionistic, expressionistic, experimental, modern, and new music, with instrumentation foreign to our ears, are all secular music -- music of the people. Opera, comic opera, and oratorio also played their roles in training our ears and psyches to react appropriately to their subtleties.

Program music uses instruments, melodies, harmonies and lyrics (where included), in support of each other to create a mood, sense of history, geography or ethnicity. Discussions of program music are frequently restricted to instrumental or orchestral music, and songs are generally excluded, except in opera and stage musicals. Personally, I consider many of my songs akin to the tone poems that are the foundation of program music. For example, my song, "The Witch," on the *Outside the Box* CD, utilizes a Bach-like Baroque passacaglia as an underlying movement to suggest the music of the era of the witch trials and deaths by fire. It is coupled with a theme reminiscent of *Beethoven's 7th symphony, 2nd movement,* a Romantic era response to the excesses of the previous age, which is married to a syncopated blues interpretation intended to speak to contemporary audiences.

My "Andalusian Bride Suite" on that same CD, belongs to the progressive rock school, considered an exception to the rule barring songs and popular music from being categorized as program music. "Ali Baba Ben Jones," on the *Odd Tales and Wonders Stories in Song* CD, utilizes samples of native East Indian instruments to suggest Rajasthan, the location in the song, and my Slim Pickens-like character voice establishes my protagonist as an American adventurer traveling through East India.

In "Don't You Care at All," on *Reconstructed Coffeehouse Blues* CD, the "instrumental break" is "played" by real-world audio recordings of helicopter gunships, machine guns, jets, rockets, and exploding napalm that provide a horrific connection with that objective reality.

Movies and TV shows depend on program music to set the mood, and when pre-recorded themes are selected, they are categorized as chase music, romantic themes or suspense cue. In our Western music heritage, composers and listeners alike, identify and are affected by the music in much the same way. Rossini's *William Tell Overture* will always be known to several generations of Americans as the theme from *The Lone Ranger*.

Richard Wagner brilliantly used what we now call *leitmotif*, a melodic theme or phrase that accompanies the appearance and reappearance of a figure or situation. I first learned to recognize leitmotif by listening to an old 78 rpm recording of Prokofiev's *Peter and the Wolf* and recognized it at once in John Williams' great white shark leitmotif in *Jaws* and the Darth Vader leitmotif in *Star Wars*.

Finally, a few words about the evolution of my specific songs and music. Over the years, I wrote many more songs than I kept. Each song, each melody contains truth and it is my task to discover that truth. Sometimes I "get it," sometimes I don't. This book testifies to the fact that even abandoned melodies may return, however battered and bruised by their journeys, and finally find their ways out into the world.

All the songs in this collection survived my creative process. Most, written years ago, are only now reaching the ears of their audiences. I know these songs all fly, but only you can say if they will find a place to roost.

01	5:14	COLD, COLD MORNING
02	2:54	THINGS AREN'T ALWAYS WHAT THEY SEEM
03	3:01	DON'T HURT ME AGAIN
04	2:57	TROPHY WOMAN
05	2:47	FOOLIN' AROUND
06	2:47	THE WAY THAT I NEED YOU
07	3:05	IT CAN'T BE RIGHT
08	2:53	I BEG YOUR PARDON
09	3:36	FEELIN' BETTER
10	2:48	ROCK N ROLL
11	3:36	END OF SUMMER (2014)

LINER NOTES, LYRICS, AND RHYMES

01. "Cold, Cold Morning" was "Bad Week" when I introduced it to The Boston Massacre in 1967. The groove was there, but the lyrics were uninspired, so it languished on an old demo until Adam heard it. We revisited it, I wrote new lyrics, and the result is this jazzy 2016 number with country-western style lyrics. (Jon DuFresne's ad lib guitar and Chris Woodcock's ad lib saxophone parts, played at different sessions, give this piece an incredible "live jam" feel.)

02. "Watch Out Woman" aka "Things Aren't Always What They Seem" was performed with the Brattle Street East on the Charles River Esplanade in Boston for the 1966 movie, *Feelin' Good*. That soundtrack cut, released on a vinyl 45 by State Records in 2017, was named the #3 single of the year by Britain's *Shindig!* magazine. This is the September 2014 studio recording by Travis and Adam Pike.

Barbara Jordan   Lauran Doverspike   Chris Woodcock

Jon DuFresne   Travis Pike in the Control Room Pickin' on his Taylor Guitar

03. Recorded in 2016, "Don't Hurt Me Again" is little changed since it was first heard in the 1966 movie, *Feelin' Good*.

04. "Trophy Woman," was "Wicked Woman" in the 1966 movie. The concept of a trophy woman goes back to ancient times, but its modern usage suggests it entered the vernacular in a cover story in *Fortune Magazine* in 1989, making this version more than 20 years newer than the original song, "Wicked Woman."

05. "Foolin' Around" apart from the addition of the saxophone part, is little changed from the original in the movie, *Feelin' Good*.

06. The original "Way That I Need You" is side 2 of the State records release performed with the Brattle Street East on the Charles River Esplanade. This version is the 2015 cut by Travis and Adam.

07. The song, "It Can't Be Right," was in the movie, but this is a new recording arranged for the 1964 German-Italian band, the Five Beats.

08. "I Beg Your Pardon," composed for *Feelin' Good*, was beautifully staged on a Swan Boat in Boston's Public Gardens.

09. Everyone in the photos (previous page) performed on "Feelin' Better." An unfinished song Travis composed after he stopped performing live, "Feelin' Better" is an all new title song for this album, so it won't compete with Travis' movie title song, "Feelin' Good," recorded by the Montclairs and released on a Pike Productions 45 single in 1966.

10. "Rock N Roll" was written in 1965 for The Five Beats in the American rock style then popular in Germany. Never before performed or recorded, that makes it the oldest "new" song on the album.

11. An "End Of Summer" instrumental was the theme for the 1973 Golden Globe Best Documentary nominee, *The Second Gun*. This version was composed in 1965 for "Teddy's" German fans, and first released with lyrics in German and English, on the 2013 *Odd Tales and Wonders Stories in Song* CD. This "bonus cut" features an orchestral accompaniment not recorded in the version on the *Odd Tales and Wonders: Stories in Song* CD.

LINER NOTES, LYRICS, AND RHYMES

COLD, COLD MORNING

Makin' my way, along the highway,
Singin' and strummin' on my Taylor guitar,
Getting' by, out in the boondocks,
Singin' and strummin' with my Taylor guitar.
But fame and fortune never came my way, and I never was a star.

One **Cold, Cold Morning**, I stopped for coffee.
The lights were on, but the joint was closed.
Four o'clock on a **Cold, Cold Morning,**
Pulled off for coffee. The joint was closed.
I had to keep the motor runnin' for the heater, but I must have dozed.

Car boiled over, fogged up my windshield,
Hot steam hissin' beneath the hood.
Steam all over, foggin' up the windshield,
Hot steam hissin' under my hood.
Well, I shut the motor down, but it kept tickin' and I knew
That wasn't good.

But then a pickup, came out of nowhere.
She'd seen me steamin,' offered a hand.
As she drove by, she'd seen me steamin.'
Said she just stopped to lend me a hand.
On that **Cold, Cold Morning**, broken down outside a roadside stand.

Nothing was open. A blizzard comin,'
Howlin' winds, snow, and freezin' rain.
Everything closed, 'cause of the blizzard,
Howlin' winds, snow, and freezin' rain.
She said to leave me stranded out there in the cold would be
Downright inhumane.

FIRST INSTRUMENTAL RELEASE

COLD, COLD MORNING (CONT'D)

That **Cold, Cold Morning,** she helped me unload,
All the stuff that was in my car.
That **Cold, Cold Morning**, she helped me move
All my stuff out of my car,
And load it in her truck bed, all except my precious Taylor guitar.

She loaded that into her cab,
As I stood by the passenger door.
She put my Taylor behind her seat,
As I waited outside the door.
But she never let me in, instead she took off in her 4-by-4.

SECOND INSTRUMENTAL RELEASE

I thought I'd freeze to death that mornin,'
But I waved down a police car.
I would have froze to death that mornin,'
But I waved down a police car.
I got through that **Cold, Cold Morning**, but they never found
My Taylor guitar.

THIRD INSTRUMENTAL TO FADE AWAY

For this song, Adam elected to play the bass line digitally direct.

LINER NOTES, LYRICS, AND RHYMES

THINGS AREN'T ALWAYS WHAT THEY SEEM

I say hey, hey, hey there, now.
Go easy, girl! I say, take care, now.
If you knew the things I know,
You'd listen to me, girl. You'd take it slow.

Hear me when I tell you I'm not tryin' to be mean,
But **Things Aren't Always What They Seem**

I say hey, hey, hey there, now.
Watch out, girl! Guys are startin' to stare, now.
Mama told me keep an eye on you tonight,
And keep you out of trouble, but stay out of sight.

So, listen to me, girl. I'm on your team.
Things Aren't Always What They Seem

(INSTRUMENTAL)

It's okay, girl. Let off some steam,
But **Things Aren't Always What They Seem**

I say hey, hey, stay with the crowd, now.
The room is hot and the music is loud now,
And just when you're thinking everything is fine,
Five and five can turn up nine.

If things get out of hand, you just haul off and scream,
'Cause **Things Aren't Always What They Seem**
No, **Things Aren't Always What They Seem**

FEELIN' BETTER

DON'T HURT ME AGAIN

If you hurt me again, I couldn't stand the pain --
If you hurt me as you did before.
Please **Don't Hurt Me Again**. What have you to gain?
I just can't take it, anymore.

Please try to be kind. Perhaps, you will find
There's still hope for us if we try,
But if being unkind, is all that's on your mind,
I'd rather not let you see me cry.

For I love you more than I could ever say.
Believe it or not, it's still true.
If you'd give me a chance, if only for a day.
Together, we might start anew.

But **Don't Hurt Me Again**. I couldn't stand the pain.
Of loving you, without you here with me.
Let me say, once again, if I've loved you in vain,
Tell me now and tell me tenderly.

It's mostly my finger-picking, but Adam added some tasty "strings."

LINER NOTES, LYRICS, AND RHYMES

TROPHY WOMAN

I never knew a woman could move me like you do
Your sexy ways drove me crazy. I fell in love with you.
Trophy Woman. Trophy Woman. You took me to school.

I told my Mom about you -- how stylish and how fine.
I told her that I loved you and was gonna make you mine.
Trophy Woman. Trophy Woman. You made me feel cool.

I told her you were reared with all the better things in life.
Then my mother warned me not to take a trophy wife,
Cause when the money ran out, it would all end in woe,
And when the shine wore off the trophy, the tarnish would show.

Well I got no more money. I spent it all on you.
I was your pawn and now you're gone, I don't know what to do.
Trophy Woman. Trophy Woman. I'm such a fool.

INSTRUMENTAL RELEASE

I never knew a woman could move me like you do.
Your sexy ways drove me crazy. I fell in love with you.
Trophy Woman. Trophy Woman. Oh, I felt so cool.

Well, I've got no more money. I spent it all on you.
I was your pawn and now you're gone, I don't know what to do.
Trophy Woman. Trophy Woman. I've been such a fool.

Trophy Woman. Trophy Woman. I've been such a fool.

Trophy Woman. Trophy Woman. I've been such a fool.

FOOLIN' AROUND

(I know you're) **Foolin' Around,**
but I won't play the fool for you, 'cause

I don't need your money, Babe. I don't need your car.
You can't buy my love, Babe. Your money don't go that far,

('Cause you've been) **Foolin' Around,**
And I won't play your fool.
(I know you're) ***Foolin' Around,***
And I won't play the fool for you

'Cause I don't need your liquor, Babe, and I don't need your place.
You can't keep my heart, Babe, with your pretty face,

Foolin' Around Chorus

'Cause I don't need your fancy cookin', Babe. I don't need your grief.
You've got no shame and when you play your game,
Your lies are beyond belief.

Foolin' Around Chorus

INSTRUMENTAL BRIDGE

Foolin' Around Chorus

'Cause I don't need your money, Baby. I don't need your car.
You can't buy my love, Baby. Your money don't go that far.

Foolin' Around Chorus

No, I won't play the fool for you.
No, I won't play the fool for you.
No, I won't play the fool for you.
I won't play the fool for you.

LINER NOTES, LYRICS, AND RHYMES

THE WAY THAT I NEED YOU

Ever lovin,' ever faithful, ever willin,' ever true.
Always right here by my side, to keep me satisfied,
That's **The Way That I Need You.**

Never cheatin,' never lyin,' always there when I feel blue,
Full of lovin' things to say, to cheer me night and day,
That's **The Way That I Need You.**

Promise that you'll never leave me, and I'll pledge my heart to you.
I want you, love you and believe me, no one else will ever do.

If you want my heart forever, just say you love me too,
By my side you'll always stay, 'cause you need me the same way,
The same way that I need you.

INSTRUMENTAL FROM CHORUS

Ever lovin,' ever faithful, ever willin,' ever true,
Always right here by my side, to keep me satisfied,
That's **The Way That I Need You.**

If you want my heart forever, just say you love me too,
And by my side you'll always stay, 'cause you need me the same way,
The same way that I need you,

Full of lovin' things to say, to cheer you night and day,
The same way that I need you.

IT CAN'T BE RIGHT

It Can't Be Right. No, no, no!
It Can't Be Right that I love you this way.
It Can't Be Right. No, no, no!
It Can't Be Right that I love you this way.
And you don't love me. Oh, no, you don't love me.

I see you. My heart stands still. I love you. And I know I always will.

It Can't Be Right. No, no, no!
It Can't Be Right that I love you this way.
And you don't love me. Oh no, you don't love me.

I tell you just what you mean to me. You say you're sorry. It can never be.

It Can't Be Right. No, no, no!
It Can't Be Right that I love you this way.
It Can't Be Right. No, no, no!
It Can't Be Right that I love you this way.
And you don't love me. Oh no, you don't love me.

INSTRUMENTAL BRIDGE

It Can't Be Right.

It Can't Be Right.
You don't love me. Oh no, you don't love me.

I know I'll love you 'til the end of time,
But you say, you just want to be my friend. Oh, why

It Can't Be Right. No, no, no!
It Can't Be Right that I love you this way.
It Can't Be Right. No, no, no!
It Can't Be Right that I love you this way.
And you don't love me. Oh, no, you don't love me.
Oh, no, you don't love me. Oh, no, you don't love me.

LINER NOTES, LYRICS, AND RHYMES

I BEG YOUR PARDON

I Beg Your Pardon, but you look so sad to me and
If you're feeling blue, need someone to
Tell your troubles to, I'll listen to you.
I'll listen to you.

I Beg Your Pardon, but you look so all alone and
I'm lonely too. Fancy meeting you.
If we talk a while, maybe you would smile
For me. Maybe you would smile for me.

INSTRUMENTAL VERSE

I Beg Your Pardon, but it looks like rain to me and
I know a place nearby, coffee and apple pie.
We could sit and talk. Will you take a walk
With me? Will you take a walk with me?

I Beg Your Pardon, but it's fairly plain to see you'd
Rather be alone. Guess I'll wander on.
What's that you say? Of course, I'll stay with you.

Travis and Adam create the piano part for "I beg Your Pardon."

FEELIN' BETTER

Just a song I wrote for a rainy day
A simple song I wrote to chase the clouds away
I didn't know if it would,
But if it made you feel the way that it should
Well I thought, if I could, I'd maybe make you feel good.

Feelin' Better! Feelin' Better! Feelin' Better, Whoo-hoo
Feelin' Better! Feelin' Better! Feelin' Better, Whoo-hoo

Just a song I wrote to sing in the rain
Just a song I wrote, 'til you're home again,
And I hope that you will like it as much as I do,
'Cause you know it's true, I wrote it thinking of you.

Feelin' Better! Feelin' Better! Feelin' Better, Whoo-hoo
Feelin' Better! Feelin' Better! Feelin' Better, Whoo-hoo

(MODULATION)

Feelin' Better! Feelin' Better! Feelin' Better, Whoo-hoo
Feelin' Better! Feelin' Better! Feelin' Better, Whoo-hoo

Just a song I wrote for a rainy day
A simple song I wrote to chase the clouds away
I didn't know if it would,
But if it made you feel the way that it should
Well I thought, if I could, I'd maybe make you feel good.

Feelin' Better! Feelin' Better! Feelin' Better, Whoo-hoo

(REPEAT UNTIL IT FADES AWAY)

ROCK N ROLL

When I hear **Rock 'n' Roll**, I get tingles up and down my spine.
Aoow! My fingers start to tappin' as the rhythm takes control of mine.
And as far as I'm concerned, that's always been a positive sign!

Well, hard drivin' **Rock 'n' Roll** isn't anything new,
But I guess I'm old-fashioned, so what am I supposed to do?
I love **Rock 'n' Roll** and I love to watch the dancers, too!

FIRST INSTRUMENTAL BRIDGE

Well, down from junior high school, high school and college too,
And if that ain't grandma out there, I don't know who.
Yeah, all 'round the world, they **Rock 'n' Roll,** they do!

SECOND INSTRUMENTAL BRIDGE

It's a tension relief valve. I hear that's what psychologists say,
But when they go dancin,' what do you suppose they play? Huh!
I plan to keep on rockin,' even when I'm old and gray.
So, Honey, turn it up! Aoow! **Rock 'n' Roll** is here to stay!
And as long as I'm around, **Rock 'n' Roll** will never fade away!
Oh, no!

THIRD INSTRUMENTAL BRIDGE TO CODA

END OF SUMMER (2014)

It's come. It's the **End of Summer.**
My homeward way, I must weave.
My darling, my heart stays with you.
Though I, myself, must leave.

Der Sommer ist leider vorüber
Unsere Liebe trotzdem nicht vorbei,
Aber Ich, Ich muss' wieder 'rüber
Und Du, Du bleibst hier, Lorelei.

INSTRUMENTAL BRIDGE

Soon, the dry leaves will chatter
All along this valley, so low
And the golden fields of autumn
Will glisten with ice and with snow.

But I'll return in the springtime.
'Til then, my love, stays with you
So watch 'til the end of winter
When I'll return to you.

INSTRUMENTAL BRIDGE

Was soll' Ich Dir noch sagen?
Schliess Deine Augen bis Zehn.
Noch'nen Kuss, Bitte, keine Fragen
Ich Liebe Dich. Auf Weiderseh'n.

01	3:36	END OF SUMMER
02	3:08	LAND OF THE GIANT BUGS
03	2:45	ALI BABA BEN JONES
04	3:20	A RED-BACKED, SCALY, BLACK-BELLIED, TUSKED, BAT-WINGED DRAGON
05	4:22	TILL THE END (THE VAMPIRE SONG)
05	2:51	OH MAMA
07	2:47	THE SORCERER'S WALTZ
08	4:50	SCREAMIN' CARETAKER BLUES
09	3:37	LOUP GAROU (THE WEREWOLF SONG)
10	3:36	THE LIKES OF YOU

ODD TALES AND WONDERS: STORIES IN SONG

My brother Adam and I produced this first album at his studio in Pasadena, California. I wrote all the songs between 1964-1974, and we began bringing them into the present in November 2012. I sang the songs and we arranged them. Only "Loup Garou" could be considered new. Originally "The Dark Old House," it was about something awful in the bayou, but since whatever awful it might be was never specified, it did not achieve the chilling effect I sought.

When I moved my family to our home in Los Angeles, we befriended our next door neighbors, Mike and Clara. (Clarabelle Smith was once Hattie McDaniels' cook.) Mike was from New Orleans, and I soon grew accustomed to his manner of speech -- a mixture of Creole and Cajun word order, delivered in English. While selecting the songs we'd record, we came across "Dark Old House." Adam asked me to play it for him. I did, and that's when I suddenly knew what haunted that "Dark Old House." A werewolf prowled its grounds. Bayou folk call it a loup garou, or rugarou, but a werewolf, by any other name, is still a classic horror, a fitting companion piece for my "Till the End" vampire song, and "Screamin' Caretaker Blues," a song I based on the most recent *Planet of the Apes*. We set the song in a New Orleans piano bar, gave it a shuffle beat, and when I mimicked Mike, dat "Loup Garou," he sprung up for true!

"Mike" Mitchell

Adam recorded, mixed, and mastered the songs, sang backup for "Ali Baba Ben Jones" and "Oh Mama," and conducted the barroom chorus for "Loup Garou." Special thanks are due Colleen Stratton, who took the role of my tasty victim in "Till the End" (The Vampire Song), voiced the role of Stephanie in "Screamin' Caretaker Blues," and sang in the piano bar crowd; Terry Hagerty, who voiced the role of Peter in "Screamin' Caretaker Blues" and also sang in the crowd for "Loup Garou;" and my wife, Judy, who voiced the role of Betty, the animal shelter owner in "Screamin' Caretaker Blues." Thanks also to Kris Snyder and Barbara Jordan, who joined the "Loup Garou" crowd

LINER NOTES, LYRICS, AND RHYMES

late (but sang their parts in time), and our last-minute volunteer, Karen Callahan, who sang the obbligato lines for the revised version of "The Likes of You." Adam and I dedicate this version of "A Red-backed, Scaly, Black-bellied, Tusked, Bat-winged Dragon" to the memory of our mutual friend, David Carr, for his brilliant piano arrangement and performance in this 1984 version for which special thanks are also due to Lonnie Snyder, Mary Moyers, Julie Long, and Michael Moores who all sang too, and to Philip Moores, whose recording of that piano demo stood up well enough that Adam could rescue it from the archives and import it so we could add the drums, tuba (and fire alarm) for this never-before-released collection of *Stories in Song.*

"Land of the Giant Bugs" and "Ali Baba Ben Jones" are straight forward novelty songs, but "The Sorcerer's Waltz," is a fully orchestrated show tune originally written for the "Red-backed, Scaly, Black-bellied, Tusked, Bat-winged Dragon," and only cut from that show because the sorcerer was too mean to sing to the dragon. "Oh Mama" and "The Likes of You" both emerged from the decade 1964-1974 covered in this book, and feature in its narrative.

Culprits are Adam Pike, Judy Pike, Terry Hagerty and Colleen Stratton

END OF SUMMER

It's come. It's the **End of Summer.**
My homeward way, I must weave.
My darling, my heart stays with you,
   Though I, myself, must leave.

Der Sommer ist leider vorüber
Unsere Liebe trotzdem nicht vorbei,
Aber Ich, Ich muss' wieder 'rüber,
Und Du, Du bleibst hier, Lorelei.

INSTRUMENTAL BRIDGE

Soon, the dry leaves will chatter,
   All along this valley so low,
And the golden fields of autumn
Will glisten with ice and with snow.

But I'll return in the springtime.
'Til then, my love, stays with you,
So watch 'til the end of winter,
   When I'll return to you.

INSTRUMENTAL BRIDGE

Was soll' Ich Dir noch sagen?
Schliess Deine Augen bis Zehn.
Noch'nen Kuss. Bitte, keine Fragen
Ich Liebe Dich. Auf Weiderseh'n.

LINER NOTES, LYRICS, AND RHYMES

LAND OF THE GIANT BUGS

I dreamt that I was shipwrecked in the China Sea,
Clinging to some wreckage barely big enough for me,
Tossed and tumbled in the surf and weak as I could be,
　Stranded in the **Land of the Giant Bugs!**

A shadow then passed over. It blotted out the sky.
I was horrified to see a giant dragonfly.
As it whirred on by me, I began to cry,
　Washed ashore in the **Land of the Giant Bugs!**

A centipede crawled toward me. I turned to run a-way.
A giant beetle blocked me. My feet, they turned to clay.
Along come a huge spider. Would I become its prey --
　Eaten alive in the **Land of the Giant Bugs?**

Arrrrgh! Trapped in the **Land of the Giant Bugs!**

A cockaroach came at me, big enough to ride.
I dove into my knapsack, grabbed the insecticide,
And sprayed him till the can ran dry and he collapsed and died.
　Could I survive in the **Land of the Giant Bugs?**

"Why not?" I thought. I can adapt. I can acclimatize.
But then I saw a preying mantis of such enormous size,
　Staring straight at me with it's gigantic, buggy eyes!
　I must escape from the **Land of the Giant Bugs!**

Ad lib to CODA: *They was everywhere! Bad bugs. Badder bugs. Fuzzy bugs. Slimy bugs. Creepy, crawly bugs. Flying, buzzing bugs. Stinging, biting bugs. INSECTS!*

BUZZING SOUND and song ends with an abrupt SPLAT!

ALI BABA BEN JONES

Runnin' through the wastelands, scared as I could be.
A crafty desert bandit was chasing after me,
'Cause I possessed a treasure chest. He'd steal my precious stones.
I'm talking 'bout the baddest man, in Rajasthan, **Ali Baba Ben Jones!**

I came to an oasis. I was so hot and dry,
I had to stop to quench my thirst or I would surely die.
A man was standing over by the row of telephones,
And it was the baddest man, in Rajasthan, **Ali Baba Ben Jones!**

I couldn't phone for help, so I turned to run away,
And bumped into the bravest man, so he professed to say.
He asked, "Who chases you?" and then he turned to dust and bones,
When I said, "The baddest man, in Rajasthan, **Ali Baba Ben Jones!**"

E-RIF INSTRUMENTAL RELEASE

I thumbed down a caravan headin' to the west,
Laden down with silks and oils and duly impressed,
I asked to see the chieftain, a man who handled loans,
And it was the baddest man, in Rajasthan, **Ali Baba Ben Jones!**

It seemed that every way I turned, I saw that awful man,
So I ran myself 'most ragged crossing Hindustan.
I finally grabbed a camel cab. It shook me to my bones.
The driver was the baddest man, in Rajasthan, **Ali Baba Ben Jones!**

E-RIF INSTRUMENTAL EXIT TO FADE OUT

(Ad lib over camel music exit) *Mr. Jones. Well, I've been looking forward to meetin' you, too. Oh yeah, box of old jewels. On consignment? Well, that'd be just fine! Oh, no. Just drop me at the bus stop.*

LINER NOTES, LYRICS, AND RHYMES
A RED-BACKED, SCALY, BLACK-BELLIED, TUSKED, BAT-WINGED DRAGON

All the dragons are extinct and it's against the law
To conjure or procure – even a dragon's claw.
That's an official decree, signed by the king of the land,
And proclaimed throughout the kingdom, by a marching band.

But this morning, something went wrong, something very hard to explain,
And the news, it quaked the earth and upset a peaceful reign.
A young warrior rode to the castle crying that the king must hear
That a dragon was on the loose. Cause for alarm and fear!

It was a **Red-backed, Scaly, Black-bellied, Tusked, Bat-winged Dragon**,
Rampaging the countryside, scourging the land.
It was a **Red-backed, Scaly, Black-bellied, Tusked, Bat-winged Dragon.**
The situation was clearly out of hand.

INSTRUMENTAL BRIDGE

He was little more than an egg when the new law was proclaimed.
Hidden away by an evil sorcerer, Long-Grin was the dragon's name!

He lives in the forbidden forest in a fortress made of stone,
And even the bravest king wouldn't venture up there all alone,
'Cause dragon's are fierce and strong, terrible to behold,
The most 'orrible creatures alive. So the story is told!

It was a **Red-backed, Scaly, Black-bellied, Tusked, Bat-winged Dragon,**
Hissing, spewing flames, smoke coming out of its ears.
It was a **Red-backed, Scaly, Black-bellied, Tusked, Bat-winged Dragon.**
Such a sight one sees, but once in a thousand years.
(And that means trouble)
One appears about every thousand years.
(I wish they wouldn't)
But one appears about every thousand years!

ODD TALES AND WONDERS: STORIES IN SONG

TILL THE END (THE VAMPIRE SONG)

(Spoken) *Listen to them! The children of the night!*

(fiendish laughter separates each complete verse)

Come here, my child. Have no fear.
You may call me "Count," for short, my dear.
Don't be afraid. I'm your friend.
I always will be **Till the End!**

This way, my sweet. We'll walk on the moor.
It's dank and eerie, here by the shore.
Take my hand. There are pits on the way,
Where various reptiles sometimes play.

Come, under my cape. You'll catch a chill.
Yes, that's better. Much better.
Over the hill is the castle of a friend of mine.
You've heard of the doctor, Frankenstein!

Malicious gossip, those stories you've heard.
He's really quite nice. Take my word!
Of course, it's true. I'm your friend.
I always will be **Till the End!**

You're feverish, dear. We'll stop to rest.
There, lay your head back on my chest.
So warm. So warm! There's a flush to your cheek.
What's that, my love? You're feeling weak?

It's true, I promised I was your friend,
And that I've been right **Till the End!**
Look up, my dear. The moon's so red.
One little kiss and now you're dead!

Spoken: *All these one night stands. I wish I could find a steady girl!*

(the fiendish laughter turns into bat-sounds!)

LINER NOTES, LYRICS, AND RHYMES

OH MAMA

BAINBRIDGE FIRE CONTROL TECHNICIANS MARCH INTRO

Oh, Mama, Oh, Ma-ma. Hey, Mama, look what you done.
Oh, Mama, Oh, Ma-ma. You took away the morning sun.
Oh, Mama, Oh, Ma-ma. Nowhere to hide. Nowhere to run.
Oh, Mama, Oh, Ma-ma. Hey, Mama, look what you done!

We were just tryin' to tell it like it is and
We were just tryin' to roll a-way the stone.
We were just tryin' to clean the cobwebs off your mind.
Out of your mind!

Oh, Mama, Oh, Ma-ma. Hey, Mama, look what you done.
Oh, Mama, Oh, Ma-ma. You took away the morning sun.
Oh, Mama, Oh, Ma-ma. Nowhere to hide. Nowhere to run.
Oh, Mama, Oh, Ma-ma. Hey, Mama, look what you done!

INSTRUMENTAL RELEASE

You wouldn't listen to what we had to say.
You were afraid that the truth would strike at home.
You thought the light of awareness would make you blind . . .
But you are so blind!

Oh, Mama, Oh, Ma-ma. Hey, Mama, look what you done.
Oh, Mama, Oh, Ma-ma. You took away the morning sun.
Oh, Mama, Oh, Ma-ma. Nowhere to hide. Nowhere to run.
Oh, Mama, Oh, Ma-ma. Hey, Mama, look what you done!

INSTRUMENTAL RELEASE

Oh, Mama, oh, Ma-ma. Hey, Mama, look what you done.
Oh, Mama, oh, Ma-ma. You took away the morning sun.
Oh, Mama, oh, Ma-ma. Nowhere to hide. Nowhere to run.
Oh, Mama, oh, Ma-ma. Hey, Mama, look what you done!

BAINBRIDGE FIRE CONTROL TECHNICIANS MARCH CODA

ODD TALES AND WONDERS: STORIES IN SONG

THE SORCERER'S WALTZ

I'll tell you a tale. It's time you were told,
A grim, grisly tale of a dragon of fame.
For he was your father, the story is his,
And so is the treasure we, one day, will claim.

It began when your grandfather, so fierce was he,
The whole forest shook with his monst'rous roar,
Was paid a great fortune to leave as may be,
The terrified peasants who kept bringing him more.

And they brought him fat sheep. They brought him fat hogs.
And since he lived to be ninety years old,
He gorged himself 'til the day that he died,
And left your father a lair full of gold.

Your father, o'erwrought by your grandfather's death,
Was hardly in shape for the terrible fight,
So the miserable peasants ran off to the king,
Who sent, straight away, his most ferocious knight.

Your father, grief-stricken, tears in his eyes
(The story, 'though sad, still must be told),
Bid me take you away, where you might be safe.
Then your father was slain, and the king got the gold!

My goddaughter, Andrea, holds one of Long-Grin's enormous claws in her hand, but is not at all afraid of the huge dragon lurking over her shoulder, because Long-Grin's not a bad sort, for all that he's a dragon, and as far as the claw is concerned, he's already grown a new one.

LINER NOTES, LYRICS, AND RHYMES
SCREAMIN' CARETAKER BLUES

Roger sings. The others don't. Phone Rings. Owner Answers.

Owner:	Hello?
Roger:	*Your herd of abandoned elephants*
Owner:	Three retired circus elephants do not make a herd.
Roger:	*Trampled down their enclosure fence.*
Owner:	Oh, my goodness! Why would they do that?
Roger:	*Perhaps they simply wished to take a stroll.*
Owner:	Is that you Roger? Where's Philip?
Roger:	*They're all playing in the watering hole.*
Owner:	Philip's playing with the elephants?
Roger:	*I'm up here in the observation booth --*
Owner:	In the tower?
Roger:	*Locked in, alone, but to tell the truth,*
Owner:	How'd you get locked in the tower?
Roger:	*Without sounding too dramatic,*
Owner:	Are you all right?
Roger:	*My situation is problematic.*
Owner:	Oh, dear . . .
Roger:	*Something outside is thumping about.*
	It can't get in, but I can't get out.
Owner:	Stephanie, can you talk to him?
Roger:	*This is not a shelter. It's a zoo!*
Stephanie:	Roger? It's me, Stephanie!
Roger:	*I came here to spend more time with you.*
Stephanie:	You knew we had this fundraiser, tonight.
Roger:	*You call this exotic atmosphere?*
Stephanie:	You told me you loved animals!
Roger:	*But I thought she'd be gone, and you'd be here!*
Stephanie:	Is that what this is all about?
Roger:	*There's a tiger prowling in the hall,*
Stephanie:	The tiger's out!?! The tiger's loose!?!
Roger:	*And Sweetheart, let me tell you that's not all.*
Stephanie:	All right, Roger. What have you done?
Roger:	*Now I keep a stun-gun handy,*
Stephanie:	For a tiger!?!

SCREAMIN' CARETAKER BLUES - 2

Roger:	*'Cause something ate up all the candy,* *Something clever unlocked all the doors;* *Something big and hairy that snores!*
Stephanie:	Sounds like my Ex. Roger, stay on the line. I'll get Peter! I'll be right back.
Peter:	Roger? Look at the bank of monitors on the console. Are the cameras working?
Roger:	*Looking! Oh, yeah, all the monitors are on.*
Peter:	Good! Now, check all the pens.
Roger:	*The ape pen's open. All the apes are gone.*
Peter:	Gone? Gone where?
Roger:	*I never trusted that bright-eyed Chimpanzee.*
Peter:	I need you to go down to the ape pen.
Roger:	*I never liked the way he looked at me.*
Stephanie:	He's locked in the tower.
Peter:	The ape?
Stephanie:	No, Roger.
Roger:	*I don't think I've made myself quite clear.*
Peter:	Go ahead. I'm listening.
Roger:	*I need candy! Get me out of here!*
Peter:	Who's Candy?
Stephanie:	He's hypoglycemic. He needs to eat something!
Roger:	*I can't eat. The refrigerator* *Is guarded by an alligator.* *Now, the apes are climbing the tower.* *It just went dark. They've cut the power!*

The Glass Observatory wall is smashed. Apes, Chimps and Monkeys howl, laugh, roar and shriek over Roger's screams . . .

Peter:	I'm calling the sheriff!
Stephanie:	Don't call the sheriff. They'll just shoot everything.
Peter:	Well?
Stephanie:	Gimme a minute! We'll have to have another fundraiser!
Peter:	Where's Philip?
Stephanie:	Philip? Are you kidding? He is so fired! FADE OUT

LINER NOTES, LYRICS, AND RHYMES
LOUP GAROU (THE WEREWOLF SONG)

SPOKEN: *I ain' no Cajun, me. But I guarontee dis song 'bout a loup garou loose in the bayou! Oo-woo! Make my skin crawl, an dat's for true. French say "loup garou." Cajun say "rougarou." Loup garou, rougarou, wolfman, werewolf, all da same ting, an' dat's bad news, any which way, hagh? Oh yeah.*

Dere's a little town near da bayou where ever one's hair gone white,
From da lady wid da ladle to da bebay in da cradle,
An you know dat cain' be right. No, *you know dat cain' be right.*

When da moon come up on da bayou, dem collar start gettin' tight,
An' even ole Mama Sadie, da voodoo lady, start in shakin' wid' fright.
Whaa, *she start in shakin' wid fright.*

Cuz dere a **Loup Garou** in da bayou and I hope wid all my might,
You be sho to take care you don't end up dere.
Don't you ever go dere at night! No, *don't you ever go dere at night!*

Da **Loup Garou** live back in da bayou,
But he come out on da moonlid night.
When he on da prowl, you can hear him howl,
Til he satisfy his appetite. Whoa, *he satisfy his appetite.*

At night da water black in da bayou, but red in da morning light,
'Cuz when he get troo, what's lef' o' you,
Feed dem gators and dey ain' polite. No, *dem 'gators just ain' polite.*

Dere a **Loup Garou** in da bayou, an' his fiery red eyes gleams bright.
Women wail an' strong wills fail, when he out on da moonlid night.
Whoa, *he come out on da moonlid night.*

Dere a **Loup Garou** in da bayou, an' I hope wid all my might,
You listen, Cher, Don' you ever go dere, an' never go dere at night!
Aw, *don't you ever go dere at night! Don't you ever go dere at night!*
No, *don't you ever go dere at night! Don't you ever go dere at night!*

SPOKEN: *I say I don' go dere, me, an dat's for true. Uh-uh!*

ODD TALES AND WONDERS: STORIES IN SONG

THE LIKES OF YOU

Introductory Obbligato

I've never seen **The Likes of You.**
Are you a dream, or a dream come true?
You're more than my imagination can conceive.
Please, let me touch you that I may believe.

Obbligato

When you come near, I feel dazed and weak.
I dare not move. I dare not speak.
I don't know why. This feeling's new.
I've never seen **The Likes of You**

Obbligato and release

Will you, like a lover's moon,
Flee the morning sun,
Or will you constant be?
Are you The One?

Don't go away. Stay near me now.
I'd keep you close, if I knew how.
If I sound strange, please trust me do.
I've never seen **The Likes of You.**
The Likes of You.
The Likes of You!

Kris Snyder

Kris came on time to record his vocal parts for the "Loup Garou" crowd.

Karen sang the obbligato lines for "The Likes of You."

Karen Callahan

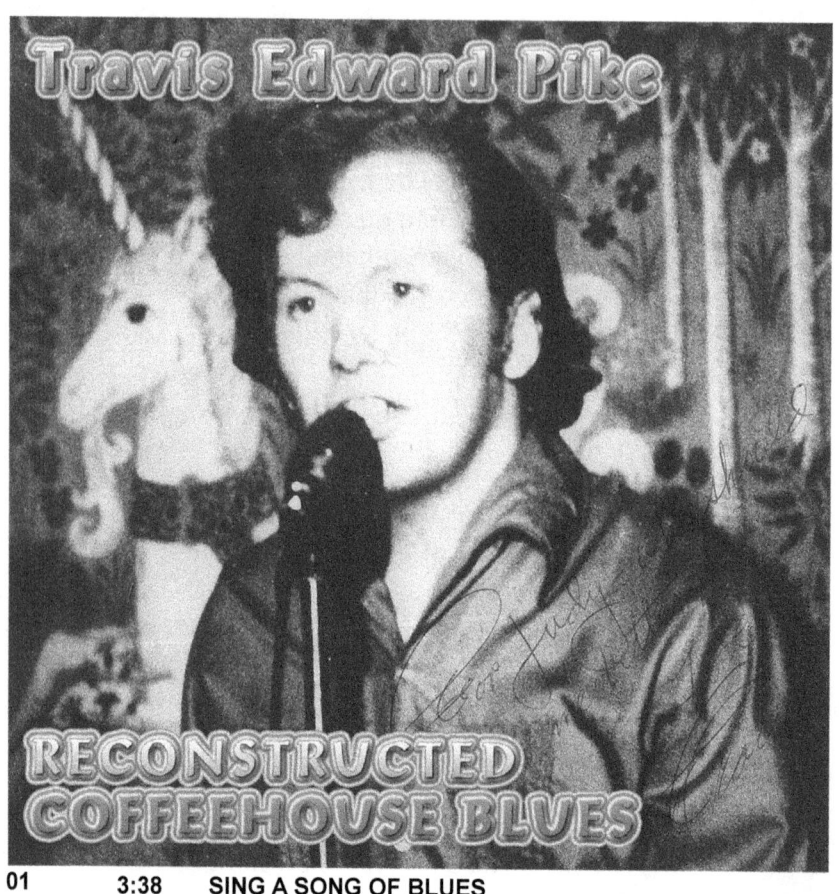

01	3:38	SING A SONG OF BLUES
02	2:54	DON'T LET ME CHANGE YOUR MIND
03	3:49	GREY DAY LADY
04	3:18	MESMERIZING, TANTALIZING, HAZEL-EYED JANE
05	2:47	SHE'S GONNA BE A WOMAN SOMEDAY
06	2:39	YOU AND I TOGETHER
07	2:50	TOMMY TEW RUN RUN
08	3:13	MIDNIGHT WALTZ
09	4:17	SHAGGY, SHAGGY BLUES
10	3:29	DON'T YOU CARE AT ALL
11	2:58	A RED-BACKED, SCALY, BLACK-BELLIED, TUSKED BAT-WINGED DRAGON

01. "Sing a Song of Blues" is dedicated to repatriated military veterans. After tours of duty overseas, many experience alienation, and have difficulty fitting into a society that seems unlike the one they left, and adjusting can be bitter and disheartening.

02. I don't know why "Don't Let Me Change Your Mind" appeals to so many, but since clinging to a lost love only results in shame and degradation, granting the former lover freedom, may provide some comfort in the notion one is alone by choice, rather than abandoned.

03. "Grey Day Lady" was inspired by a coffeehouse incident. A young woman entered, child in tow, and settled in a dark corner. The child was silent, the mother in tears. Were they abused, hungry, or just in out of the rain? They left before I finished my set, so I never knew.

04. "Mesmerizing, Tantalizing, Hazel-eyed Jane" another product of my 1965-66 New England coffeehouse scene, was composed about the waitress at Mark Edward's "Sword in the Stone" coffeehouse in Boston's Back Bay. Tall and lovely, Jane's undulating walk was probably a by-product of carrying trays of coffee while she wended her way between the tables. Always and only Mark's lady, she was, nevertheless, a visual joy to behold for patrons and performers alike.

05. "She's Gonna Be a Woman Someday" sprang from a visit with a friend to a girl's house where the younger sister tried in vain to get the suitor's attention. A "third wheel," I listened to the little one's tale and entertained her with a few of my own, making it a thoroughly enjoyable afternoon. The pianist is David Pinto, an extraordinary talent and founder of the Academy of Music for the Blind.

06. "You and I Together" is about being with my brother, Adam, whose diligence and attitude made this musical venture a joyful experience.

07. "Tommy Tew Run Run" evolved from my coffeehouse days. As "Three Girls," it was about a notorious, fictitious rake, but in prepping this version, the "Three Girls" became metaphors for ships, and the tale of the notorious Rhode Island pirate emerged, as from a fog bank.

LINER NOTES, LYRICS, AND RHYMES

The "Fresh launched" lady, which Tommy Tew attempted to loot in November, 1695, resisted, and Tew was disemboweled by a cannon shot, an appropriate end for either Tew or my original cad.

08. "Midnight Waltz" is a memory of the aftermath of a party on Beacon Hill, when I discovered my ride had already left. I hobbled down to the all-night diner on Cambridge Street, where the song ends, hitched a ride to the Boston side of the wind-swept Mystic River Bridge, and crossed on foot to get back to Chelsea Naval Hospital.

09. "Shaggy, Shaggy Blues" is the most genuinely authentic "blues song" on this CD. It goes back to my earliest repertoire for the hospital wards and coffeehouses, and my performance hasn't changed, but with Adam's bass, piano and guitar parts, it is now finally, fully evolved.

10. "Don't You Care At All" is dedicated to all American and allied forces who served in Vietnam. A favorite of my friend, Chuck, who was in basic training in 1968 during the Tet Offensive. Walter Cronkite's call for an end to America's role in the Vietnam conflict, followed, but our withdrawal was still years off. Most who have heard it agree it reflects perfectly that divisive era in American history.

11. 1984's recording of "A Red-Backed, Scaly, Black-Bellied, Tusked, Bat-winged Dragon" was remastered for this "bonus" version, shortened to the length it was when the Tea Party played it live, with the addition of an accordian part that gives it an amusement park feel.

I did a lot of finger-picking on this CD, with Adam playing everything else except the piano part in "Gonna Be A Woman Someday" and the accordian part in "The Red-backed, Scaly, Black-bellied, Tusked, Bat-winged Dragon." both played by David Pinto.

The parts of the waxing and waning protesters were sung by Lauran Doverspike, Barbara Jordan, Kris Snyder and a number of others to whom I am grateful, but who shall remain anonymous. (The voice of the newscaster on the separate singles version of "Don't You Care At All" is Joe Kondash.)

SING A SONG OF BLUES

Sing a Song of Blues, crawlin' over my mind,
Ugly kind of blues, creepin' up from behind.
Low-down evil blues, sneakin' under my skin.
Mean wicked blues, tryin' to kick its way in.

I'm a stranger in your town -- everywhere I go.
My whole world's been shattered in ways you'll never know.
I came back, but back to what?
A home that was no home, so now I wander – now I roam.
Sing a Song of Blues

INSTRUMENTAL BRIDGE

Looking for a place to rest, somewhere I can heal.
Somewhere that's more than just a bed and a hot meal.
If there's nothing here for me -- nowhere I can stay,
Tell me so and I'll go on my way.

Sing a Song of Blues, creepin' into my soul.
Ugly kind of blues, tryin' to take control.
Meanest kind of blues, cuttin' right to the bone.
Low-down evil blues, when you're always alone.

Adam flat-picked the rhythm guitar part for "Sing a Song of Blues."

LINER NOTES, LYRICS, AND RHYMES
DON'T LET ME CHANGE YOUR MIND

Don't let my heart influence your mind.
You've made all your plans, surely, clearly defined.

Don't let my tears make you hesitate.
Wasn't it you who said, "It's over now, it's too late?"

I should have known not to trust in you,
But I had a dream of my own -- a dream that'll never come true.

Don't let what I say, give you pause at the door.
You've already on your way. It's doesn't matter anymore.

Don't Let Me Change Your Mind.
Don't Let Me Change Your Mind.
Don't Let Me Change Your Mind!

I pick it and sing it. Adam's does everything else, and I like it!

RECONSTRUCTED COFFEEHOUSE BLUES

GREY DAY LADY

Grey Day Lady, why are you so sad and blue.
Grey Day Lady, I've had my bad days too.
It's not the end. Your heart will mend.
Shall I call a friend for you?
Grey Day Lady, is there something I can do?

Grey Day Lady, is there someone I should phone?
Grey Day Lady, it's no good weepin' all alone.
I see you cry. I hear your sigh.
You give me shivers when you moan.
Grey Day Lady, is there someone special I should phone?

Instrumental Bridge

Grey Day Lady, let me help you, if I can.
Grey Day Lady, I don't know how this all began.
You had a row. It's over now. Take a bow. Make a new plan.
Grey Day Lady, you deserve a better man.

I pick and sing this one, too, but it's really Adam's bass and keyboard that bring this "Grey Day Lady" out of the shadows.

LINER NOTES, LYRICS, AND RHYMES

MESMERIZING, TANTALIZING, HAZEL-EYED JANE

Saw somebody walking, coming down the avenue.
Turned my head around, stood up to get a better view.
The mini-skirted sight I saw commenced to broil my brain.
Mesmerizing, Tantalizing, Hazel-eyed Jane.

Her long-legged, undulating walk is something else to see.
A grown man can only moan and gawk. Take it from me.
She's enough to make an able man start raising cane.
Mesmerizing, Tantalizing, Hazel-eyed Jane.

She turns me on. She's got such shapely hips,
When she walks by my heartbeat skips.
Her eyes are bright. Her hair is brushed. She's always in style.
Did you see her playful little smile? Woohoo!

INSTRUMENTAL BRIDGE

Mesmerizing, Tantalizing, Hazel-eyed Jane.

She turns me on. She's got such shapely hips.
When she's nearby, my heart does flips.
Her eyes are bright. Her hair is brushed. She's always in style.
There it is again, that playful little smile!

Tall and lovely, sweet and sexy, oh she holds her head up high.
Everybody stares at her as she goes strolling by.
I try to catch her eye as she goes by, but I just try in vain.
Mesmerizing, Tantalizing, Hazel-eyed Jane.
Mesmerizing, Tantalizing, Hazel-eyed Jane.
Mesmerizing, Tantalizing, Hazel-eyed Jane.

THE "SHE'S GONNA BE A WOMAN SOMEDAY" SESSION

David Pinto asked me to sing along as he played, to help get him into the mood. I said okay, and asked Adam to record my scratch-track too. That's how we got the performance we ultimately used on the album -- David plugged in to the console, Adam engineering, and me, in the booth, singing it "live" -- an inspired session.

Best of all, I finally recorded the song, just as I had imagined it.

LINER NOTES, LYRICS, AND RHYMES

SHE'S GONNA BE A WOMAN SOMEDAY

PIANO INTRO

She may not be such a knockout to you,
But she's a total gas to me.
You like 'em older, taller, and stacked.
Huh, take my advice, it's free!
You ignore her 'cause she's not twenty-one,
But there's one thing that I have to say.
She may just be a little girl now,
But **She's Gonna Be a Woman Someday.**

Don't think she won't remember. She will!
She'll know you didn't treat her right.
When she gets older, you think she'll forget
Your condescension and slight. Huh.
How you ignored her, how you shined her on.
Well she won't. She'll make you pay.
'Cause she may just be a little girl now,
But **She's Gonna Be a Woman Someday.**

PIANO BRIDGE

Would it hurt you to say hello,
To listen when she talks to you?
All these fine ladies were once little girls,
But then they grew and grew! Oh yeah!
Go ahead. Act like a fool.
When she grows up she'll send you on your way,
And you'll remember then what I said, way back when,
'Cause **She's Gonna Be a Woman Someday.** *(I'm gonna tell ya . . .)*
She's Gonna Be a Woman Someday. *(You better believe it!)*
She's Gonna Be a Woman Someday.

RECONSTRUCTED COFFEEHOUSE BLUES

YOU AND I TOGETHER

We'll go walkin.' We'll go strollin.' **You and I, Together.**
Through the country, gently rollin,' **You and I, Together.**
Oh, the sights that we will see, trekkin' through this land.
Me with you, and you with me, we'll lay down in the sand.

If we come across a stream, here, and we get the notion,
We can stop to fish or dream, or go on to the ocean.
This is the only way for us. It's great to be free.
No schedule to meet. No cause for fuss. As free as the sea.

We can watch the boats come in, and mind the seagull choir.
We'll have dinner from a tin, cooked on a driftwood fire.
We've still got a little time, to do us what we want to.
No deep thoughts to fog our minds, just goin' where we're gone to.

We'll go walkin.' We'll go strollin.' **You and I, Together.**
Through the country, gently rollin,' **You and I, Together.**

This is the only way for us. It's great to be free.
No schedule to meet. No cause for fuss. As free as the sea.

We'll go walkin.' We'll go strollin.'
You and I, Together.
Through the country, gently rollin,'
You and I, Together.
You and I, Together.
You and I, Together. *Oooo.*

FADE AWAY

LINER NOTES, LYRICS, AND RHYMES

TOMMY TEW RUN RUN

I sing of a darling of uncertain renown.
When I came alongside, she let her hair down.
She claimed to be a princess, bound for Araby,
But all she had upon her, she bestowed on me.

**Tommy Tew Run Run. Tommy Tew Run Run.
Tommy Tew Run Run. Tommy Tew Run Run!**
To me, the dark-eyed darling surrendered her pride,
But I didn't ask the lady to be my bride.

Another came to view, sharp as a pin.
I drew alongside. She welcomed me in.
Generous and gentle, she be well-bred.
She gave me all she had to give, or so she said.

**Tommy Tew Run Run. Tommy Tew Run Run.
Tommy Tew Run Run. Tommy Tew Run Run!**
For her fond affections, I had risked my very life,
But I didn't want the lady for to be my wife.

For there's another, still, that I'm bound to get.
Fresh launched, she hasn't learned how to please me yet.
To win the precious prize, I'll play gentle and kind,
But teach her soon and well enough what's on my mind.

**Tommy Tew Run Run. Tommy Tew Run Run.
Tommy Tew Run Run. Tommy Tew Run Run!**
For her sweet attentions, though I'll risk everything,
I'll not be giving the lady a wedding ring.

**Tommy Tew Run Run. Tommy Tew Run Run.
Tommy Tew Run Run. Tommy Tew Run Run.**
Tommy run!

MIDNIGHT WALTZ

Walking the dark, damp streets of the city,
The musty perfume of its mist-kissed air,
The clop-clop of my footsteps, a car in the distance.
I sense eyes upon me. I know she is there.
Midnight

Here and there, in a window, a light remains burning.
Sometimes in the darkness, blue windows glow,
And from open windows, the sound of a TV.
Still, someone watches. She sees me, I know.
Midnight. Midnight.

INSTRUMENTAL BRIDGE

Here and there, a glow in a darken'd doorway,
The smell of tobacco, a lover's embrace,
A shuffle, a sigh, an admonishing whisper.
I search all the windows, but can't see her face.
Midnight. Midnight.

An old man sits alone in an all-night diner.
The glow of a streetlight on a gumwrapper glistens.
The old man is reading tomorrow's newspaper.
If she can't see me, still, somewhere she listens.
Midnight. Midnight. Midnight!

SHAGGY, SHAGGY BLUES

I feel so lowdown in the morning.
I feel so lowdown in the night.
I feel so lowdown all day long -- 'n' that ain't right
And I feel worried when I wake up.
Yeah, I know that something's wrong.
I've got the **Shaggy, Shaggy Blues**. Baby, you're gone.

Well, I wander all around, dear,
To all the places that we'd go,
And I wonder what went wrong -- 'n' yet, I know.
I've got nobody left to guide me,
'Cause beside me, there ain't you.
I've got the lowdown misery, **Shaggy, Shaggy Blues**.

INSTRUMENTAL BRIDGE

I've got the **Shaggy, Shaggy Blues**. Baby, you're gone.

Well, I wander all around, dear,
To all the places that we'd go,
And I wonder what went wrong -- 'n' yet, I know. Whoa, I know!
I've got nobody left to guide me,
'Cause beside me, there ain't you.
I've got the lowdown misery, **Shaggy, Shaggy Blues**.

RECONSTRUCTED COFFEEHOUSE BLUES

DON'T YOU CARE AT ALL

Remember how the little children cried,
When the cable came that said their Daddy'd died.
Saigon reports "change is in the tide."
Now you think that there are things,
Matters more important to recall.
Don't You Care at All? Don't You Care at All?

Our casualties are numbered by the score,
But even so, we've slaughtered ten times more,
And any day now, we will win the war.
But now the curtain's slowly drawn. The window's gone.
We're up against the wall.
Don't You Care at All? Don't You Care at All?

AUDIO FX AND INSTRUMENTAL BRIDGE

Politicians start a purge each year.
They tell us what new demons we must fear,
And so we band together and we cheer.
But still the world, maliciously,
Keeps on spawning villians great and small.
Don't You Care at All?
Don't You Care at All? (Don't You Care at All?)
Don't You Care at All? (Don't You Care at All?)
Don't You Care at All? (Don't You Care at All?)
Don't You Care at All? (Don't You Care at All?)
Don't You Care at All? (Don't You Care at All?)
Don't You Care at All? (Don't You Care at All?)
Don't You Care at All?

LINER NOTES, LYRICS, AND RHYMES
A RED-BACKED, SCALY, BLACK-BELLIED TUSKED, BAT-WINGED DRAGON

All the dragons are extinct and it's against the law
To conjure or procure – even a dragon's claw.
That's an official decree, signed by the king of the land,
And proclaimed throughout the kingdom, by a marching band.

But this morning, something went wrong,
Something very hard to explain,
And the news, it quaked the earth and upset a peaceful reign.
A young warrior rode to the castle, crying that the king must hear
That a dragon was on the loose. Cause for alarm and fear.

It was a **Red-backed, Scaly, Black-bellied, Tusked, Bat-winged Dragon,**
Rampaging the countryside, scourging the land.
It was a **Red-backed, Scaly, Black-bellied, Tusked, Bat-winged Dragon.**
The situation was clearly out of hand.

He was little more than an egg when the new law was proclaimed.
Hidden away by an evil sorcerer, Long-Grin was the dragon's name!

He lives in the forbidden forest in a fortress made of stone
And even the bravest king wouldn't venture up there all alone
'Cause dragon's are fierce and strong, terrible to be hold
The most 'orrible creatures alive. So the story is told!

It was a **Red-backed, Scaly, Black-bellied, Tusked, Bat-winged Dragon,**
Hissing, spewing flames, smoke coming out of its ears.
It was a **Red-backed, Scaly, Black-bellied, Tusked, Bat-winged Dragon.**
Such a sight one sees, but once in a thousand years.
(And that means trouble)
One appears about every thousand years.
(I wish they wouldn't)
But one appears about every thousand years!

01	2:48	IF I DIDN'T LOVE YOU GIRL
02	2:48	OKAY
03	2:43	WORRIED SICK
04	2:48	CAN'T YOU SEE
05	3:32	ONE-TEN BLUES
06	3:01	STAY BY ME
07	3:20	WHAT'S THE MATTER WITH YOUR MIND
08	3:45	IN YOUR EYES
09	2:58	I'LL DO ANYTHING I CAN
10	3:18	YOU GOT WHAT I NEED
11	2:54	OH MAMA (2014)

LINER NOTES, LYRICS, AND RHYMES

In 1967-1968, the original Travis Pike's Tea Party featured lead guitarist/third vocalist Karl Garrett, Phil Vitali on drums, Mikey Joe Valente on electric bass, Juris "George" Brox as second vocalist and rhythm guitar, and singer-songwriter and rhythm guitarist, Travis Pike. Adam and I have attempted to play these songs today, as much like the band played the originals some 50-years ago. And we succeeded. I know, because I was there.

01. The first cut on the CD is a fresh recording of "If I Didn't Love You Girl," side one of the 1968 recording released on the Alma label. Arguably more psychedelic in concept than rock style, its background vocals contradict the lead vocal, reflecting the ego-preserving schizophrenia of first love.

02. "Okay" was one of the first rock songs in the band's repertoire. It offers excuses, rather than apologies — even going so far as to imply that the girl's unusually high standards are all that made the vocalist's misbehavior seem inappropriate. It's a bad excuse and he won't get away with it . . . unless the girl is crazy about him.

03. "Worried Sick" was inspired by a drum head replacement. In such situations, I usually entertained the crowd with my stories in rhyme while the equipment was repaired, but that night, George started strumming and singing "Goodnight Irene." Taken unawares, there was little Karl and I could do, but join in. It went over so well that I composed "Worried Sick." Never performed after the group's California migration, it will be new to all but their most loyal New England fans.

04. "Can't You See" is a refreshing broken-hearted love song in that it doesn't threaten or wish ill upon the purportedly responsible party in the failed relationship.

05. "One-Ten Blues" is less remorseful than mournful, dealing with a personal loss so tragic and profound that a recovery is unlikely, perhaps even impossible.

06. "Stay By Me" is a rocking, powerful plea for a stable relationship based on love and history.

07. On the other hand, "What's the Matter with Your Mind" is an equally rocking, disillusioned lover's primal scream -- as likely a projection of his disturbed state of mind, as of hers.

08. "In Your Eyes" beautifully addresses the hurt, anger and potential relief inherent in the breakup of an ill-fated romance.

09. "I'll Do Anything I Can" is one of those promises made out of desperate, adolescent infatuation, but I have to wonder if "anything" will ever be enough to win this particular gal -- or any other, for that matter. Experience suggests a vague "anything" hasn't much of a chance against a steady job.

10. "You Got What I Need" is a rocking celebration of primal, post-adolescent hormonal activity run amuck.

11. "Oh Mama (2014)," first released last year in *Odd Tales and Wonders: Stories in Song*, is a new, more authentic-sounding version of one of my most outstanding hard rock tunes. It's unclear what, exactly, Mama did, but it resulted in a catastrophe that could be personal, but could just as easily have global ramifications.

With Adam's help, Travis is starting to sound like the entire Tea Party!

LINER NOTES, LYRICS, AND RHYMES

IF I DIDN'T LOVE YOU GIRL

I - - - didn't love you girl
I wouldn't cry all night, **If I Didn't Love You Girl**
I - - - - didn't love you girl
And I wouldn't sigh all right, **If I Didn't Love You Girl**
    I - - - - didn't love you girl
No, I wouldn't cry all night, **If I Didn't Love You Girl**
If you didn't mean everything to me, I wouldn't care at all
              everything to me, I wouldn't care at all
                        I wouldn't care at all

You - - - - really loved me girl
You wouldn't do what you do, if you really loved me girl
You - - - - - really loved me girl
You would be true, through and through, if you really loved me girl
    You- - - - really loved me girl
No, You wouldn't do what you do, if you really loved me girl
If I didn't think there was hope for you, I wouldn't care at all
               there was hope for you, I wouldn't care at all
                       I wouldn't care at all

INSTRUMENTAL BRIDGE

I - - - didn't love you girl
I wouldn't cry all night, **If I Didn't Love You Girl**
I - - - - didn't love you girl
And I wouldn't sigh all right, **If I Didn't Love You Girl**
    I - - - - didn't love you girl
No, I wouldn't cry all night, **If I Didn't Love You Girl**
If you didn't mean everything to me, I wouldn't care at all
               everything to me, I wouldn't care at all
                       I wouldn't care at all
          If I Didn't Love You Girl,
          If I Didn't Love You Girl,
          If I Didn't Love You Girl!

TRAVIS EDWARD PIKE'S TEA PARTY SNACK PLATTER

OKAY

Okay, so one time I was wrong,
But girl you know it's been so long,
Since I met anybody who thinks like you.
So try to see my point of view.

Come back with me. Come back with me. Come back with me.
(Oh, please!)
Cause I - have been searchin' for someone - like you
                                      I - - - - - have been searchin'
And I - think I love you. I mean to say, I really do!
  I - think I love you. I mean to say, I really do!
    think I love you. I mean to say, I really do! **Okay!**

INSTRUMENTAL BRIDGE

Okay, so I was rough on you,
But understand what I've been through.
I didn't mean to make you cry.
I'll make it up. At least, I'll try!

Come back with me. Come back with me. Come back with me.
Cause I - have been searchin' for someone - like you
                                      I - - - - - have been searchin'
And I - think I love you. I mean to say, I really do!
  I - think I love you. I mean to say, I really do!
    think I love you. I mean to say, I really do! **Okay!**

INSTRUMENTAL BRIDGE

Okay, so one time I was wrong,
But girl you know it's been so long,
Since I met anybody who thinks like you.
So try to see my point of view.

Come back with me. Come back with me. Come back with me.
Okay!

LINER NOTES, LYRICS, AND RHYMES

WORRIED SICK

Since I had to leave you. *Since I've been gone.*
I've been so lonely. *Oh so long.*
Darlin,' I've missed you *all of this time.*
When I get home, *will you still be mine?*

Well I'm **Worried Sick** *and scared to death -- lonely as I could be.*
Yeah, I'm **Worried Sick** *and scared to death that you won't wait for me!*

Oh, you know I love you, *and I've been true.*
I'm so broken-hearted, *alone without you!*
I never got a letter, *in all of this time.*
When I get home, *will you still be mine?*

Well I'm **Worried Sick** *and scared to death*
That you've found someone new
Yeah, I'm **Worried Sick** *and scared to death, waitin' to hear from you!*

INSTRUMENTAL RELEASE

I wish I'd never left you, *but I had to go*
Tell me what's been goin' on. *I gotta know!*
Did you lose my address, *or didn't you care?*
I've been gone three days now. *I'm tearin' my hair!*

'Cause I'm **Worried Sick** *and scared to death and lonely as I could be.*
Yeah, I'm **Worried Sick** *and scared to death, you won't wait for me!*
And I'm **Worried Sick** *and scared to death*
That you've found someone new.
Yeah, I'm **Worried Sick** *and scared to death, waitin' to hear from you!*
Worried Sick!

CAN'T YOU SEE

Can't You See I'm weary?
Can't You See *I'm down?*
Can't You See *my heart's been broken,*
By your runnin' 'round?
Can't You See?

And now, I'm through with tryin.'
Things can never be the same.
Seems you think that love is just a game.
You've been cheatin.' You've been lyin.'
We both know it's true.
I'll get by better *without you.*

INSTRUMENTAL BRIDGE

Can't You See it's over?
Can't You See *it's passed?*
Can't You See *that though I've cried,*
Now I've cried my last?
Can't You See?

You know I tried to love you,
But I can't go on.
The time has come for me to move along.
So I'll go and know that one day,
I'll find someone true,
And hope that someday, *you will too.*

LINER NOTES, LYRICS, AND RHYMES

ONE-TEN BLUES

INSTRUMENTAL INTRO VERSE

All the colors and all the lights,
All the girls and all the sights,
Can't spare you the lonely nights with the blues.
'Cause when your baby's up and gone,
And you must face the lonely dawn,
No one else knows what's goin' on except you.

You can go where the music's loud,
Walk under skies without a cloud,
And still be alone in a crowd with the blues.
For a love that lived in your soul,
A kind of blues like a deep dark hole,
And no one knows that you've lost control except you.

People as busy as bees in their hives,
Each tryin' to live each other's lives,
All seekin' solace in beat down dives with the blues, yeah.

One-Ten Blues! Oh, woman, about these blues . . .
I'm gonna tell you about this low-down misery,
Evil blues. Yeah. **One-Ten Blues!**

Adam doubled on lead guitar for this one.

STAY BY ME

Girl, I can't say he's no good.
All I want is for you to see,
He's been doin' all that he could,
To try to steal your love from me,

And I say girl, *I want you to think about it.*
Think about the things we had.
They weren't so bad, and if it makes you sad,
Darlin,' **Stay By Me! Stay By Me!**
Stay By Me! Stay By Me!

I love you still. That's no surprise.
And we both know we'll never forget
The love we shared. It's still in your eyes.
Don't make a choice that we'll both regret.

I say, girl, *I need you to think about it.*
Slow down and think it through.
It's all up to you. He don't love you like I do.
Darlin,' **Stay By Me! Stay By Me!**
Stay By Me!

Oh, Girl, *I need you to think about it.*
Slow down and think it through.
It's all up to you. He don't love you like I do.
Darlin,' **Stay By Me! Stay By Me!**
Stay By Me! Stay By Me!

Darlin,' **Stay By Me! Stay By Me!**
Stay By Me! Stay By Me!
Aoow, **Stay By Me!**

LINER NOTES, LYRICS, AND RHYMES
WHAT'S THE MATTER WITH YOUR MIND?

(Phone Rings Twice.)

    I try to call you for a date, but you're out late,
    And that ain't nothin' new.
    If I call you on the phone and you're not home,
    Don't think I'm gonna wait for you. Oh no!

    Aow, *Baby,* **What's the Matter with Your Mind?**
    If I decide to go out, you know *I'm sure to find*
    Someone else who knows *how to treat me right*
    I won't be stayin' home, alone, *another night.*

    You say you'll be around, but I have found
    I can't believe a word you say.
    You're so busy bein' cool, makin' guys drool,
    You get lost along the way. I say hey!

    Aow, *Baby,* **What's the Matter with Your Mind?**
To say your brain is badly wrinkled's just my way of *being kind.*
It's obvious you think you're something else and I should *wait on you.*
I got bad news for you, baby. I've done all the waitin' *that I'm gonna do!*

    INSTRUMENTAL BRIDGE

    You won't believe I'd talk this way, that I would say
    The things I've said to you.
    Well, I'm not so numb to not know where you're from
    Is where you're always goin' to. Oh, yeah!

    Baby, **What's the Matter with Your Mind?**
What's this all about? I'm gettin' out. *It's time we redefined,*
What I am to you and you to me and this *insane game we play.*
    Well, I'm done. It's no fun, and this is one time
    You won't have it your way.
And now, I'm hanging up, 'cause there ain't nothin' more for me to say.

TRAVIS EDWARD PIKE'S TEA PARTY SNACK PLATTER

IN YOUR EYES

I thought I knew my love, but you've changed.
Your kiss is cold, and your eyes.
I look at you my love. You're so strange.
You look so bold, and your eyes.

Your eyes tell me a story I didn't want to know.
Your eyes tell me a story – a story filled with woe, but not for you.

I know you've found somebody new.
Why didn't I know? I hadn't a clue.
You're breaking my heart,
Without a single tear.
It's all over now.
That much is clear.

INSTRUMENTAL BRIDGE

Your eyes tell me a story
I didn't want to know.
Your eyes tell me a story
A story filled with woe,
But not for you.
I know you've found somebody new.
Why can't I find a love that's true?
You're breaking my heart.
Without a single tear.
It's all over now.
You've made that clear.

No reason now to stay, my love.
I can see the look **In Your Eyes.**
I'm leaving now.
There's no need to shove.
I can read a book **In Your Eyes,**
In Your Eyes,
In Your Eyes.

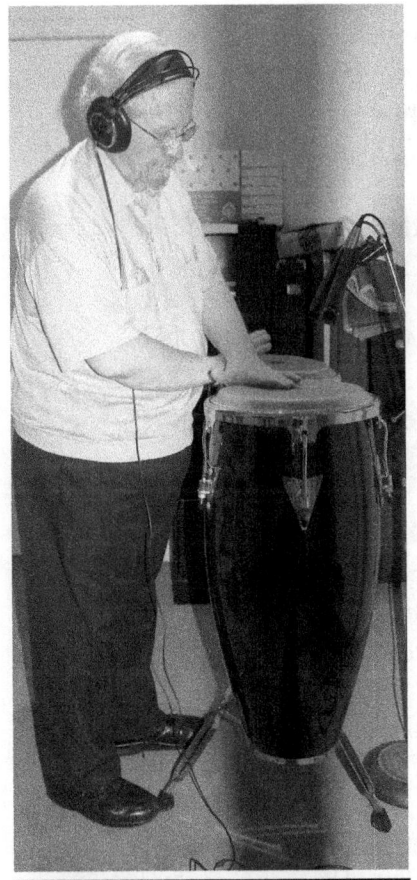

Travis played the congas.
Adam played everything else.

LINER NOTES, LYRICS, AND RHYMES

I'LL DO ANYTHING I CAN

I can't be all things to you. *No, I can't be.*
No matter how hard I try, *I'm still only me.*
You'll find there are many things that *I can never do,*
But you know that if I could I'd *do them all for you.*

Yes, **I'll Do Anthing I Can.**
Yes, **I'll Do Anthing I Can.** I'm your man!

If you need money, honey, *I'll get it for you.*
And if it's lovin' you need, well, *I can do that too.*
I'll work. I'll beg. I'll borrow – *anything for you.*
Just tell me what you want. *There is nothing I won't do!*

And **I'll Do Anthing I Can.**
Yes, **I'll Do Anthing I Can.** I'm your man!

INSTRUMENTAL BRIDGE

I'll Do Anthing I Can.
Yes, **I'll Do Anthing I Can.** I'm your man!

I can't be all things to you. *No, I can't be.*
No matter how hard I try, *I'm still only me.*
But if you're ever lonely, *need someone to rely on,*
I'll come a-runnin' if you *need a shoulder to cry on!*

'Cause **I'll Do Anthing I Can.**
Yes, **I'll Do Anthing I Can.** I'm your man!

I'll Do Anthing I Can.
Yes, **I'll Do Anthing I Can.** I'm your man!

YOU GOT WHAT I NEED

You Got What I Need.
I'll follow where you lead.
Oh, don't be a tease.
I'm begging baby, please.

Sighin' for your lovin' uh-huh!
Cryin' for your lovin'
Yeah!

You could do me right.
C'mon, make it tonight.
Oh, I need you. Can't you see?
I say girl, bring your love to me!

Cryin' for your lovin' uh-huh!
Dyin' for your lovin.' Yeah!

You, you turn me on with ease.
Then you turn me off and freeze.
I say girl, you know that I love you.
Tell me why *(Oh why?) (Oh why?)*
You do me like you do!

'Ayow Girl, you know **You Got What I Need.**
I'll fall down on my knees and plead for you, *(For you!) (For you!)*
If that's what I have to do. *(For you!) (For you!)*

Ayow! You come on strong, string me along,
I know you think you're, oh, so clever, *(so clever) (so clever)*
But this can't go on forever. *(and ever) (and ever)*
This can't go on forever! *(Never!) (No, never!)*
Nothing lasts forever!

LINER NOTES, LYRICS, AND RHYMES

OH MAMA

BAINBRIDGE FIRE CONTROL TECHNICIAN'S MARCH INTRO

Oh, Mama, Oh, Ma-ma. *Hey, Mama, look what you done.*
Oh, Mama, Oh, Ma-ma. *You took away the morning sun.*
Oh, Mama, Oh, Ma-ma. *Nowhere to hide. Nowhere to run.*
Oh, Mama, Oh, Ma-ma. *Hey, Mama, look what you done!*

We were just tryin' to tell it like it is and
We were just tryin' to roll a-way the stone.
We were just tryin' to clean the cobwebs off your mind.
Out of your mind!

Oh, Mama, Oh, Ma-ma. *Hey, Mama, look what you done.*
Oh, Mama, Oh, Ma-ma. *You took away the morning sun.*
Oh, Mama, Oh, Ma-ma. *Nowhere to hide. Nowhere to run.*
Oh, Mama, Oh, Ma-ma. *Hey, Mama, look what you done!*

INSTRUMENTAL BRIDGE

You wouldn't listen to what we had to say.
You were afraid that the truth would strike at home.
You thought the light of awareness would make you blind . . .
But you're so damned blind!

Oh, Mama, Oh, Ma-ma. *Hey, Mama, look what you done.*
Oh, Mama, Oh, Ma-ma. *You took away the morning sun.*
Oh, Mama, Oh, Ma-ma. *Nowhere to hide. Nowhere to run.*
Oh, Mama, Oh, Ma-ma. *Hey, Mama, look what you done!*

INSTRUMENTAL BRIDGE

Oh, Mama, Oh, Ma-ma. *Hey, Mama, look what you done.*
Oh, Mama, Oh, Ma-ma. *You took away the morning sun.*
Oh, Mama, Oh, Ma-ma. *Nowhere to hide. Nowhere to run.*
Oh, Mama, Oh, Ma-ma. *Hey, Mama, look what you done!*

BAINBRIDGE FIRE CONTROL TECHNICIAN'S MARCH CODA

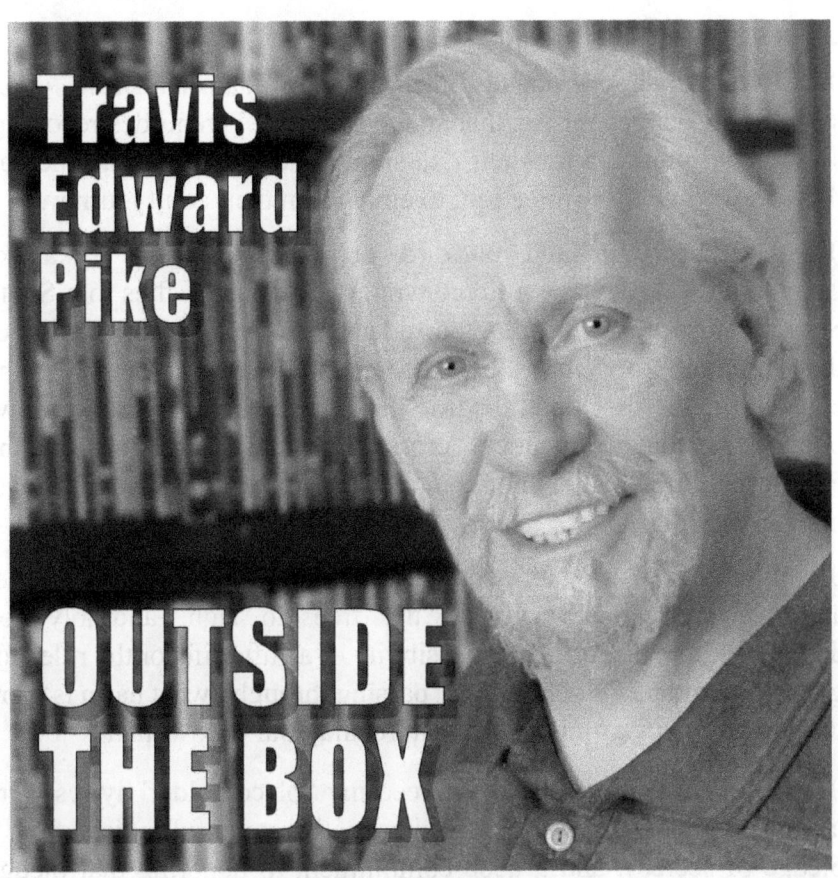

01	7:35	ANDALUSIAN BRIDE SUITE
02	3:02	PUKAPUKA GAGADOODY
03	2:52	FLYING SNAKES
04	2:59	ONLY YOU AND ME
05	3:04	OTHERWORLD MARCH
06	5:18	WITCH
07	2:53	PSYCHEDELIC MELTDOWN
08	2:47	GOTTA BE A BETTER WAY
09	3:20	FRIEND IN FRESNO
10	3:08	LOVELY GIRL I MARRIED
11	3:37	STAR MAKER

LINER NOTES, LYRICS, AND RHYMES

01. Originally a tone poem, I later turned "Andalusian Bride" into a song for my daughter, Lisa, then nine-years-old. Parents desire loving, secure environments for their daughters, but recognize that one day they must leave that protection, to embark on their adult journey.

02. The New England blizzard of 2015 inspired "Pukapuka Gagadoody." To escape a fierce winter, a Bostonian flies to a South Seas paradise. King Neptune considers the overflight an evasion of the "initiation" undergone by passengers and crews who cross the equator for the first time aboard ships. The "beach party" follows published accounts of nautical "crossing the line" ceremonies, and the Polynesian Pupu platters noted in the song make entirely appropriate hors d'oeuvres.

03. "Flying Snakes" addresses the divide between subjective belief and objective reality. Snakes do "fly," trees do "sigh," and holy men do lie. Without disputing the possibility of an afterlife, or the rules for gaining admittance, if one is just 'passing through,' what harm is there in living a life in harmony with nature and your fellow man?

04. We liked this melody, but agreed my "place holder" lyrics were lame. I composed new lyrics dealing with a youthful indiscretion, a pledge of secrecy, and a deep commitment to honoring that pledge and "Only You and Me" emerged. Songs about getting carried away by desire are nothing new, but I know of no other quite like this one.

05. I composed my "Otherworld March" in the early seventies, when I was still contemplating a return to live performances. I intended it for a grand entrance, a choreographed showpiece with dancers writhing and swirling across a fogbound stage from which I would emerge.

06. "Witch" was composed in 1973 for my rock musical, *Changeling*. I had researched the delusion of witchcraft and witch trials during the 30 Years War, when Biblical authority sanctified torture and witch-burnings. Tragically, the horrors of that Central European war between Catholics and Protestants (1618-1638), seems now to plague Shi'ite and Sunni Muslims as modern terrorists cite verses from the Koran to support their atrocities against "Westerners" . . . and each other.

07. The melody for "Psychedelic Meltdown" was the second movement of a tone poem based on Joan Miro's 1924 painting, *Harlequin's Carnival*. Now, its lyrics deal with the deadly folly of recreational drug use.

08. "Gotta Be a Better Way" warns against precipitous action based on claims and counter-claims by opposing parties. Allegations require investigation, and if proven, adjudication and remediation. Democracy requires an educated, accurately informed, and involved electorate.

09. "Friend in Fresno" describes a road trip leaving Burbank in the early morning, to have lunch with a friend in Fresno, then returning, a trip totalling 450 miles in one day, and ending in rush hour in L.A.

10. I wrote "Lovely Girl I Married" for my wife, Judy, as we approach our 50th Anniversary. It's a simple song about mature, enduring love, but no one seems to be writing such songs, so at 73, I decided I would.

11. Radio play was once the key to record sales, and DJ's chose what to play. Is there a modern paradigm? "Star Maker" is about trying to find a way for an old retread, like myself, to get some traction in a music industry fanatically youth-oriented, and driven by the internet.

For this album, Adam and I played most of the instruments, analog and sampled, heard on this recording, with Adam shouldering most of the load. I sang or spoke all the male vocal parts.

Additional musicians on this CD include my grandsons, Robert Gunner (French Horn), and Daniel Gunner (Trumpet), who both played parts in the "Andalusian Bride Suite," and my long-time friend, David Pinto, founder of the Academy of Music for the Blind, who played the harpsichord and pipe organ parts for "Witch."

Karen Callahan, Lauran Doverspike, and Colleen Stratton shared the vocal parts on "Witch" and "Psychedelic Meltdown." Lauran and Colleen also performed on "Flying Snakes" and Lauran provided the sole vocal support for "Friend in Fresno."

LINER NOTES, LYRICS, AND RHYMES

Deciphering "The Andalusian Bride Suite" was tough. Regardless of their point of entry, all the parts started on page one. Had the sections been lettered, it wouldn't have mattered so much that, in the half century since Travis composed it, *he forgot where they entered!*

OUTSIDE THE BOX

"Have you tried starting it here? See if that works . . ."

These two handsome lads are my grandsons; Robert Maxwell Gunner on French Horn, and Daniel Gregory Gunner on Trumpet. In December 2015, they were both in music programs at their Middle School. During Christmas Vacation, I invited them to play on my recording of "The Andalusian Bride Suite." They practiced their parts, then came in and laid down their tracks. This happy grandpa loved every minute of it, and could not be more proud of them.

LINER NOTES, LYRICS, AND RHYMES

ANDALUSIAN BRIDE SUITE

Prelude:

There has always been sunshine in your garden,
Your many friends to keep the clouds at bay,
And they all wish you well in your garden,
Watching over you to guide you when you stray.

Still, there's more to living.
More and more you feel lonely. You feel sad.
You, you feel the need to be giving,
And the wall around your garden drives you mad.

Safe in their love, their enchantments about you,
You set yourself free. Life can't go on without you.

There's a gate in the wall around your garden,
And beyond, a world of wonder, strange and wild,
For a goddess is ever a woman,
And the Fey have seen the woman in the child.

You slip out the gate, their enchantments about you,
Seeking your fate. Life can't go on without you.

Say goodbye to the unicorn, who stands alone, in the garden, crying!

Coda

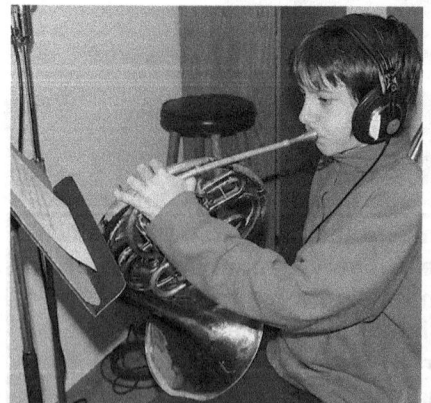

Their first recording session, and "Max" and "Dan" nailed their parts.

PUKAPUKA GAGADOODY

I flew out of icy Boston on a wicked winter's day,
Headin' for the South Pacific. I just had to get away.
Once there, aboard a war canoe, set out across the sea,
To where an island paradise had been reserved for me.
There was a party on the shore, as the sun sank in the west,
And a gal named Amphitrite said I was her special guest.
Davy Jones tended the fire. He was planning a surprise,
But I couldn' tell just what, 'cause the smoke got in my eyes.

Pukapuka. Gagadoody. Whadda-lodda-pupu!
Rarotonga. Kawabonga. Shabba-dabba-doo-doo!
Pukapuka. Gagadoody. Whadda-lodda-pupu!

Well, I started feelin' woozy, watchin' Amphitrite dance,
And I woke up soakin' in a tub in just my underpants.
Then out of all that smoke old King Neptune appeared,
A trident in one hand and snarlin' through his beard,
That he and he alone was master of the bounding main,
And me, a slimy polliwog, trespassed on his domain,
When I dared to cross his ocean in that native war canoe,
Without his leave, required for all passengers and crew!
(Chorus)
I told him, "Crossin' the equator in a plane is not a crime,"
But Neptune is the final judge in matters maritime.
Well, I wasn't boiled in oil. Neptune proved a decent sort.
He pardoned me when I signed on and joined his Royal Court, so . . .
(Chorus x2)

LINER NOTES, LYRICS, AND RHYMES

FLYING SNAKES

INTRO:

I've seen snakes fly, trees cry and holy men lie!

Your life may be a mystery. You just appeared miraculously,
Well, if you say so.
You live in your reality, but if it seems unreal to me,
Perhaps I'm just slow,

But *I've seen snakes fly, trees cry and holy men lie!*

*Your after-life is groovy. I've seen it in a movie. Yeah!
But it seems while you still live here,
You've something more to give here. Yeah!*

PSYCHEDELIC INSTRUMENTAL BRIDGE

Spoken:	You say that you're just passing through
Spoken:	And that may work just fine for you
Spoken:	But should that prove to be untrue
Spoken:	What harm would then come to you

If you spent a little time, helping us to hold the line, *before you go.*
I don't just ask for me and mine. You tell me that you're doing fine,
Well, *if you say so,*

But *I've seen snakes fly, trees cry and holy men lie!*

*I do believe you're clever, bound to live forever. Oh!
But I've got mortal things to do and I don't ask so much of you,
But one thing you should know*

I've seen snakes fly, trees cry and holy men lie!
Lie!
Lie!
Lie!

ONLY YOU AND ME

If you remember me, don't be shy. Come say hello.
If you don't, I'll know why, and no one else need ever know.
Only You and Me.
Only You and Me,
Will know we were lovers.

The moments we shared were never meant to be,
But those magic hours, still belong to you and to me.
Only You and Me.
Only You and Me,
Know we were lovers.

Though I can't forget, the sweet scent of your hair,
I'll never forget, what you once made me swear.

We'll part strangers now, and be strangers evermore,
And should we meet again, we'll never have ever met before.
Only You and Me.
Only You and Me.
Only You and Me,
Will know we were lovers.
Once we were lovers, we two.

I can fix it if you punch me in here.

LINER NOTES, LYRICS, AND RHYMES
OTHERWORLD MARCH

 The "Otherworld March," being entirely instrumental, never had lyrics, but it supported an ambitions program. I composed it when I was attempting to put together the group I called Majick. Whether live or filmed, it was meant to be the prelude to our curtain opener in concert venues. It would begin with the rumble of drums and colored fog spreading across the stage. Enter the dancers twirling and writhing through the fog, violently crashing into each other, sometimes to embrace, sometimes with murderous intent -- all the violent emergence of life on this world evolving as cultures clash, fight for survival, for dominance over each other, and for dominance over nature. Then failing and starting over, each time advancing an illusion of dominance, and each time reduced to ashes in a never-ending cycle of destruction and renewal until, in this age, the fog parts as Majick rises into view, revealing the sorcerer and sorcery behind the masks of god, the creator-illusionist, not a god, but a man reforming creation to suit his desires.

 Once on stage, my opening number was to be "The Fool" -- Truth, Reason, and Magic, all in one, not a god, but a man. My song "The Fool" is today more evolved than ever before, the revelation of the *Changling's Return*, is not that he changed from what he was into something else, but having sipped from the Cauldron of Inspiration, remembered his origins, and knew himself for the first time in his current incarnation. But that's another story. On this CD, I'm content to have the "Otherworld March" be the prelude to "Witch."

OUTSIDE THE BOX

WITCH

INQUISITOR (Spoken): *In pains and in anxieties dost thou bear children, woman, and toward thy husband is thine inclination, and he lords it over thee. And do you not know that you are an Eve? The sentence of God on this sex of yours lives in this age: the guilt must, of necessity, live too. You are the devil's gateway. You are the unsealer of that forbidden tree. You are the first deserter of the Divine Law. You are she who persuaded him whom the devil was not valiant enough to attack. You destroyed so easily, God's image – man. On account of your desert – that is –death, even the Son of God had to die.*

> They said she had beguiling lips, and shapely figure too.
> She had coal black hair and eyes of deepest blue.
> They said her wanton conduct would never ever do.
> They bound her down and stood around, and watched as the fire grew.

> She cried, "Dear neighbors, hear me! Somehow you've been deceived
> I've never done a wicked thing!" She nearly was believed,
> But all her guile was wasted, and so she swore they'd rue
> The day they burned her life away and cheered as the fire grew.

> A woman dare not be so fair and not be wicked too,
> Their law implied and justified they laughed as the fire grew.

INQUISITOR (Spoken): *We, the judges and jury of this Supreme High Court, have finally recognized it just that the accused, because of her evil doings, should be punished with fire from life to death, and we herewith anathemize, sentence, and condemn her thereto. May God have mercy on her soul.*

> The sun was swallowed by black clouds. The sea began to pound.
> The tempest tore the cliffs away. Her neighbors all were drowned,
> Save a black-haired, blue-eyed little girl, and therein lies the clue.
> Leave it be good brothers for you know not what you do.

(Continued on page following.)

LINER NOTES, LYRICS, AND RHYMES

WITCH (CONT'D)

The child she dare not be so fair and not be wicked too,
But before you strike the flames of hell, remember -- you'll burn too!

INQUISITOR (Spoken:) *The infection of witchcraft is often spread by a sort of contagion to children by their sinful parents when these try to find favor with their devils, for the greed of Satan was ever limitless and insatiable, thus, when once he has entered a family, he will never give up his foothold, except with the greatest difficulty. And it is one among many sure and certain indications against those accused of witchcraft, if one of their parents was found guilty of this crime. Wherefore we, having the fear of God before our eyes, have caused to be written this our definitive sentence and according to the lawful precepts of revered theologians and jurists, piously pronounce and formally sentence the accused to . . .*

    This session was actually the third time David Pinto recorded the harpsichord and organ parts of "Witch" for me. The first time was for *Changeling* in 1975, the second, for *Morningstone* in 1987, and this time, in 2016, for *Outside the Box*. Our rhythm tracks made the song easy for him to follow, but he asked me to play the passacaglia for him, so I did. And then he showed me how it should be played . . .

OUTSIDE THE BOX
PSYCHEDELIC MELTDOWN

Phantoms passing through your mind, visions in your brain,
Create a world of fantasy where everybody's sane.

Took the handout, glanced inside it. Had to find a place to hide it,
Where no one would ever have a clue.
Called the number just to try it, didn't really plan to buy it.
Said I should come by, since I was new.

Star-illuminated ceilings, darkened rooms for darker dealings,
And our special blend of herbal tea
Exotic joys and psychic healings, freedom to explore one's feelings,
Everything provided for a fee.

INSTRUMENTAL RELEASE

Try our capsules, juices, tablets, and psychedelic creams.
Expand your mind and you'll soon find your life becomes your dreams.

Bought a cream so I could try it, somewhere secret, somewhere quiet,
Somewhere where no one would ever know.
On a roof, above the city, where the lights shine bright and pretty,
Overhead the sky begins to glow.

INSTRUMENTAL RELEASE

This cream makes me feel fantastic, light and downright protoplastic,
Like I could rise up and touch the stars.
This is way beyond all praising. It's a feeling quite amazing,
Reaching down from here to touch the cars.

THUD, SHATTERED GLASS, CAR ALARM.

LINER NOTES, LYRICS, AND RHYMES
GOTTA BE A BETTER WAY

I used to worry 'bout pollution --
Meltdowns and toxic spills,
Until they told me it was under control,
And sold me some kind of pills,
That made it seem that everything was fine,
Until they closed the mills,
And now I'm lucky to be working at all,
But I'm behind on my bills.

Gotta Be a Better Way. *There's* **Gotta Be a Better Way**

They got me runnin' like a rat in a wheel, loaded up on caffeine,
Working harder than ever before, long hours just routine.
I keep an eye out for something else -- for something in-between.
Don't want to get blindsided again, by something unforeseen.

Gotta Be a Better Way. *There's* **Gotta Be a Better Way**

You say the time has come for movin' on. Whoa! I say take it slow.
The constitution gives us legal means to change the status quo.
In deep and unfamiliar waters, beware of dangers below.
That golden shore may look real fine from here,
But there may be an undertow.

Sometimes you think you know what's goin' on.
Sometimes you haven't a clue.
Sometimes you can't believe a word you hear.
Sometimes you know it's true.
Sometimes it's nothing but the same old thing,
Dressed-up like something new.
Sometimes I wonder if I'm losin' my mind.
Sometimes I wonder 'bout you!

Gotta Be a Better Way. *There's* **Gotta Be a Better Way.**

FRIEND IN FRESNO

Fuel injection, tuned to perfection,
I love my new classic wheels.
If I have my way, we'll hit the highway,
To get a sense of how it feels.
But where to go? I think I know.
What say we go see Shay!
A destination, by my estimation,
About four hours away! *(Hey!)*

We've got a **Friend in Fresno.**
Do we have her new address? No.
We'll call her up when we arrive.
Anticipation growing,
Now we know we'll be going,
Northbound on Interstate Five.

Gas up in Burbank. Gotta have a full tank.
Don't want to run out on the way.
The traffic's light. Skies are getting bright.
Whew! Looks like a beautiful day.
We're startin' to climb, making good time,
Up and over the grapevine.
Once down below, don't have far to go,
Till we turn off on 99.

We've got a **Friend in Fresno.**
Lunch won't be fancy dress, no.
Burgers, chicken or fried rice.
Or maybe Quesadilla,
With a glass of Manzanilla,
Or maybe pizza by the slice. *(That's nice!)*

(Lyrics continue on page following.)

LINER NOTES, LYRICS, AND RHYMES

FRIEND IN FRESNO (CONT'D)

Shay is sure to say whatever's on her mind.
On that we may depend.
She's elemental, but highly refined.
We couldn't have a better friend.

Meet her by the Tower. Only have an hour.
Not much time for exploring.
We drive through town with the top down,
You know we're all-out touring.
Shay loves the car, but we can't go far.
There's so little time to visit.
We have to go so we take a photo,
But that's not the same thing, is it?

We've got a **Friend in Fresno.**
Did we miss her? Yes, I guess so.
And it's been a lovely day.
But now we're feeling glum,
Because the time has come,
We have to say goodbye to Shay.

In Bakersfield I stop off,
Check the oil and then top off,
For the trip back to L.A.
This one goes in the files,
Four hundred and fifty miles,
Fresno and back in the same day. (Oh yeah!)
Back in time for rush hour in L.A!

(Was that the plan?)

OUTSIDE THE BOX

LOVELY GIRL I MARRIED

I remember the first day that we met,
That first day when your smile blew me away.
Look at you now. Your smile is still the same,
Even though your hair has turned to gray.

You're still here -- still the girl I carried
Across my threshold long ago,
The **Lovely Girl I Married.**

Now we're getting on,
Seems we're slowing down
As time flies ever faster than before.
You by my side, your hand in mine,
We're together,
And I don't ask for any more,

As long as you're here!
The same girl I carried
Across my threshold long ago,
The **Lovely Girl I Married.**

You're still here!
Still the girl I carried
Across my threshold so long ago
The Lovely Girl I Married.
The Lovely Girl I Married.

The photo that proves the tale. You can barely see Adam's head at Judy's right elbow, as she cuts our "wedding cake," but that's Adam, singing "Happy Birthday" to her.

LINER NOTES, LYRICS, AND RHYMES

STAR MAKER

Hey *(hey, Mr. DeeJay)*, play my song for me.
Hey *(hey, Mr. DeeJay)*, please, play my song for me.
We'll give you an interview. Anything you want us to.
Anything that we can do, you see, you're the . . .

Star Maker, *star breaker.* What will it take to make a break for me?
Star Maker, *star breaker.* You've got the power to let it be.

Hey *(hey, Mr. DeeJay)*, c'mon, play my song for me.
Hey *(hey, Mr. DeeJay)*, won't you play my song for me?
Before you do your next live show, put us on the radio.
We'll come out and do your show for free!

INSTRUMENTAL RELEASE:

Star Maker, *star breaker.* You say there's nothing that you can do.
Star Maker, *star breaker.* Who holds the power, if it's not you?

Hey *(hey, Mr. DeeJay).* Who picks the songs you play?
Hey *(hey, Mr. DeeJay).* Don't you *even* have a say?
Tell us, is it really true, someone hands a list to you?
If that's true, please tell us who today, is the . . .

Star Maker, *star breaker.* Who should we talk to? Who should we see?
Star Maker, *star breaker.* Who's got the power? Who holds the key?

Star Maker, *star breaker.* If there's really nothing that you can do,
Star Maker, *star breaker.* Who holds the power, if it's not you?

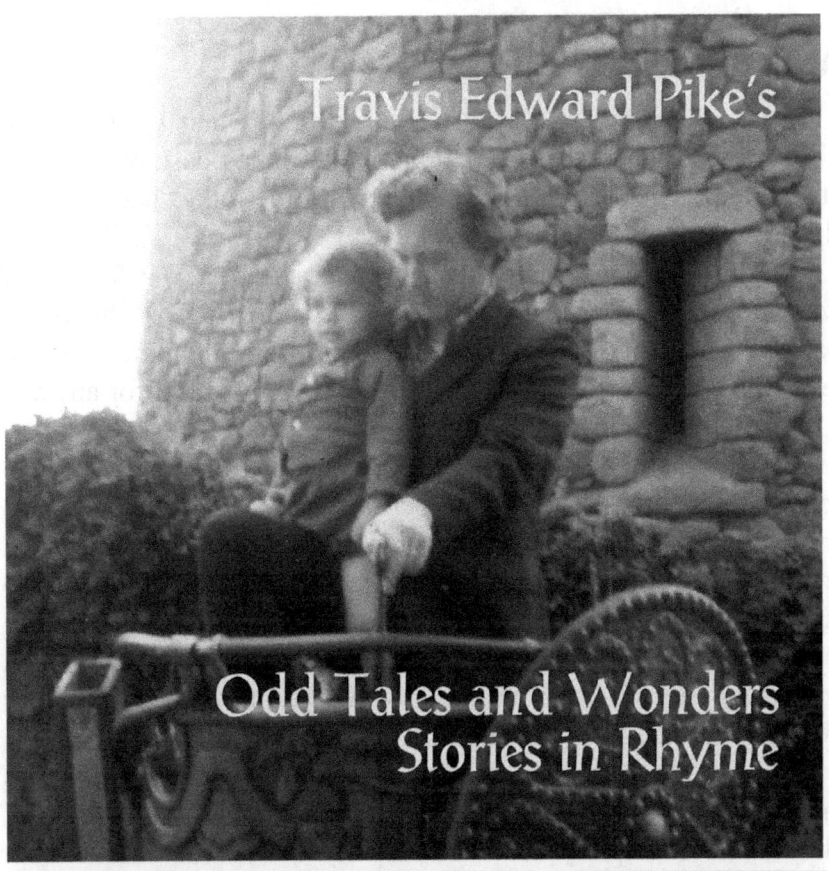

Travis Edward Pike's
Odd Tales and Wonders
Stories in Rhyme

In this section we depart from our CD Liner Notes format to discuss each Story in Rhyme as it appears on the disc.

01	9:03	SANTA'S MAGIC	316
02	3:50	A TWAIL'S TALE	324
03	5:37	THE ODDWOK AND THE MARBUCK	329
04	3:37	THE GLOMLOP AND THE QUARK	334
05	2:29	KRIMMS	338
06	2:44	THE LORI	341
07	2:45	THE PEERLESS GOTH	345
08	4:23	THE TWADDLE AND THE GURCK	348

An interpretation of The Twaddle and the Gurck — 353

ODD TALES AND WONDERS: STORIES IN RHYME
SANTA'S MAGIC

I wrote *Santa's Magic* in 1968, for our first Christmas in California. With our extended families on the East Coast, we pioneers felt isolated. This rhyme that I shared with the folks "back home," helped us bridge the gap.

Santa's Magic was published under the title *The Wonderful Magic of Santa Claus* in the Fall, 1973 edition of *OPUS* by the Media Board of California State Polytechnic University, Pomona under a special caveat, which allowed me to retain my copyright for any and all future publications.

When telling a story, the storyteller's voice, gestures and expressions are only part of the performance. The audience also contributes, whether horrified and trembling in terror, inspired and bursting with pride, sympathetically reduced to tears or compelled to laughter, cheers and shouts. A recording of a story should fully engage the imagination of its listeners, but distractions -- a phone ringing, a barking dog, even a well-meaning host interrupting to offer food or drink may pull the listener out of the story and the spell be lost.

Since I will not be present when the recording of Santa's Magic is played, I relied on audio devices dating back to the days of radio drama to keep my audience properly enthralled. In the audio realm, nothing says Christmas Eve quite as decisively as sleigh bells. I added them to the trusty tone-poem I composed, a sonic appreciation of Joan Miro's 1924 painting, *Harlequin's Carnival,* which I came to appreciate in a 20th Century Art course at CalPoly. I think it conveys both the spooky, magical mood of Santa's nocturnal visit, and provides a calliope of celebration and joy for Christmas morning.

Thinking back to my childhood, I recalled the enchanting Department Store Christmas window displays in downtown Boston and remembered that nothing kept our cold little noses glued to that store window more than watching the dizzying collection of toy trains. For me, nothing says Christmas morning quite like the sound of a toy train whistle as its locomotive drags its cars around the track -- and another dollop of "Harlequin's Carnival" just added to my sonic delight.

SANTA'S MAGIC

On Christmas Eve, gathered
In nearby Hancock Park,
Three children from New England,
Bright eyes gleaming in the dark.

"Does it seem like Christmas Eve to you?"
Whispered the eldest child.
"There's still no snow and the forecast
For tomorrow is 'fair and mild.'"

The second eldest answered,
"Well, we've got our Christmas tree,
With lights and balls and tinsel.
Now, that's real Christmasy."

"We got a lot of Christmas cards,"
Admitted the eldest child.
"And Grandma sent us Christmas cookies,"
Said the second boy, and smiled.

"And our socks! Don't forget our socks!
We finally got them hung . . ."
"Shhh! Not so loud or we'll get caught."
"And the Christmas carols we've sung,

And Dad brought home the turkey,
And Mom's been cooking and cooking!"
"Let's get to bed." "I can't go to sleep!"
"He won't come, if anyone's looking."

"If you wake up first, you wake me up!"
Said the second and jumped into bed.
"Whoever wakes up gets everybody up!"
(That's what the eldest said.)

ODD TALES AND WONDERS: STORIES IN RHYME

"You, too!" said the second to the youngest,
Just to be sure that he'd heard,
For all the time his brothers had talked,
The youngest had said not a word.

The youngest boy climbed into bed
And thoughtfully rubbed his nose,
And pulled on his ears, and hugged his knees
And artfully wriggled his toes.

Then he asked, in a voice that quavered,
Filled with doubt and woe,
"How can Santa land his sleigh
On a roof that has no snow?"

At first, both his brothers were dumbstruck,
But then, the eldest child,
Who, eight years old, knew everything,
Sat up in bed and smiled.

"Don't be ridiculous!" said he, with a grin,
"What a silly thing to say.
In Southern California,
Santa won't come in a sleigh."

"He won't come in a sleigh," the second agreed.
Said the first, with considerable poise,
"He'll prob'ly come in a big rig."
"Yeah! Filled top to bottom with toys!"

"Out here, Santa comes in a big rig.
'Member we went to the store
And Santa asked us what we wanted?
'Member the whiskers he wore?

SANTA'S MAGIC

If you were worried, you should've asked him.
He would have told you how."
Said the eldest child. "Now, go to sleep.
He's on his way right now!"

"How's he drive a big rig up on the roof?"
The little one wanted to know.
"He won't drive it up," the eldest boy said.
"The reindeers will give it a tow!"

"That's it, boys! Now, no more noise!"
Said their Dad, who'd appeared at the door.
"Get to sleep, if you want Santa to come.
Now, I don't want to hear any more!"

The children slammed their eyes shut,
'Til their father walked off down the hall,
But then, when they were quite sure he'd gone
And wouldn't hear through the wall,

The second boy said, "See what you did?"
"Be quiet! It's all right.
Just go to sleep!" said the eldest.
And the youngest said, "Good night!"

Despite the excitement, the older boys
Were asleep in less than a wink.
But the youngest boy couldn't sleep at all.
All he did was just lay and think.

"Santa Claus doesn't drive a truck.
He just only has a sleigh.
And back home, there's always plenty of snow,
'Specially on Christmas Day.

And even if it melts by morning,
It always falls during the night.
And Santa can land on the least little snow —
Even if it snows real light."

Oh, how he fretted and tossed and turned,
For he just could not understand
How, lacking snow on the rooftop,
Santa's sleigh could land!

Of course, he believed that Santa would come,
After all, they'd been good little boys
And mostly didn't fight or cry,
And mostly shared their toys.

So, he felt quite certain that Santa would come,
But he just had to know
How Santa Claus could land his sleigh
On a roof that had no snow.

So, quietly, he crept out of bed
And went down to the Christmas tree.
Then he crept behind the draperies,
Where he could wait and see.

"Quick! Quick, wake up! He didn't call us!
He's already up and gone!"
"What time is it?" "It's five past six!
Get up quick! C'mon!"

Both older boys donned slippers and robes.
Then, the eldest one thoughtfully said,
"We'd better wake up Mom and Dad.
They're prob'ly still in bed."

SANTA'S MAGIC

"Mom? Mom? Wake up! Wake up, Dad!
It's already Christmas day!"
"Oh, what are you two doing up?"
"Go back to bed! Go play!"

"But it's already Christmas morning!"
"Where's . . ." "He's already gone to the tree!"
"I wonder if Santa found our new house?"
"I hope so!" "C'mon! Let's go see."

Together, they went to the parlor,
Where, to both boys' enormous glee,
They found the youngest boy asleep,
Curled up 'neath the Christmas tree.

"Now, there's a sight!" said their father.
Said their mother, "He looks so sweet.
Oh, quick, take a picture before he wakes up."
But the child woke and sprang to his feet.

"Mommy! I saw Santa!" he yelled.
"He does it with magic, you know!"
"What do you mean?" his mother asked.
"I mean about the snow!"

"Snow?" asked his Dad, "in Los Angeles?
It couldn't have snowed last night."
"But, Dad, Santa Claus has magic.
I know it with all my might!"

"With all your might?" his father laughed.
"That's quite a lot, I guess!"
"Did you really see Santa?" the second boy sneered
And the youngest answered, "Yes!

ODD TALES AND WONDERS: STORIES IN RHYME

And he doesn't drive a big rig,
And he does just have eight reindeers,
And he only just has a great, big sleigh."
And his eyes brimmed bright with tears.

"So, how did he land his 'great, big sleigh'
Without any snow on the roof?"
Asked the eldest boy and the middle boy said,
"Yeah, we're waiting to see some proof!"

"It's secret magic," the youngest boy said.
"I'm not allowed to say."
"Oh, right!" said the first. Said the second,
You never saw Santa. No way!"

"Perhaps you were dreaming," his mother said.
"Yeah. You made it all up in your sleep!"
Said the middle boy and the eldest boy grinned
And the youngest boy started to weep.

"Now, look, boys," said their father,
"After all, you were both still in bed,
As you should have been —" "I got my bike!"
Well, that's what the youngest boy said.

And from that moment on, the discoveries
Of who got what and from whom
And whose toys were best and all of the rest
Of Christmas day filled the room.

For Santa Claus had come, indeed,
And there seemed no end to their toys
And their stockings were filled to the tippity tops,
For they really had been good boys.

But how Santa landed on a roof,
Without snow, in a sleigh,
Only the littlest boy ever knew
And he would never say.

ODD TALES AND WONDERS: STORIES IN RHYME
A TWAIL'S TALE

    This little rhyme is the main reason for the disclaimer on this CD. It's not as grim as some of Grimm's fairy tales, but it can be quite frightening to younger listeners. In fact, some years ago, one little boy's mother complained that this story gave him nightmares and kept both of them up all night long. Since then, my performances for audiences in middle school and up have become more dramatic and with the addition of sound effects, more frightening than ever before. So, especially for storytellers and parents who read aloud to their children, I composed an alternate ending for younger children.

    A Twail's Tale is a fable by definition. The animals speak and behave like human beings. The villain of the piece is the Avaritch. Its only vocalization is its shrill, horrific cry. It is an entirely fabulous, gigantic bird of prey, possibly related to the Roc, a mythical creature known from medieval Asian literature. I tried to play the Purple Stang the way I imagined the marvelous old character actor, C. Aubrey Smith might have done, complete with rattling teacup. The heroic Twail is a simple everyman who stumbles upon an unfolding drama and suffers its terrible consequences.

    I much prefer this story's original ending, especially when you consider the popularity of the children's song "Great Green Gobs of Greasy, Grimy Gopher Guts," but I've included an alternate ending, coming tight after the original that may be more appropriate for a very sensitive younger child.

A TWAIL'S TALE

Now, every Kindrell knows this tale,
Yet again, must it be told —
The tale of the Stang and the Oprus
And the Twail, courageous and bold.

The Stang and the Oprus sat at tea
And what a strange pair they made —
The Golden Oprus and Purple Stang,
In a downy forest glade.

Their conversation had turned to wax
And melted into the sand,
And soon they'd dozed contentedly,
For the afternoon was grand,

But when the chill of evening struck,
The Stang awoke to find
The Golden Oprus had gone and left
Her beautiful tea set behind.

"Without so much as a 'by your leave,'"
Muttered the Stang, and the Twail,
In that instant, came into view
At the bend in the forest trail.

"Without so much as a 'by your leave,'"
Repeated the Stang aloud.
"Beg your pardon," muttered the Twail.
"I'm the Twail," he said, and bowed.

"She's left her tea set, one shoe and her hat.
Now, don't you find that odd?"
Asked the Stang, and the Twail, amazed,
Could only blink and nod.

ODD TALES AND WONDERS: STORIES IN RHYME

"The day seemed ordinary enough.
We'd both come here for tea . . ."
"Both?" puzzled the Twail as he looked around.
"Yes. The Golden Oprus and me.

Oh, by the by, I'm the Purple Stang
And my friend has just disappeared,
Without hat or shoe or tea set!"
And at these three items, they peered.

"Alas!" cried the Twail, "We must flee at once!"
"Flee?" cried the Stang, "But why?"
"These signs in the grass! We must hide, alas,
Or we, too, will surely die!"

"Oh, dear, oh, dear!" fretted the Stang,
"Do you mean there's been foul play?"
"There's simply no time to explain, just now,
But here, we dare not stay!

You'll be safe in yon heather, Stang,
But for me," said the Twail, "'Tis folly.
Still, there's a chance I might be saved
If I can reach yon holly!"

"But it's so far away!" squawked the Purple Stang,
"Isn't there somewhere near?"
"Oh, do come along!" cried the courageous Twail,
"One thing's certain. We dare not stay here!"

And dragging the Stang, the Twail dashed away
To the heather, thick and low,
But it lost precious time on account of the Stang
Being frightened and clumsy and slow.

A Twail's Tale (the original tragic (scary) ending)

With the Stang tucked away in the heather,
The Twail turned tail to run,
But in that instant, the Avaritch rose,
Blotting the setting sun.

The Twail was as fast as a Twail could be,
But the Avaritch faster still.
The Twail hadn't reached the holly bush
When the Avaritch dove for the kill,

And clasping the Twail in its terrible talons,
Rose with a horrible cry,
As, circling, ever higher, it flew
Into the darkening sky.

And yet, the dying Twail called back
To the Stang, horrified below,
"Remember the Golden Oprus and me
And tell everyone you know . . .

Behold the awesome Avaritch.
Behold and then beware,
The Avaritch with eyes of doom
Whose shadow casts despair."

ODD TALES AND WONDERS: STORIES IN RHYME

A Twail's Tale (the less tragic alternate ending)

The Stang cried out in horror!
The Twail turned, the better to see,
But that twist caught the Avaritch by surprise
And the Twail, of a sudden, broke free!

The Avaritch screamed as it wheeled in mid-air
And flew after its plummeting prize
But the Twail dove right into the holly bush
A maneuver both daring and wise,

For the Avaritch, dreading the holly's thorns,
Turned and flew off with a shriek!
As the Twail settled down to catch its breath
Feeling dizzy and giddy and weak,

The Stang called out, "I say there, Twail,
Are you hurt?" And the Twail answered, "No.
But do, you, keep one eye on that darkening sky,
And learn well, lest you come to woe!

Behold the awesome Avaritch.
Behold and then beware,
The Avaritch with eyes of doom
Whose shadow casts despair."

THE ODDWOK AND THE MARBUCK

In this fable, the creatures are relatively well-defined. I imagine the Marbuck to be a near relative of the American Pronghorn. As for the Oddwok, it might be a muskrat, although there are any number of candidates. Many, otherwise not particularly smelly animals, smell bad when their fur is wet. We know this is a fable because the animals talk. Most of our sound effects are readily recognizable, but unless you grew up around raccoons, the strange snorting noises the Oddwok makes, though present in nature, may be totally unfamiliar.

A Spanish proverb claims that "What belongs to everybody belongs to nobody." Lands set aside for public use are frequently trashed by that same public, and people who jealously maintain their private property, may think nothing of littering, defacing or wrecking public property. Tax money is required to hire crews to clean up trash and repair vandalized restrooms, windows, doors and park benches.

I hope listeners consider the attitudes of both characters. Youngsters tend to be sympathetic to the Oddwok. To them, it seems more disabled than nasty. Some even defend its repulsive and destructive behavior as justified by the Marbuck's atitude.

At the risk of being tossed out of the egalitarian salad, I relish the language in the outraged Marbuck's tirade. Yes, it's abusive and intimidating, but don't we all resent it when our day at the beach or picnic in the park has been disturbed by noisy or unruly interlopers. The Marbuck never suggests that another, clean, well-behaved creature (a lovely Mardoe, perhaps), would not be welcome to share its retreat, but many seem to think the Marbuck's behavior stems from a selfish desire to keep the Quockomo pool to itself and fail to consider that it might be moved by an unselfish desire to preserve the beauty and tranquility of its environment.

Does the Marbuck represent Order? Does the Oddwok represent Chaos? *The Oddwok and the Marbuck* is no picnic, but it provides wonderful food-for-thought and conversations with youngsters, many of whom fear going to public parks and playgrounds. Try steering the conversation one way or another. You may find their reactions surprising and enlightening. I always do.

ODD TALES AND WONDERS: STORIES IN RHYME

THE ODDWOK AND THE MARBUCK

As elegant a Marbuck came
As ever sought to cool
Itself 'neath the shade of a Quockomo tree
And drink from a Quockomo pool.

It thought it might well rest itself,
And where's a better place?
So, it sat by the edge of the Quockomo pool
And studied its handsome face.

Such beautiful eyes. What a regal nose.
Such nobleness of chin!
But, as if to deliberately spoil its repose,
An Oddwok blundered in!

It splashed with its paws and squealed out loud
And made ripples that spoiled the mood,
Of the Marbuck, that cried, "Oh, this is outrageous!
How thoughtless! How selfish! How rude!"

"What's that you say? I don't hear too well.
Were you addressing me?"
Asked the nearsighted, odd little Oddwok
As it blinked and tried to see.

"By what right do you come sully my pool?"
The haughty Marbuck replied.
"Oh, there you are!" the Oddwok grinned,
And swam to the Marbuck's side!

"No! No! Go back! You'll muddy it up!"
Cried the Marbuck in despair.
"Now see what you've done, you nasty beast.
It simply isn't fair!"

THE ODDWOK AND THE MARBUCK

"Brrr! Just let me shake myself.
Everyone seems so busy, these days.
It's seldom one gets a chance to chat,"
Said the Oddwok, with vacuous gaze,

Directed, by chance, at the left forefoot
Of its reluctant host.
"Is that awful smell you?" gasped the Marbuck.
"I'm better informed than most,"

Continued the odd little Oddwok.
"Now, what shall the discourse be . . .
The beauty of a summer's day
Or, perhaps, philosophy?

To me, one's as good as another.
Tell me, have we met before?"
"Most decidedly not!" snapped the Marbuck,
Indignant to its core.

"Oh, my goodness! You're way up there!
You must think I'm out of my mind,"
Snickered the near-sighted Oddwok,
(It was very nearly blind.)

"I'm afraid my eyesight is rather poor.
Would you bend down closer to me?
I didn't realize you were quite so large,
But if you bend close, I can see,"

Continued the odd, little Oddwok,
But the Marbuck just could not bear
To bring its nose any closer
To the Oddwok, squatting there.

ODD TALES AND WONDERS: STORIES IN RHYME

"What makes you think," the Marbuck cried,
"That I'd want to talk to you?
You're loathsome, small, ugly and smelly
And noisy . . . and boring, too!

You're the most despicable creature
I've ever set eyes upon
And my day will surely stay ruined
Even long after you've gone!

You've come and muddied up the pool
And now, the whole place smells like you!
Look, even the Quockomo's wilted!
Oh, this will never do!

You're such a detestable creature
That the longer that you remain,
The worse you befoul this once pleasant place!"
Raged the Marbuck, so graceful and vain.

Then the Oddwok replied in a tone that was snide,
"Oh my! Aren't you lah-dee-dah?
Begging your pardon, might I inquire,
Just who do you think you are?

I'll stay here and bathe as long as I please.
This whole region is public domain.
If you don't like the mud, or the noise, or the smell,
I suggest that you not remain!"

"I certainly shan't!" the Marbuck fumed
And rose to be on its way,
But the Oddwok turned sly. With a glint in its eye,
It said, "No. Perhaps you should stay.

THE ODDWOK AND THE MARBUCK

You were here first and fair is fair.
Let's face it. You go with the place.
I've never before seen a creature like you —
So refined and so full of grace."

"Well, you see what you've done," the Marbuck whined.
"It's a shame!" the Oddwok agreed.
"You might have stayed on the other side,"
Said the Marbuck. Said the Oddwok, "Indeed!

Just look at me and then look at all this.
No, it holds no attraction for me.
You can keep your stinking, muddy old pool
And your wilted Quockomo tree!"

And snickering again, the Oddwok dove in
And swam back to the other side,
Which act, spiteful and small, and not nice at all,
Makes it awfully hard to decide

Just which creature was right. If the Oddwok,
That's the end of the Quockomo tree,
And the lovely, crystal clear Quockomo pool
And whatever serenity

That little world offered. The Marbuck,
To be sure, would keep it pristine,
But exclusive and private -- all to itself --
Though well-maintained, quiet and clean,

But I wonder, if you or I, one day,
Wished to rest 'neath the Quockomo tree,
And drink from the beautiful Quockomo pool,
Would the Marbuck allow you or me?

ODD TALES AND WONDERS: STORIES IN RHYME

THE GLOMLOP AND THE QUARK

The Glomlop and the Quark was always meant to start a dialogue. Cogs in the wheels of evolution, the characters shall prosper or perish according to their abilities to adapt.

Topics of discussion might deal with the consequences of greed and ambition, illustrated by the Quark's attempt to have the Glomlop for breakfast, although the creature would seem to be large enough to feed several Quarks, and it might be that the Glomlop might have plans of its own. Or maybe a discussion could arise about the dangers inherent in exploring the unknown, illustrated by the Glomlop's visit ashore, where a hungry Quark awaited him. In the chain of evolution, where does the Quark fit in? If the theory of evolution is valid, its ancestors came ashore much earlier. What might have awaited them, before they learned to fly?

Be prepared. Centuries ago, Tertullian (c. 160 - c. 225 AD), claimed religious faith was incompatible with reason. Reason and observation are at the root of evolutionary theory. This tale has provoked heated arguments between people who fervently believe in Intelligent Design (that a Creator God made the universe, the Earth and all that is in it), and others who, as fervently, espouse evolution. The viewpoints are considered irreconcilable, and the storyteller is not present, so it will be up to the host to steer the conversation toward a less confrontational discussion.

I don't know why the two viewpoints are so far apart. Could not evolution exist by the Will of God? I find most youngsters are fascinated by this sort of thing and not at all shy about vocalizing their opinions. And their alternatives show, conclusively, that imagination is a wonderful thing, and one can certainly imagine a whole lot more than one can prove, and that faith requires no proof. Belief in the imaginative revelation of the mystery is suffficient. And that may be said of both sides of the controversy.

THE GLOMLOP AND THE QUARK

A Glomlop left its murky lair
And slithered toward the shore,
Which, over and above unusual,
Had never been done, before.

The nearer to land the Glomlop came,
The stronger the ocean's call.
Rolled and tumbled in the surf,
It barely got there at all,

But it clung to a rock in the pounding waves,
As slowly the sea withdrew,
Until it emerged, triumphant,
In a world completely new.

For the first time in the Glomlop's life,
It felt the wind's soft kiss.
It couldn't return to the cold, dank deep
Without knowing more of this.

Slowly, its new world brightened
And though the light hurt its eyes,
It gazed for the first time upon the sun
And basked in its warm surprise.

A Quark awoke to the first glow of dawn
And leaving its sheltering nest,
Hopped to the edge of the sea ravaged cliff
Where, joining all the rest,

It gazed at the bountiful feast below
Stretched out on the gleaming sand
By the generous morning tide,
As wide as the eye could command.

ODD TALES AND WONDERS: STORIES IN RHYME

It huddled in its feathers
As slowly the morning sun
Drove the cold, dank night away
And, as this task was done,

The Quark surveyed the morning's fare
And, with lust-shrouded eyes,
Selected those tidbits and morsels
Of the most generous size.

The Glomlop, blinded by the sun,
Found the heat too great to bear,
And slowly turned to go back to the sea
And the cool of its murky lair.

But, suddenly, sharp talons seized its flesh!
'Twas the Quark, in pursuit of a feast.
It had pounced on the unwary Glomlop,
But the powerful, deep sea beast,

In turn, fastened on the Quark with such force
That it barely had strength to draw breath,
And locked in the Glomlop's awful embrace,
The Quark learned the cold fear of death!

As the day wore on, the Glomlop,
Blinded by the brilliant sun,
Growing stiffer and drier, exposed on the rock,
Feared that its life was done.

Its adventure had brought it such torment,
Such horror and terror and woe,
It might have surrendered itself to the Quark,
Had it not grown too stiff to let go.

THE GLOMLOP AND THE QUARK

And unable to break the Glomlop's grasp,
The Quark watched the bountiful sea
Begin, again, its relentless assault
And struggled the more to break free.

It seemed, with the spray of each incoming wave,
That the fate of the Quark had been sealed,
But in fact, as the Glomlop grew moist again,
Its fierce grip began to yield.

At last, the wretched Quark wrenched free.
It fluttered away, 'cross the shore
And achingly scaled the sea ravaged cliff
To be cautious, ever more.

And the tide roused the land-weary Glomlop.
And it slithered back into the sea,
And while things were never quite ever the same,
They were as they ought to be.

Adam selects and places FX tracks prior to mix.

ODD TALES AND WONDERS: STORIES IN RHYME

KRIMMS

Krimms have little to say, although they babble incessantly. Should one stop for breath, you realize their prattle was an effort to appear to be communicating, without actually communicating anything at all. With nothing but noise to contribute, were it not for politics, I suspect they would have succumbed to natural selection long ago.

So Krimms giggle, wail, moan, whimper, gobble up the pies and pastries they send flying across the room, and that seems to be all they do. The deep-pitched Gart and noisy Shrill are equally unintelligible. I know. I created their "voices" in the recording booth.

Using separate tracks for each, the noises they make suggest "conversations," actions, and reactions of all the characters, but until they are placed in a meaningful context it remains nothing but noises.

To orchestrate it into a series of recognizable events, Adam and I started by placing crashes of breaking glass and a number of wet, sloppy "splats" strategically throughout the tale, then placed all the creature reaction sounds in relation to those audible cues. In a noisy restaurant, when a waiter drops a tray, the room goes silent until the source of the noise is identified, and then the room noise returns to its previous level. Everything else you need to know about Krimms, you will learn from their foolish, beleaguered host.

Krimms was especially popular at a birthday party for an 11-year-old, who thought it would make a fascinating and funny, randomized digital food-fight game. He was probably right, but unlike the host in this silly tale, no responsible adult would ever let it, or a Krimm in the door.

KRIMMS

Krimms are unusual creatures
Of a most disturbing sort.
If invited to tea, first they giggle with glee,
Then wriggle and sniggle and snort.

If you're filled with dismay by this early display,
You'll soon wish you'd not spoken at all.
You've good cause to fret, for there's worse to come, yet.
You might as well hire a hall!

By bidding just one single Krimm to tea,
You've invited a multitude more,
For he'll ask a friend — and that friend ask a friend —
In the end you'll be hosting a score!

Should it stop at that, you'll be lucky.
But if your Krimm knows a Gart,
He'll bring the Gart, too! Then what will you do
When the two start to tear things apart?

Oh, they're really quite rude. They've no manners at all!
They'll complain about all the fare.
But you're fortunate still, if they don't bring a Shrill.
Oh, a Shrill will quite likely be there!

In a mournful tone, the Shrill will moan
That there's fungus all over the floor.
You'll just frustrate your brain if you try to explain
It's a carpet, she sees — nothing more.

Tea will be slopped on the tablecloth.
Pastry projectiles will fly.
Just try staying polite, while they bicker and fight.
Oh, whatever you do, don't serve pie!

ODD TALES AND WONDERS: STORIES IN RHYME
KRIMMS

I've entertained Krimms, not once, but three times.
Believe me, I know what I say.
When it's over that night, they appear so contrite,
You invite them again, straight away.

The last time, the poor things looked ever so sad
As they chorused, "Oh, never again."
Resist those wiles, those tears, those smiles,
Third time and you're one in ten.

I found myself making apologies.
I confess it. I'm one of the nine.
But greater fool, me. They're not coming to tea.
I've invited them back to dine!

Travis telling the story in 1974.

THE LORI

The Lori and *The Peerless Goth* were first published in *OPUS 17*, Spring Quarter, Vol. 9 No. 2 © 1973 by the Media Board of California State Polytechnic University, Pomona, with the caveat that the rights granted were for the single publication, and that all other rights, including the copyright, remained my property.

The *Opus* Faculty Advisor suggested I might illustrate them, if I could get the drawings in by the end of the day. I managed to do drawings for *The Lori*, but in documentary film fashion, rather than depict what the narrative rhyme had already covered, I illustrated the result. As for the Lori, being unable to find one is not the same as proving they no longer exist. In my treatment, their story is told by one of the Lori, who, when revealed, disappears.

This short rhyme covers a broad expanse of mythical time and cultures, so Adam and I used audio shorthand for the effects tracks. We created the civilization of the Lori through an ever-expanding universe of artisans at work, building an audio civilization of sculptors, builders and musicians.

The end of their civilization came suddenly and, as stated in the rhyme "no single horn sounded a warning." This is a reference to the Ragnarok of Norse mythology, which was supposed to be announced by a blast of Heimdall's horn. The disaster was beyond imagining, perhaps a coronal mass ejection that reached Earth.

"Disaster" literally means an unfavorable aspect of a star or planet and suggests the horror came to Earth from outside, as do all the upward turned faces found on cycladic idols. In Greek myth, Apollo's son, Phaethon, "borrowed" his father's chariot (the Sun), and unable to control its horses, came too close to Earth, setting the atmosphere aflame. If myths are tales invented to explain the inexplicable, the myth may be based on a genuine catastrophe.

The immediate aftermath is represented by a howling California firestorm, and the sounds of the four galloping horses representing my version of the Four Horsemen of the Apocalypse, galloping into the cannonade, trumpet calls and musketry of an ongoing battle.

ODD TALES AND WONDERS: STORIES IN RHYME
THE LORI

They're gone. You won't find a single one.
They've been extinct for some time.
Oh, every so often you'll hear one survived
In some wild and exotic clime,

But it's nonsense, pure and simple.
They've been gone for many a year.
Demand a more detailed account and you'll see
Just how quickly they all disappear.

Hence, I'm quite certain there are none left.
They've all perished and gone,
But they did exist, some time ago,
In a distant, clearer dawn.

Their trade was in the arts and crafts —
Their sculpture beyond belief.
Their paintings and illustrations
Brought the abstract to bold relief.

Actors, they were, and writers,
Composers beyond compare,
And architects and weavers
And musicians with music to share.

Throughout the world, their poetry enhanced,
In most ingenious ways
Both common ideals and the wisdom of kings,
In those golden, forgotten days.

THE LORI

No single horn sounded a warning,
But the earth began to buck
And the seas to rise toward burning skies,
On the day the disaster struck.

Winter on winter with never a sun,
Their forests all stripped and bare,
Their herds all dead, no grain for their bread,
A world of dread and despair

Beyond their most awful imaginings,
Beyond what their craft could forestall,
Beyond all the arts of their glorious race,
Far beyond any reason at all.

Then on came War, all blood and gore,
Pestilence, on a famished steed,
Death rode triumphant in their wake
And leading them all was Greed.

Dark ages, then. Men surrendered their souls
And turned to plunder and war.
What little we learn of the Lori is found
In myth and fable and "lore."

And so, in the end, it has fallen to us,
To pick up the torch and go on.
Our own values and ethics, desires and dreams
Must define us. The Lori are gone.

ODD TALES AND WONDERS: STORIES IN RHYME
THE LORI

These illustrations in CalPoly's *OPUS 17*, Spring, 1973, are in the style I proposed for the animated Universal TV Special.

THE PEERLESS GOTH

I am especially fond of *The Peerless Goth,* companion piece to *The Lori* in that Spring Issue of CalPoly's *OPUS* Quarterly. Coaches, contractors, bandleaders, scoutmasters, producers, directors, shop foremen or anyone else who has ever had to manage a crew will know exactly what I mean. Years ago, I performed it at a party hosted by my friend, composer, arranger and keyboard virtuoso, David Pinto. After a magic act, David introduced me. I looked at him, as if unprepared, and began with the Drang's shrill, whining protest, "Why me?" The stunned crowd fell silent, but I had their complete and undivided attention as I calmly continued, "why should I be the one to go?"

I finished the rhyme to a standing ovation, but in fact, most of my audience had been standing the entire time, as the crowd was larger than the room and seating was sparse.

Although my father was one of television's pioneers, as I was growing up, radio was still king, and radio dramas held us all in thrall. The stories and vocal characterizations, enhanced by sound effects, fired our imaginations, so storytelling, especially when sound effects are included, takes me back to my childhood (in a previous century), when I used to sit, or lie on my belly in front of our old upright radio set, hypnotized by the yellow glow of the radio dial, embarking on vicarious audio adventures that inspired my imagination.

The question that confronted Adam and me was how to create an audio atmosphere that set up the Peerless Goth's situation for the listener. The solution was to set the action in a factory and cast the Peerless Goth as the shop foreman. The action takes place in the foreman's office as, one by one, the disgruntled employees go to work. Shortly after each leaves the office, you hear another machine start out on the factory floor. This amazingly simple audio device handled all the audio effects superbly.

And the rest of the story, you know.

ODD TALES AND WONDERS: STORIES IN RHYME
THE PEERLESS GOTH

"Why me?" said the Drang, in a sulky mood.
"Why should I be the one to go?"
But the Peerless Goth only closed its eyes,
Which dismissed the matter, you know.

So, the Drang fetched up its grundle
And went herrilly on its way,
But not without a sour snout
And more that it dare not say.

The Cuspis offered no complaint
And quietly went to its chores,
But its hard-pressed lips gave its soul away,
For such tasks, it simply abhors!

"I won't! I won't!" raved the Ugly Grunch.
"I'll never do it, again!
This is positively the very last time!"
And it, too, went herrilly fenn.

"So! Now, at last, you've come to me,"
Said the Frice, "but do as you may,
I'm really quite self-sufficient, you know.
I needn't do as you say!

It's just lucky for you, that this time I will,
But be warned that you stand alone,
For I side with the Ugly Grunch and the Drang,
And the Cuspis is only on loan!"

THE PEERLESS GOTH

Thus, it progressed for some period of time
And the Goth kept the system intact,
And the work was done, and new tasks assigned,
But the Goth grew disgusted. In fact,

Finally, the Goth, in a fit of its own,
Vanished right into thin air
And the Drang, and the Frice, and the Ugly Grunch
And the Cuspis could find nothing there!

Oh, how they cried in ecstasy,
"We're free to do as we will!"
"What shall it be?" they cried, in glee,
But there came a sudden chill,

For they hadn't a single thing to do
Until, with much foam and froth,
They arrived at this brilliant conclusion.
They'd seek another Goth.

Oh, at last, everything had been settled.
The new Goth was very bright.
Everything began with a brand new zeal,
Until, on a sultry night,

"Why me?" whined the Drang, in a sulky mood.
"Why should I be the one to go?"
But the Peerless Goth only closed its eyes
And the rest of the story, you know.

ODD TALES AND WONDERS: STORIES IN RHYME

THE TWADDLE AND THE GURCK

The Twaddle and the Gurck is a deliciously chilling fable, meant to be performed aloud and heard by its audience. If you are unfamiliar with Lewis Carroll's *Jabberwocky*, this particularly odd tale may seem to be utter nonsense. Indeed, "twaddle" is a genuine word in the English language meaning "nonsense," but onomatopoetically speaking, which is to say, where the sounds of the words are supposed to suggest their meanings, this piece generally works brilliantly with live audiences. But for this tale, all the elements of the storyteller's arts come into play. Tone of voice, facial expressions, posture and gestures, as well as the intrinsic sound of the words spoken, whispered, shouted or wailed, all contribute to the audience's experience of the tale, which meant that offering it as a recorded piece, without the benefit of a live storyteller's performance, posed the greatest challenge of all these narrative rhymes.

I used the word experience, rather than understanding, since the tale is not in English (or any other known language). Wherever I perform it, I always try to find a few willing volunteers (or better still, a few fans already familiar with the piece), to enlist their aid in the responsive refrain. I hand out copies of the "words," coach them on pronunciation, strongly suggest they memorize their parts for the sake of the presentation and hope for the best.

I introduce *The Twaddle and the Gurck* as a story the audience probably learned at their mothers' knees and invite the audience to join in the refrain. After the first two quatrains, just about the time the audience is deciding I'm putting them on, I come to the first refrain. I chant the words slowly, ponderously, to help my volunteers stay with me. Imagine, the effect, when half a dozen people, strategically placed throughout the room, suddenly begin reciting the nonsense refrain, as if they really had learned it at their mother's knee!

"Cai, if an Illy cry "Dunair,
Cai, if an Owsie lie zerutch,
Cai, if an Elwith sigh "Ferair!"
A Twaddle gare is overmuch."

THE TWADDLE AND THE GURCK

It occurred to me that I've been telling this story for so many years that it's remotely possible some may have, in fact, learned it at their mother's knee. Soon, either way, nearly everyone is muttering along, embarrassed by their ignorance of the rhyme and, no doubt, feeling neglected by their mothers. At the very end, after the first three lines of the refrain, I hold up my hands for silence and speak the all-important final line alone.

"But ne'er a Twaddle for Gurck too much."

The Twaddle and the Gurck is told entirely in an Otherworldly tongue that sounds almost maddeningly familiar, yet remains incapable of objective translation, because the meanings of the words are entirely subjective, conveyed not by definitions, but by the feelings and emotions the words awaken in the listener, rather like Chinese.

I have more than a passing familiarity with a number of languages and the sounds they employ for verbal communication. The language in *The Twaddle and the Gurck* draws liberally from all of them, but mostly from English, German and Latin.

To illuminate this Otherworldly tale, it was important to establish its ambience. To do so, Adam and I used the sound of wind whispering through a forest glen to set the battle scene. The approach, growls, and roars of the attacking Twaddle mingle with the cries of the overmatched Woof. We even added a hissing fuse of black powder that fizzles out as Umberling's whifferpoof fails and he falls to the ferocious Twaddle.

Finally, as the Twaddle devours the fallen Woof, (the soundtrack includes the bones crunching in its salivating jaws), a swift, powerful blow from an edged weapon is heard and by the sound of it, takes the Twaddle's head clean off! That is not only the end of the Twaddle, but the end of the story, signaled by that last changed line in the final refrain, which you should have learned at your mother's knee.

(Yes, this one could give impressionable kids and their parents sleepless nights, too.)

ODD TALES AND WONDERS: STORIES IN RHYME

It takes a vivid imagination to fully comprehend this otherworldly adventure, but Adam's audio effects are enormously helpful.

THE TWADDLE AND THE GURCK

Full tane and twilly were the Woof,
But their pockenthatch lang queerily denn.
Sighed Imberlick, "Lass hoe nee soof!"
And Umberling gas worrily, "Venn!"

The Twaddle cam and gye the twack.
The Twaddle, gare and capricocious,
The Twaddle, ratch and lapfernack
And, inciderilly, ociferocious!

Cai, if an Illy cry, "Dunair."
Cai, if an Owsie lie zerutch.
Cai, if an Elwith sigh, "Ferair."
A Twaddle gare is overmuch.

THE TWADDLE AND THE GURCK

The Twaddle cam and gye the twack.
Noo, nee full twilly were the Woof.
The Twaddle cam. The Woof fie back,
And Umberling fail his whifferpoof.

The pockenthatch lang sterilly denn.
The tane and twilly Woof were doon.
Noor Imberlick gang herrilly fenn,
And the Twaddle sang ferloon.

Cai, if an Illy cry, "Dunair."
Cai, if an Owsie lie zerutch.
Cai, if an Elwith sigh, "Ferair."
A Twaddle gare is overmuch.

Imberlick cam an the floroo.
He leg his werrilly doon and shree.
The ruferfull Woof lang gore and due,
And cam a Gurck by oversee.

The Gurck ree, "Hoe!" and "Rasperoo?"
And Imberlick then sare his core.
The Gurck aire to and sare, "Cai, noo?"
But Imberlick could nee fermore.

Cai, if an Illy cry, "Dunair."
Cai, if an Owsie lie zerutch.
Cai, if an Elwith sigh, "Ferair."
A Twaddle gare is overmuch.

ODD TALES AND WONDERS: STORIES IN RHYME

The Gurck rang haze and ree, "Noo, nye.
I irre nay from ratch and twack.
The Twaddle, so, by me ferdye!"
And Imberlick ree, "No! Ferback."

The Gurck, by fare an omniroo,
An absolissimus ruferfull say,
With coperociousness terroo,
Noo figgery ruse his way.

Cai, if an Illy cry, "Dunair."
Cai, if an Owsie lie zerutch.
Cai, if an Elwith sigh, "Ferair."
A Twaddle gare is overmuch.

The Twaddle lang full saferee,
But everso, its fearilly ratch
Clang a farrowless lapferee
And goo the sperrilly doon for zatch.

But the Gurck, with oralless fay,
Cam the Twaddle from the roo
And, with overtwack ferslay
The garrilly Twaddle who ratch neroo.

Cai, if an Illy cry, "Dunair."
Cai, if an Owsie lie zerutch.
Cai, if an Elwith sigh, "Ferair."
But ne'er a Twaddle for Gurck too much.

THE TWADDLE AND THE GURCK: AN INTERPRETATION

Whenever I perform *The Twaddle and the Gurck*, I am asked what it means and what language it is, and while I sincerely hope you will read it aloud and let the sound of the words inform you through your subconscious, (or better still, buy and listen to the CD), I offer the following interpretation as a concession to the limitations of the written word.

Before I begin, I should mention that there are those who contend that since "twaddle" is a genuine word meaning "nonsense," one should consider a Twaddle to be nothing more than a nonsense monster created to frighten children. All well and good, unless and until one actually shows up, in which case, it will suddenly become an Otherworldly flesh-eating monster called a Twaddle by its victims, and hardly "nonsense." What it calls itself, I don't know. It may not even have a sense of "self." And if you think a Twaddle is nothing but nonsense, I strongly suggest you think so from a safe distance.

Personally, I do not recommend searching through English dictionaries for the meanings of foreign or alien words, especially if I know in advance that it is the sound of the word, in combination with the words around it and the vocal expression of the speaker that is intended to convey its meaning. In truth, the meaning may only be understood in some deep recess of some primal level of our consciousness, but if you listen attentively, you may be surprised at how close you come to a shared "understanding" of the entire piece.

Still, for those addicted to specific translations (they will never master Chinese), there is a sort of link between the British Army Ghurkhas and the Gurck in our story, not historically or genetically, but certainly generically. Ghurkhas, Nepalese soldiers and mercenaries, served mainly in the British Indian Army, and later in the Indian Army, with honor and distinction in many far-flung military operations and regions of this world. There is no real relationship between the Ghurka soldier and the lone Gurck wandering through Otherworld, but some are determined to compare the two, even down to the imagined weapon the Gurck uses to "overtwack" the Twaddle, suggesting it must be similar to the trademark khukuri, the forward-curving Nepalese knife used by the Ghurkhas -- and that may be so.

The following is one interpretation, but *The Twaddle and the Gurck* is open to others. Be warned. It is a tale of Otherworld. Behavior quite natural there may be reprehensible to people from this world, but you must remember that this world's social covenants often ignored or overlooked here, do not exist in Otherworld. In this interpretation, I sought to reveal this gruesome adventure from the perspective of this world and I fear that for some, it may cast the minions of Otherworld in an unfavorable light, but as one of their most famous bards once said, "Truth serves not. It is its own unbending master," and nothing less than "the truth, the whole truth and nothing but the truth" is acceptable if the tale is to be told at all.

The first verse states:

"Full tane and twilly were the Woof,"

The Woof are a tribe of like creatures, small and vulnerable taken one at a time, but more formidable when arrayed to do battle. In English, we would expect "tane and twilly" to refer to their numbers, or to their size and disposition, but in the language of Otherworld, it conveys a sense of both.

"But their pockenthatch lang queerily denn."

Despite their numbers and readiness, they lack "pockenthatch," which translates well as morale or confidence. This is modified by the phrase pertaining to their pockenthatch, reporting that it "lang queerily denn" or strangely subdued, yielding the sense that despite their numbers, preparedness and weapons, morale was low. One might even go so far as to say they were filled with dread and foreboding.

"Sighed Imberlick, 'Lass ho nee sufe.'"

Imberlick, leader of the Woof, friend to Umberling, another significant Woof, seems to be invoking divine intervention. The

THE TWADDLE AND THE GURCK: AN INTERPRETATION

sense is "Let something (horrible) not happen," possibly a simple charm against disaster, but indicative of a belief in some arcane and mysterious power.

> *"And Umberling gas worrilly, 'Venn!'"*

Umberling's response is clearly an attempt to strengthen the efficacy of the charm, much as people in this world, in similar circumstances, might say "So mote it be!"

> *"The Twaddle cam and gye the twack,*
> *The Twaddle, gare and capricocious,"*

The voracious, gore-encrusted Twaddle attacks, deriving demonic delight from its murderous onslaught . . .

> *"The Twaddle, ratch and lapfernack*
> *And, inciderilly ociferocious!"*

The Twaddle, with swift, death-dealing claws, is easily the most ferocious, mindless and sophisticated killer in all of Otherworld. And so, to the refrain . . .

> *"Cai, if an Illy cry 'Dunair!'*
> *Cai, if an Owsie lie zerutch.*
> *Cai, if an Elwith sigh 'Ferair,'*
> *A Twaddle gare is overmuch."*

"Cai" translates directly as "woe," and each following phrase has to do with what would inspire woe in this Otherworldy realm. It is certainly an occasion of woe if an Illy cries "Dunaire!" An Illy is a gentle creature whose sorrow would melt the hardest heart. As for an Owsie, a playful creature much loved and in demand by the minions of Otherworld as pets, all would mourn an Owsie "zerutched," its life squished out in the middle of the road. Even as you love and treasure your kitty or puppy (as well you should for they make excellent pets for earthly folk), surely you can imagine the depth of sorrow experienced by the denizens of Otherworld at the sight of a dead, or worse still, mortally injured Owsie. And of the Elwith's mournful sigh, known to herald the death of someone close, there is no need to speak.

But as ever awful these terrible events may be, nothing is more woeful than the arrival, in your vicinity, of a "Twaddle gare," for the Twaddle is an insatiable killer, and the deaths it deals, full of slashings and tearings and rippings and rendings and dismemberments are all too horrible to contemplate. There has never been a more terrible and terrifying monster than the Twaddle, and even in the violent Otherworld, it is considered the ultimate evil, killing for pleasure, a creature outside Nature itself. And so, back to the story.

> *"The Twaddle cam and gye the twack.*
> *Noo, nee full twilly were the Woof."*

Under the Twaddle's relentless assault, the hapless Woof are rapidly diminished in every respect.

> *"The Twaddle cam. The Woof fie back."*

For the third time, a report of the Twaddle's onslaught, but this time, both the ranks and the spirit of the overwhelmed Woof are broken.

> *"And Umberling fail his whifferpoof."*

Alas, a terrible fate befalls Umberling. Was Umberling's last stand intended to cover the escape of Imberlick? If Imberlick was the sacred king of the Woof, probably so. He was certainly a notable. He pronounced the invocation. And when brave Umberling's whifferpoof failed, did that result in the headlong flight of the Woof?

It has been suggested that "Umberling" is as much a rank or position as a name, and should be translated as "Underling," but I

THE TWADDLE AND THE GURCK: AN INTERPRETATION

believe Umberling was a creature of some importance, perhaps even second in command. After all, he is the only other Woof whose name is known to us.

What, exactly, is or was a whifferpoof? My first inclination, indicated here by the sound of a black-powder misfire, was to translate it as a muzzle-loading blunderbuss, with a flared barrel, a shotgun, of sorts, inaccurate at long range but devastatingly deadly at close range. But a "whifferpoof" might as easily refer to a blowgun, perhaps capable of firing a poison dart that might bring down a Twaddle at close range, because I imagine a Twaddle as having a thick hide that at a distance the dart might not be able to penetrate.

I reconstruct the moment this way. As the ranks of the Woof begin to collapse, Umberling heroically steps forward. The Twaddle turns its attention to Umberling and advances. Umberling stands his ground, and only when he feels the beast's hot breath on his face, does he raise his whifferpoof.

It matters little if his whifferpoof is a blunderbuss, blowgun or light saber. In the critical instant the weapon fails, and Umberling is slain. For those who walk the warrior's path, there is nothing more disheartening than the failing of one's whifferpoof at the moment of confrontation. Realization, resignation and certain death follow.

"The pockenthatch lang sterrilly denn.
The tane and twilly Woof were doon."

Never mind their morale: their bodies lay strewn across the bloody field of battle, utterly destroyed.

"Noor Imberlick gang herrilly fenn,
And the Twaddle sang ferloon."

Only Imberlick, alone of all the Woof, escaped the field, his mind unhinged by the horrors he witnessed, his heart weighed down by unfathomable grief. And the Twaddle then croaked out its victory song, which is about what you'd expect a Twaddle to do. And so, the now familiar refrain . . .

> *"Cai, if an Illy cry 'Dunair!'*
> *Cai, if an Owsie lie zerutch.*
> *Cai, if an Elwith sigh 'Ferair,'*
> *A Twaddle gare is overmuch.*
>
> *Imberlick cam an the floroo.*
> *He leg his werrilly doon and shree."*

Imberlick finds his way to a brook, collapses beside it and weeps for his fallen comrades.

> *"The ruferfull Woof lang gore and due,"*

Notwithstanding the adjective "ruferfull," to which we shall return, it seems clear that the Woof are all dead, underscored by the Otherworldly "due" which conveys that dreadful sense of finality.

> *"And cam a Gurck by oversee."*

And a Gurck happened along and saw Imberlick collapsed by the edge of the brook below.

> *"The Gurck ree 'Hoe!' and 'Rasperoo?'"*

The Gurck greeted Imberlick and asked why he wept.

> *"And Imberlick then sare his core."*

And Imberlick told him. To "sare his core" is to spill his heart out, subjectively conveying the terrible gist of the story, if not every detail, which he would not have known in the heat of battle, anyway.

> *"The Gurck aire to and sare 'Cai, noo?'*
> *But Imberlick could nee fermore."*

Alerted to the arrival of the monstrous Twaddle, the Gurck pressed Imberlick for more details, but Imberlick was unable to go on with the terrible account of the one-sided battle.

THE TWADDLE AND THE GURCK: AN INTERPRETATION

"Cai, if an Illy cry 'Dunair!'
Cai, if an Owsie lie zerutch.
Cai, if an Elwith sigh 'Ferair,'
A Twaddle gare is overmuch."

The terrible truth of the refrain is becoming ever more clear.

"The Gurck rang haze and ree, 'Noo nye!'
'I irre nay from ratch and twack!'"

The Gurck, in a bloodthirsty rage, shouted "This cannot stand!" "Ratch and twack" (carnage and slaughter), were not unknown to him, and he feared them not!

"'The Twaddle, so, by me ferdye!'"

Bold talk. The Gurck vows to slay the Twaddle, to kill it to death! It may sound silly to you, but not to Imberlick.

"And Imberlick ree 'No! Ferback'"

Imberlick implores the Gurck not to interfere, to "stay out of it." Does he seek to protect the Gurck from a terrible fate, or might some more terrible catastrophe occur if the Gurck attempts to slay the Twaddle and fails? The Twaddle's killing spree was the result of its joyful pursuits. What horror might ensue if the Twaddle was threatened or angered?

"The Gurck, by fare an omniroo,"

At last, a description of the Gurck. Now, "omniroo" easily translates as "master," but to be "by fare" a master is quite beyond simple mastery. It is an honorific reserved for the unrivalled best in any given field.

"An absolissimus ruferfull say,"

Absolutely, which is just how I translated it. And a "ruferfull say," as well. A "say" (probably related to "sage") implies wisdom, or perhaps, in this instance, merely connotes a thorough knowledge of whatever art the Gurck possesses.

It is not easy to translate adjectives like "ruferfull." What can it mean to be so full of "rufer," anyway? It doesn't sound like a particularly heroic attribute at all. "Ruferfull" may be related to "ruffian," or worse. "Rough" might be in there, too. Now if it's rough like in the "Rough Riders," that would have a heroic connotation, but rough might also suggest "hot-tempered" or "ill-mannered," which may not be particularly welcome in polite society, but hardly disqualifying in the battlefield.

The question as to the Gurck's character is still unsettled. Is the Gurck a sheriff, a park ranger or a cold-blooded killer? Does he side with the Woof that justice might prevail, or to gain notoriety? Or is he going after the Twaddle to protect his "turf" from a potential competitor? Whatever his reason, the Gurck's decision is to act!

> *"With coperociousness terroo,*
> *Noo figgery ruse his way."*

With a terrible "ability to cope," to plan the destruction of his adversary, the Gurck "figures" to overcome the Twaddle through some subterfuge, through a "ruse" of some sort. Wouldn't a hero put his faith in the justice of his cause and confront the beast head on? Not a Gurck. Although he's alone, "figgery" might suggest a conspiracy. It is widely held that some Otherworldly creatures have bicameral brains that only rarely communicate with the other side and are perceived as separate entities or even the voice of God.

> *"Cai, if an Illy cry 'Dunair!'*
> *Cai, if an Owsie lie zerutch.*
> *Cai, if an Elwith sigh 'Ferair,'*
> *A Twaddle gare is overmuch."*

If there is one thing of which we may be certain, it is that there will surely be enough woe to go around.

THE TWADDLE AND THE GURCK: AN INTERPRETATION

"The Twaddle lang full saferee . . .
But everso, its fearilly ratch"

The Twaddle reclined, confident in its deadly prowess, but even though the creature was at ease, its fearful "ratch" (almost certainly its carnage wreaking claws) . . .

"Clang a farrowless lapferee . . ."

Tore up everything within reach. This may refer to a nervous twitch, brought on by a state of constant readiness.
"And goo the sperilly doon for zatch!"

And in so doing, continued to mindlessly destroy even tiny, unseen creatures and their rare, exotic habitats.

"But the Gurck, with oralless fay,"

Which is to say, the sheriff (or park ranger or mercenary), without so much as an audible breath, much less a word of warning . . .

"Cam the Twaddle from the roo,"

Snuck up on the Twaddle from behind . . .

"And, with overtwack, ferslay . . ."

This does sound like cold-blooded murder. True, the Twaddle was a monster and had to be destroyed, but you see what I mean about it not being a fair fight. In fact, no fight at all. The Gurck snuck up on it and slit its throat, or with "overtwack," cut off its head! Whether you consider the act brave or cowardly, this was nothing more than an execution.

"The garilly Twaddle who ratch nerroo."

Garilly or not, it wasn't likely to go around ratching anything after that, was it? And so, to the final refrain . . .

"Cai, if an Illy cry 'Dunair!'
Cai, if an Owsie lie zerutch.
Cai, if an Elwith sigh 'Ferair,'
But ne'er a Twaddle for Gurck too much!"

In the end, the entire tale boils down to this dramatic alteration of the last line of the chorus. The Gurck's rule seems to be that you do whatever it takes to fulfill your mission and stay alive to go home at the end of the day. It's no good trying to change it. Otherworld is an honest place and its minions are wont to "tell it like it is."

So endeth the tale of the Twaddle and the Gurck.

THE TWADDLE AND THE GURCK: AN INTERPRETATION

A FINAL NOTE ABOUT
THE TWADDLE AND THE GURCK

In July 1999, I attended the National Storytellers Conference in San Diego, where I signed up to tell a single tale at the Story Swap for Storytell ListServe members and prepared *The Twaddle and the Gurck*. It was late when I was called to perform. The audience was tired and restless, so I decided to change the program and tell the shorter and more readily understood, *Peerless Goth*. I announced my program change and my mind went blank. I could not remember how *The Peerless Goth* began. Not only that, but I couldn't remember any of my other rhymes. After a few awkward moments, with no choice but to accept my fate, I told *The Twaddle and the Gurck*, which woke up most of the crowd and went over as brilliantly as ever.

When I finished telling my tale, the late, great street poet and storytelling icon of Harvard Square in Cambridge, Massachusetts, known affectionately in the community as "Brother Blue," leaped to his feet, applauding my performance, shouting "That's like Lewis Carroll, isn't it? Like Jabberwocky?" I answered that it was and he applauded all the louder. By the time Brother Blue finished lauding my effort, everybody was wide awake. And that was my delightful, memorable, live introduction to the StoryTell ListServ population of the National Storytelling Network.

I love performing it. Whether you find reading or listening to it amazing, amusing or a complete waste of time, is for you to say.

www.ingramcontent.com/pod-product-compliance
Lightning Source LLC
Chambersburg PA
CBHW060450170426
43199CB00011B/1153